Praise for *Evidence of Inquiry*

"Jessica Vance has done something truly remarkable with *Evidence of Inquiry: Exploring, Questioning, and Documenting with Learning Walls*. She has written a book that is both deeply rooted in theory and powerfully practical—a perfect reflection of an inquiry stance on learning. With clarity and insight, Jessica offers multiple entry points into understanding what learning walls are and how they serve as dynamic tools for reflection, planning, and making connections. This book is an invaluable guide for educators seeking to craft spaces that communicate 'the story we want the learning to tell.' She helps us focus on what matters most as we shape a culture of inquiry where curiosity and meaning-making thrive. A must-read for any educator committed to fostering agency and deep learning!"

—Anne van Dam, education consultant

"Twenty-five years ago, working in schools in New Zealand, I attended a staff meeting held not in a staff room, but a classroom. The principal opened the meeting by asking us to gather around the learning wall, while the host teacher shared challenges and successes of her students' current learning story. It has been wonderful to read Jessica Vance's detailed and thoughtful book in which she honours this powerful practice and brings it to a new generation of teachers. Drawing on her teaching experience and celebrating the work of many other fine educators, Jessica reminds us that visible, public, co-constructed documentation can power up learning for both students *and* educators. The benefits of this kind of documentation are beautifully articulated. *Evidence of Inquiry* will not only deepen your understanding of learning walls and equip you to create and use them, but it will also deepen your understanding of the pedagogy of inquiry itself."

—Kath Murdoch, teacher, consultant, and author of
Getting Personal with Inquiry Learning

"Jessica Vance has written a real game-changer for leaders and teachers who value deep, reflective learning, curiosity, and collaboration. Whether you're new to learning walls or already using them, this book is packed with simple, practical strategies and real-world examples that will bring how to build learning walls to life. You'll find quick wins as well as key grapple points, like how to involve students and keep walls meaningful over time. More than just a classroom tool, it's a way to embed a culture of learning across your school, build connected community, and drive team collaboration."

—Becky Carlzon, community designer, Learning Pioneers and PressPlay

"Documentation is more than just a record—it's a powerful practice that brings students' thinking to life and captures the unfolding story of learning in our classrooms. Yet, learning how to document effectively can sometimes feel daunting. With practical wisdom, expert insight, and inspiring examples, Jessica Vance becomes a trusted guide, leading readers step-by-step through the process of creating Learning Walls—and, more importantly, using them as dynamic tools to enrich and extend student thinking."

—Ron Ritchhart, EdD, director, Cultures of Thinking Foundation

"Jessica Vance's *Evidence of Inquiry: Exploring, Questioning, and Documenting with Learning Walls* offers a comprehensive and insightful exploration into the power of learning walls as a cornerstone of inquiry-based education. Rooted in the author's experiences as a classroom teacher, coordinator, and leader, this book serves as a practical guide for educators at all levels seeking to transform their learning spaces and deepen student engagement.

"Vance encourages us to see learning walls as an opportunity for dynamic, co-constructed spaces that document learner voice and provide evidence of the learning process. She positions them as integral to fostering a student-centered assessment practice that builds confidence and provides evidence of understanding. The book serves as a catalyst for transforming learning spaces into dynamic environments that truly reflect the inquiry process."

—Rachel French, author, educational consultant, and workshop leader

"Educational literature is replete with terms like active learning, inquiry, student centered, ongoing assessment, reflection, visible thinking, self-assessment, and reflection. *Evidence of Inquiry* offers an eminently practical method for integrating these ideas and bringing them to life in classrooms. Jessica Vance describes the use of learning walls as a means of actively engaging student inquiry and meaning-making while concurrently chronicling the process of their learning.

"The learning walls that Vance describes reflect process and product, input and outcomes—all revealed through student voices. Numerous examples with illustrative photographs confirm the applicability of this method across grades and subject areas. I'll conclude on a personal note: Would I want my four young grandchildren in classrooms in which their teachers understood and effectively applied the learning wall process as Vance describes it? Absolutely!"

—Jay McTighe, co-author of the *Understanding by Design®* series

Leading with Inquiry Series

Evidence of Inquiry

Exploring, Questioning, and Documenting with Learning Walls

Jessica Vance

Editing and Layout by My Writers' Connection
Artwork by Ryan Bear

Published by Elevate Books EDU

Library of Congress Control Number: 2025907309
Paperback ISBN: 979-8-9913909-6-5
eBook ISBN: 979-8-9913909-7-2

To the countless classroom teachers and school leaders who, with an open mindset and a willingness to playfully explore this documentation practice, join me in asking,

I wonder what would happen if . . . ?

Also by Jessica Vance

Leading with a Lens of Inquiry
Cultivating Conditions for
Curiosity and Empowering Agency

Typical models of training and professional development focus on telling. It's a model that far too often trickles down to classrooms where the traditional way of "doing school" limits the way educators teach and students learn. Fortunately, there is a better way to learn: through wonder, agency, and inquiry. From *Leading with a Lens of Inquiry*, administrators, educational instructors, and peer leaders learn how to cultivate learning spaces that ignite curiosity and inspire critical thinking in adult and student learners alike.

Download additional resources and learn more
at LeadingWithInquiry.com.

Contents

Foreword by Trevor MacKenzie xiii

Part 1: Roots of Wonderings 1

Chapter 1: What Is a Learning Wall? 9

Chapter 2: Tenets of Equitable Evidencing 25

Part 2: Building a Learning Wall 45

Chapter 3: Find a Blank Space 49

Chapter 4: Set an Intention 63

Chapter 5: Retrieval (Part I) What's Worth Knowing? 77

Chapter 6: Retrieval (Part II) Me vs. We 95

Chapter 7: Make Connections 121

Chapter 8: Leave Space for Wonder 155

Chapter 9: Co-Construct for Personal Meaning 197

Part 3: Stories of Learning Journeys 249

Stories of Co-Construction 251

Stories of Skill, Competency, and Approaches to
Learning (ATLs) Development 277

Stories of Teacher Agency 297

Stories of Conceptual Understanding 325

Stories of Assessment 339

Stories of Virtual and Digital Learning Walls 363

Concluding with a Call to Action 375

Bibliography 379

Acknowledgments 383

More From Elevate Books EDU 386

About the Author 393

About the Illustrator 394

Foreword

Inquiry can be a nebulous thing. Imagine sitting around a table in the staff lounge with three of your colleagues and one asks *what is inquiry?* I would wager that among the four of you, there would be four differing definitions of what *inquiry* means. The research tells us this is the case. Pour over the many articles about the effect of inquiry on learning and you'll see a tale of two stories. Some of the research suggests that inquiry has a low effect size and paints a bleak picture of the potential of inquiry when it comes to teaching and learning. When one looks closely into this body of work, it becomes clear that much of it amounts to little more than "exploring big questions" with "free research time" and lots of "students learning about what interests them the most." This sort of kicking your students into the deep end of inquiry with little to no curricular ties is sure to be disastrous from the start. In my experience, both students and teachers feel anxious, overwhelmed, and uncertain with this *free-rein learning*.

On the other hand, some of the research suggests that inquiry, when scaffolded and intentionally planned towards curricular outcomes, has a practical significance when it comes to teaching and learning. When teachers plan for inquiry through co-designing with students, identifying curricular outcomes, and engaging in experiences that are agentic in nature and across time, lead to a progression of learning, undeniably positive things happen. Students have experiences wherein they feel competent, confident, and to a certain degree, in control of their learning. There is a shared dynamic in the classroom between teachers and students, a dynamic that shifts the learning from hierarchical to inclusive and invitational. This progression requires explicit planning and intentionality that we must embrace if inquiry is to be fruitful and worth our efforts.

To help plan with this progression in mind, I propose that we think of teaching as having two impacts on students and their experiences in school: learning is agentic or learning is disengaging. When learning is agentic, students feel empowered and see that their ideas and perspectives are critical in the building of new learning. They have an active role in the thinking, the planning, and the decision making in the classroom in an ongoing, supported, and authentic manner. Their questions are honoured, their curiosities are leveraged, and their voices are heard.

When learning is disengaging, students are complacent and disinterested in what they are learning about. The dynamic in the classroom is teacher controlled and hierarchical. Students fall into the trap of easy learning, looking for the path of least resistance and quick ways to get tasks done. Over time, many disengaging experiences lead to disenchantment. When this occurs, many students just don't see the point of school.

We can map this out in a simple yet powerful graph. Our vertical axis represents this continuum of agency (top) and disenchantment (bottom). Our horizontal axis represents growth over time. When teachers plan towards agency with a progression of experiences in mind, we see more competent and confident students who are, over time, able to take on the heavy lifting of learning. This is not merely thin slicing or breaking things down into smaller chunks. Planning for a progression means considering strategies that build on one another to help students be more successful in inquiry. Let's call these *above-the-line strategies*.

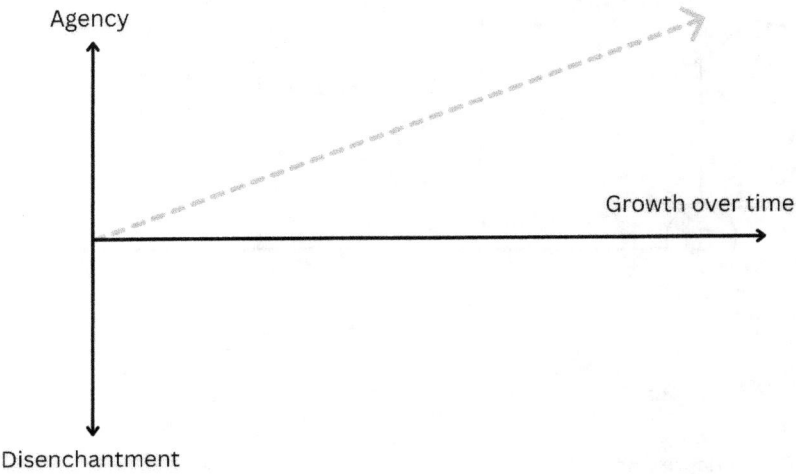

Let's take a close look at co-designing with students as an example of an above-the-line strategy and progression. A good way to introduce students to co-designing early in the school year might be to build the essential agreements or norms for learning together. This experience would be close to the coordinate plane and act as the first point of co-design for us to build from with our students (labelled 1). A step up our progression slope might be to co-design indicators for specific skills and competencies for inquiry. We can build a list of descriptors or behaviors for strong collaborators, thus designing a point of reflection, self-assessment, and target for growth in collaboration. This experience would be further up the progression slope, a nice addition to the previous co-design experience with students (labelled 2). A step up from here could be to co-design success criteria with students. In identifying the desired targets and outcomes with our students, they gain a clearer and deeper understanding of how to grow given the parameters of learning that are actively building with their teacher. This third experience would be the furthest up the progression slope (labelled 3), a point that if we jumped too fast or too soon towards, many students would feel anxious and overwhelmed.

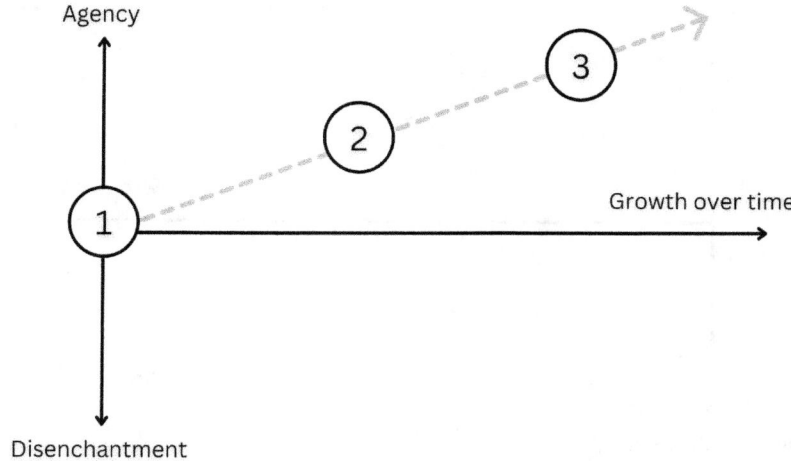

Now let's focus on below the line strategies. A series of disengaging experiences can have a negative effect on student agency, competency development, empowerment, and interest. When stacked up against one another and when disengaging experiences become the norm, students slowly become disenchanted with their schooling experience. The longer students experience learning that is below the line, the more hesitant, uncertain, and unsuccessful they'll be when they encounter an above-the-line strategy. Consider this: When the teaching is most often composed of below-the-line strategies, it is quite difficult to come back to an above-the-line experience. The closer we are to disenchantment, the harder it is to get back to agency.

There is a rich opportunity in getting critical about above-the-line and below-the-line strategies. Spending time reflecting on our practice, deepening our inquiry repertoire, becoming better versed in frameworks, routines, and protocols that support agency and curiosity will take us far when it comes to our commitment to remaining above the line in our teaching. Conversely, noticing when disengagement occurs and what teaching strategies that we are utilizing during these times will help us avoid disenchantment.

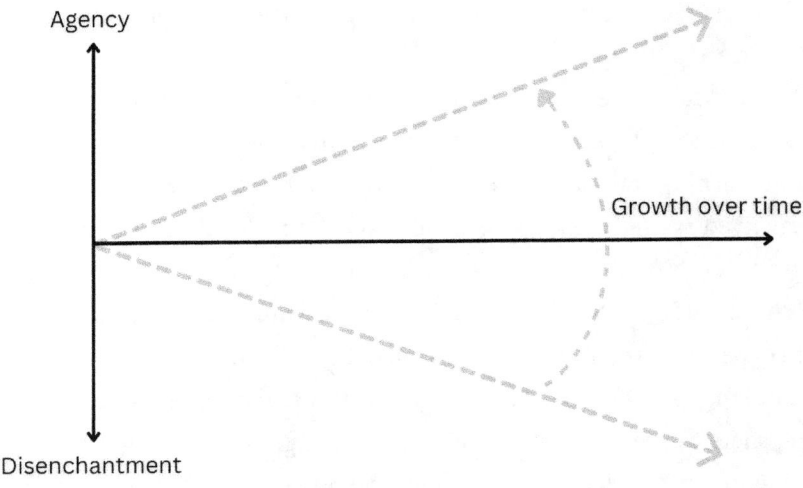

Learning walls and the rich evidencing and documentation practice that comes along with them are powerful examples of above-the-line strategies. Building a learning wall with your students, when done well, includes many agentic experiences. When done well, learning walls engage the teacher and students to co-design and co-plan, using the evidence of learning that is visibly documented to prompt reflection and shape next steps. When done well, learning walls invite students to get on their feet, move their bodies, and get physically engaged and, in turn, cognitively engaged. When done well, learning walls call on students to switch on their critical thinking, reflection, collaboration, curiosity, and many other competencies, ones that are difficult to tap into when teaching below the line strategies. When done well, learning walls shift teacher planning to be well informed and timely as the creation of universal supports occurs in real time with students as opposed to outside of class time and away from them.

It is quite easy, however, for learning walls to become a below-the-line experience for students. It happens when the spaces are too teacher controlled and void of student involvement. Or when we fail to use the space that learning walls provide for deep thinking and reflection, or shortchange students by not leveraging their ideas to plan next steps. These are pitfalls to avoid.

Jessica Vance's *Evidence of Inquiry: Exploring, Questioning, and Documenting with Learning Walls* offers us a blueprint for above-the-line learning walls and experiences. The book is brimming with practical, lived examples that have been used in a variety of schools, contexts, grade levels, and subject areas, from our youngest learners to our high school students. Vance's framework for learning walls allows teachers to experience their own progression of agency, one that allows them to take small steps toward big change. An abundance of photos that allow teachers to see into classrooms around the globe, learning walls *done well* are on full display throughout the book. Jessica's vast experience in supporting schools on their inquiry journeys shines brightly as she shares stories from classrooms she has taught in, coached, and supported. She leaves no stone unturned, making every effort to guide us on our own learning wall journey as we are invited to reimagine how we can use the spaces in our classrooms to support inquiry. In a world in desperate need for empowered youth, deep thinkers, and agents of curiosity, *Evidence of Inquiry* helps us all stay above the line.

Trevor MacKenzie
Author of the *Inquiry Mindset* series

Part I

Roots of Wonderings

*F*ollow *your learners.* This phrase is repeated often in the inquiry community. The words summarize what we value as inquiry educators and highlight how this pedagogical approach differs from the traditional systems many of us experienced as students.

Follow your learners. These are the words we say to ourselves when reflecting on the data gathered through assessments, observation, and the evidence and wonderings presented by our learners.

Follow your learners. This simple reminder quiets the noise of trying to "do it all" while balancing new initiatives that are still working their way toward clarity. It's the advice we give *ourselves*, and it invites us to lighten the perfectionist tendencies of educators who hope that practice will one day "make perfect."

Follow my *learners.* That's exactly what I did in writing this book—a book I hadn't planned on writing. I had other plans, ideas that had been stewing for a different story that I wanted to share for my second publication. I had an itch to draft a children's book and was only beginning to put pen to paper to brainstorm the plot and characters when my learners (educators like you) made it clear that they needed something very different from me. That revelation surfaced over time—in workshops, in requests for partnerships from schools that were eager to revisit key elements of their learning spaces, and in the inquiry cultures they were nurturing. It came through direct messages and comments that popped up after I playfully shared my personal practice of vertical documentation on Instagram. It showed up week after week in one-on-one coaching and planning sessions with teachers and leaders, in which we pulled up our chairs to their learning walls to reflect on what we saw before launching into action.

A curiosity was brewing, and I couldn't help but notice the increased interest as I heard the same kinds of questions time and time again. The questions were the evidence that I needed to *follow my learners*.

So I did what any experienced inquiry educator does: I listened harder. I asked more questions. I jotted down notes. I spent even more time in classrooms. I filled notebooks and snapped photos. I sat with the evidence, tinkered with ideas, and built several learning walls with a variety of focuses and lengths.

Slowly, the trends in the artifacts before me took shape. I saw piqued interest in data and evidence, a shifted access and equitable invitation toward learning, a surprising flex of agency in spaces and systems that were typically scarce, and sizable changes in school culture and mindsets around learning. Listening to my learners was taking me somewhere special; I just had to keep following where it led me.

I didn't do all of this research and reflection solo, of course. Inquiry works best with others, after all. Other educators joined me in this quest to explore documentation. I pitched ideas their way and asked them to share their experiences. I invited myself into classrooms so I could sit alongside learners of all ages to gain perspective about learning walls in action. I watched students and educators engage and interact with their learning in new ways. Together, classroom teachers, other inquiry leaders, and I reflected on the impact of learning walls on their communities. We discovered trends, made adjustments, and followed creative outlets to unearth refreshed ways of looking at our vertical spaces. I also called on thought partners to help me verbally process what I had observed. They proved to be critical to the works as they lifted up barriers, identified common themes I initially overlooked, made suggestions, and asked even more questions.

Documentation and evidencing of learning isn't a concept that's mine alone. My well-worn copies of Mark Church and Ron Ritchhart's publications, *Making Thinking Visible* and *The Power of Making Thinking Visible*, as well as my time as a primary years program (PYP) classroom teacher and coordinator launched me on this journey. These books and experiences gave me the confidence to try new thinking routines, fumble through questioning protocols, and dutifully collect sticky notes from exit tickets and end-of-unit reflections. If you read my first publication, *Leading with a Lens of Inquiry*, you know those stories and are well aware of my growth as a leader. The prompts and questions I share in that book are intended to help *you* document your thinking and process of learning regarding how you can lead with a lens of inquiry.

Since then, I've spent more time in the early years classroom studying the research and pedagogy that underpins a play-based approach to teaching and learning. I've found new books and blog posts from educators who are well versed in authentic documentation. Working alongside classroom teachers, superintendents, program coordinators, and other school leaders, I've built hundreds of learning walls. These collaborative spaces and the lingering questions that emerged from them became the provocation for a shifted focus in my writing and an addition to the school of thinking that I hold so dearly in my practice. This book summarizes the coaching conversations, theories about the human need for meaning-making a process of thinking about our thinking, collections of unexpected kinds of data, and actions that reflect the values of a constructivist approach to teaching and learning.

Honoring and celebrating the process of learning is a key component to building, maintaining, and leveraging the impact of learning walls—vertical spaces where thinking, ideas, wonderings, and evidence are collected by a community of learners. This book explores the learning process and will guide you along your own journey of building a learning wall. I've organized this book to scaffold your inquiry journey, but I anticipate that you'll find your own way around this book. My hope is that you'll see yourself and your students in the stories and will find examples of learning walls that give you the start you need.

Part One: Roots of Wondering sets the stage for our thinking before diving into how to build a learning wall. In this section, I'll introduce the core tenets of a learning wall. We'll use these as the framework for deeper understanding of purpose, intention, and routine. While you might want to jump into immediate action and implementation, the depth and complexity of these tenets are foundational as they clarify the differences between traditional classroom displays or bulletin boards and learning walls. When you finish reading Part One, you will have the checklist you need to get started on a new learning wall or to reflect on one you have been building.

Part Two: How to Build a Learning Wall is structured around the sketchnote, *How to Build a Learning Wall,* which serves as your roadmap for co-construction and authentic documentation. You'll notice that the stages of building a learning wall are not siloed actions to blindly check off of a list. The strategies presented here are rooted in imperfect but authentically active learning walls, offering practical ways to interpret and apply each step of building a learning wall. The steps are seamlessly interwoven, enabling a smooth shift, both in mindset and approach to documenting learning. It is important to keep in mind here that the learning walls included in this book were captured at varied stages within the cycle of inquiry while being co-constructed by educators and students across different contexts and levels of professional experience. I invite you to stay curious and be inspired by these fantastic educators! You'll find prompts to support your reflection, new tools to nudge you forward, and resources that link you to continued research and experts in the field of inquiry. Hands-on learning is powerful, so I encourage you to build or edit your learning wall as you read this book. Consider sharing your process of learning and reflection by snapping a photo or grabbing some video evidence. Use the hashtag #learningwalls to be a part of the conversation around authentic documentation!

In Part Three: Telling Stories of Learning Journeys, you'll meet more than twenty different educators from around the world whose stories bring the tenets of a learning wall to life. Each individual shares their firsthand experience with co-constructing a learning wall alongside their learners, including the challenges they encountered along the way and the aha moments that changed the direction of learning. The learning journeys they share highlight reflections of student agency, rich formative assessment practices, as well as crucial moments in which relationships and competencies shone brightly. These vignettes showcase a variety of perspectives, years of expertise, and different levels of experience with inquiry. The diverse approaches to starting and maintaining a learning wall pull back the curtain on their thinking and how they respond to and use student evidence. Draw inspiration from these educators and allow them to inspire you. This section also includes reflective templates, photos of learning walls, and examples of evidence to collect. With these resources and a long list of new thought partners, you'll be well equipped to leverage the power of learning walls.

This book is more than just the words that fill each page. As you read, I'll ask you to pause and reflect and to flip back to previous sections and reread them with a different lens. My hope is that you will take immediate action, using the links to the resources and the wisdom of other experts add to the knowledge and depth of complexity inherent to an inquiry-based approach to teaching and learning.

Before I send you on your way, let's engage in a retrieval exercise to begin a process of documentation of your own learning and reflection. Set a timer for two to three minutes and respond to the questions that follow. The exercise provides an opportunity to slow down long enough to take stock of what's uniquely important to you and creates an artifact of what's currently drawing your attention. Use the space provided here or grab a sticky note or inquiry notebook if that's more your style! Add your own questions as you jot down the roots of what's next for your practice.

- What do you need to know to help you get started with building a learning wall?
- What stories do the walls of your classroom tell?
- How are you currently using space, or the environment, as the third teacher?
- What does your current documentation look like?
- In reflecting on your current learning walls, who is doing the heavy lifting: is it you, is it your students, or is it done collaboratively?
- What is something you hope to gain from reading this book?
- What are the current barriers or challenges you feel when it comes to your documentation process?

In the Reggio Emilia approach, educators say the learning environment is the third teacher (after parents or guardians and the classroom teacher). This means that the learning environment is a crucial space to show wonder, curiosity, ideas, values, pictures, stories, etc. that are being told on a daily basis in the school setting.

As you read the rest of this book, pause periodically to revisit the notes you jotted down. Notice how your learning brings clarity and confidence. Consider what new wonderings emerge because of your learning. Tab sections of this book, dog-ear pages you want to return to often, and take your learning off these pages by applying it to your own setting and circumstances. Whether you are a school principal, classroom teacher, curriculum coordinator at the district level, or an instructional coach, I know you will see yourself and your practice in the pages before you and will find new ways to lead and learn with a lens of inquiry. It's time to begin a new journey of inquiry together!

Sometimes things are just better in color! Use this QR code to access a pdf of full-color images of all the learning walls shared with you in this publication.

Chapter 1

What Is a Learning Wall?

In my first book, *Leading with a Lens of Inquiry*, I shared many stories with readers. Stories of failures and frustrations, stories of wonder and awe, stories of challenges overcome, and stories about the process we stumbled on as mindful inquiry leaders. One particular story I fondly look back on now is how our administration team began to rethink how we were nurturing a school that valued inquiry, including our physical spaces.

> We, too, returned to these artifacts of learning as we prepared for individual coaching sessions or brainstormed action plans to support district initiatives. Along with our anecdotal notes, we viewed this documentation as valuable data that informed our next steps with our learners. We could analyze these displays as we continually reflected on what was needed to meet the teachers where they were, differentiating the ways we approached our roles, leveraging time in the way that best served the growth of all learners.

Having this space also lent itself to collaboration across the campus. When teachers would drop by the office, something on the bulletin board invariably drew their interest. Prompted by their curiosity about what they saw, they would ask questions based on another artifact of learning we had intentionally placed from another grade level.

—Leading with a Lens of Inquiry

Since writing that book, I've continued to work with educators and leaders around the globe as we reflect on the role and impact that space has in the overall culture of learning we're trying to nurture. Using the learning environment as a *third teacher* is nothing new. The concept stems from contemporary theories and the well-respected research of Reggio Emilia. It's the pedagogical stance that views space as an integral part of planning and calls on educators to consider the potential that the physical environment has on influencing students and inviting them to the learning.

Tapping into the valuable role of space, we consider the following questions:

- How does the physical space encourage students' agency?
- How is learning built into the environment?
- What learning opportunities are created by changing the space?
- How do the different spaces foster a sense of belonging and community?

With this approach to teaching, we see provocation stations anchored with an essential question that invites the exploration of loose parts. Carefully arranged furniture that nudges students to discuss and further synthesize larger concepts with their peers. Secondary classroom teachers rethinking displays, choosing to use them as carefully curated selections of artifacts that challenge older students to stretch their thinking and take a more active role in the process of learning. But these wall displays are much more than student sketches, preprinted posters, or wallpapering of student work. They are snippets of the learning that capture thinking, highlight current and past wonderings, and anchor bigger ideas around connected concepts such as perspective, identity, or systems.

The walls in these learning spaces tell stories that are centered around the student. They propel agency. They reflect the pedagogical mindset and teaching stance of inquiry.

These walls are learning walls.

So, *what exactly is a learning wall?* How are learning walls different from the displays commonly seen in school buildings and collaborative workspaces? How do learning walls honor the foundational research of Reggio Emilia and nudge us to lead and teach with an inquiry mindset?

When I asked my thirteen-year-old son, Londyn, to define a learning wall for me, he nonchalantly and yet quite confidently stated, "An improvement on a wall." The simplicity in his answer to the question that launches this book is quite revealing and invites us to consider what that might look like in different contexts—in *your* unique context.

As with inquiry itself, the responsiveness and creative ambiguity of learning walls make them challenging to define. Although the entirety of this book is meant to deepen your understanding of what learning walls are and their function within our classrooms, I think it's best that we start with what learning walls are *not*.

Learning walls are not a collection of teacher-created anchor charts.

Walk into any classroom, and you're bound to find charts stapled to walls and pinboards filled with big ideas and topics to explore. From phonics sound patterns that support emerging readers to strategies that help students approach a complex word problem in math to a list of social-emotional learning (SEL) skills intended to foster a growth mindset, anchor charts are meant to support the overall growth and development of student thinking. The intention in tacking these onto walls is to allow students to refer to them. But how often do our students actually reference and use these to support their thinking? How often do these anchor charts stay up well beyond the term's end, eventually becoming a wallpaper that blends into the background of learning?

By definition, anchor charts are meant to *anchor* learners' thinking. Typically, although not always, co-constructed with a group of learners, these charts might document a class conversation or experience. Even when co-constructed, anchor charts rely heavily on teacher curation and control. A collection of these on a wall presents the message that wondering and sorting the topics being explored has no space within the learning environment. Instead, they present the topic or material in a neat and organized way, affirming that *this* is the only way to approach or think about it.

Learning walls may include or display anchor charts—but in a way that may not look so tidy. Instead of neatly curated, clean, laminated sheets of large paper, the anchor charts you might find on learning walls rely on student voice. Marked with revisions or crossed-out ideas, they show how the inquiry has unfolded. Anchor charts on learning walls are just one of many types of artifacts being displayed.

Learning walls are not wonder walls.

A wonder wall may be a start to capturing learner curiosity and should be included as an aspect of a learning wall, but a wonder wall is *not* a learning wall. Wonder walls are a fantastic structure that inquiry leaders can use to leverage questioning, but they only tell *part* of the learning story. We take scholars' questions from our classroom wonder wall and add them to the classroom learning wall to model how questions connect and drive our next steps.

Learning walls are not stagnant.

Our role as inquiry educators requires that we pause regularly to consider exactly how we are responding to learners. We must adapt our lesson plans, throwing out the preprinted worksheets and making space for hands-on experiences that allow learners to explore and play with their thinking. This shift opens up opportunities to let small groups of students revisit big ideas and creates time for collaboration in which they can question, process, sort, and extend their thinking.

Like our teaching, learning walls are not stagnant. They reflect the ebb and flow of student inquiries.

Learning walls are the dynamic third teacher in the room.

Learning walls expand a learning narrative that's easily read by anyone viewing them.

Learning walls are not a collection of one product.

Learning walls tell the collective story of a learning journey. A final draft of a persuasive writing assignment, a sheet of chart paper with a class-generated list of academic language, student reflections, or a sorted collection of sticky notes are single products gathered to evidence the story being told. On their own, however, they are only part of the larger puzzle. Learning walls contain a variety of artifacts that display the process of thinking, meaning-making through the lens of wonderment, and different learners' voices.

Learning walls are not solely the final product.

Parents are often invited to view showcased celebratory exhibitions of the hard work completed by students and teachers. Classroom teachers spend hours arranging displays of their students' summative thinking with the intention of highlighting the purpose of the work. These traditional displays, most commonly found in school hallways and classroom walls, which fail to show the rich feedback and multiple attempts it took to achieve the final product, send the message that learning only occurs at the end of a unit of inquiry. Unlike the differentiation expressed on learning walls, these final product displays reinforce values of compliance and comparison.

Learning walls are not meant to be marked, graded, or used as summative assessments.

Inquiry teachers place value on creating equitable and inviting spaces that nurture independent learners who feel confident in sharing their knowledge and understanding. These collaborative structures can be used during peer-to-peer feedback sessions and to co-construct success criteria generated before beginning work on a larger project or writing assignment. All of these inquiry moves are part of a rich assessment practice that puts learners at the center. A student-centered assessment practice fosters confidence in learners because they have a clear understanding of the success criteria and feel proud of what they create because they have had a voice throughout every part of the learning process.

Gathering and mindfully displaying artifacts from different parts of the learning process, including evidence from formative assessment, doesn't happen at the expense of the inclusive culture we are trying to construct. Learning walls help our scholars see the thinking process, which emboldens them to take risks and stretch their thinking. In contrast, graded assignments naturally lead to a comparative culture. Showcasing a teacher-selected collection of graded assignments accelerates this process. Learning walls are a tool to support learning as well as our assessment practice, but they are never be marked or graded.

Learning walls are not Pinterest worthy.

Let's face it: *Pinterest-worthy* and *picture-perfect* displays have no place in the messy process of inquiry learning. Something can be visually enticing but completely void of authenticity. The desire for social media "likes" erroneously places value on appearance rather than learning. Beyond that, striving for Pinterest perfect is unsustainable in a profession that constantly teeters on the edge of work–life balance. Do a quick Pinterest search and you'll find plenty of learning walls structured with an inquiry cycle or similar structure. Many are color coordinated, and they have perfectly aligned artifacts and preprinted or teacher-created labels. They evoke a false sense of flawlessness in the process of learning.

Learning walls are not teacher controlled.

As we shift our understanding of our role as inquiry teachers, we gain expertise in knowing just how much or how little to lean in and do the heavy lifting. Keeping our learners and curriculum in mind, we navigate the balance of who is controlling the learning. Unlike a traditional bulletin board display, learning walls are not teacher controlled. Rather, they are a curation of evidence from a variety of experiences. We must use our experience and knowledge of the content to determine what's important to display. As with many new routines, structures, or classroom practices, inquiry teachers may be the lead curator or guide. As such, our role is to share and model reflective thinking and use powerful questions and protocols to help students think about their thinking. This is how we leverage our spaces to support students as they learn about their learning.

Learning walls are not manufactured or preprinted posters.

Whether it's an 18 × 24-inch sheet of paper plastered with district goals and unit standards or a mass-produced poster with subject-specific vocabulary, there are some must-haves in every learning space. These resources, created without the individual learner in mind, are designed to appeal to and be used by a wide audience. Manufactured and preprinted posters lack learner voice and individuality and rarely reflect the depth and complexity of topics and concepts being explored.

Learning walls are not one size fits all.

Each learner is different. With that in mind, we differentiate our lessons by providing heavier-handed scaffolds for some students, different manipulatives for others, and a variety of learning resources and materials that align with learners' interests and needs to equitably build the knowledge needed to confidently approach learning. Some artifacts, structures, and elements of learning walls will resemble one another, but as with our students, no one learning wall is the same as another. Each wall displays the thinking, personal connections, and unique wonders as the community of learners unpacks big and small ideas.

Now that you've read about what a learning wall *is not*, take a moment to jot down some key takeaways or ideas you'd like to remember when you are preparing to design your next learning wall.

Making Thinking Visible

Learning is a process differentiated to the individual. It's not a simple input/output system that always warrants the same results. We need tools and resources that help us connect with our learners with an authenticity that only comes when we are truly attuned to the moment. We respond with carefully crafted questions to stretch our learners' thinking or provide feedback based on our experience about what we know works best for different styles of learning. Learning walls are tools to support the process of learning and, more importantly, the process of thinking.

Harvard's Project Zero and the work of Ron Ritchhart and Mark Church highlight the power of making and *keeping* thinking visible. The thinking routines thoroughly explored in their publications and resources call on those facilitating the learning to first pause and reflect and consider what types of thinking are needed to support and develop in their learners. Inquiry teachers then look at their curriculum standards to evaluate what may best scaffold toward that type of thinking.

Their body of work nudges us toward a different type of documentation than we're perhaps used to within our practice. There are no blackline masters to photocopy or print. Instead, the routines are a structure that we leverage as a tool to frame the thinking and ideas being explored. We choose an open-ended medium such as chart paper, whiteboard, or a digital tool to make learner thinking visible. With the focus now on the process of thinking, we're able to more easily model an interest in learner ideas and flex essential skills and competencies such as curiosity and collaboration. No matter which routine you choose, you'll notice that making thinking visible is grounded on the same core tenets:

- Questioning
- Modeling an interest in ideas
- Constructing understanding
- Listening
- Documenting

These tenets ensure that your practice continually puts your learners at its center and aligns with the principles of constructivism, the foundation for a pedagogical approach that's rooted in inquiry. Learning walls reflect these same values, nurturing a sense of belonging and learner voice that highlights a commitment to shifting the narrative of learning in our classrooms from teacher controlled to co-designed.

So, *what are learning walls?* Learning walls are co-constructed spaces that reflect the process of learning with collections of carefully selected artifacts that are rich in student voice and thinking. Learning walls communicate the critical thinking and connections learners make as they tune into new ideas and gather evidence that helps them construct new understandings. A learning wall is an accessible documentation tool that empowers the classroom environment.

Although inquiry-based learning discourages checklists, common terminology describing key features of effective learning walls is helpful. Each description that follows is multifaceted. We'll delve deeper into these aspects after discussing the principles of gathering evidence equitably; for now, let's examine what learning walls are.

Learning walls tell a learning narrative.

Whether we're exploring a unit of inquiry over several months or have a condensed timeline and focus that lasts only a handful of weeks, learning walls tell the full story. Like a traditional narrative, there is a beginning, middle, and end that encompass the journey. The critical elements, in this case artifacts and evidence of learning, are revealed slowly over time to paint the picture of learning. Each lesson has the potential to contribute to the learning wall.

Learning walls are co-designed and co-constructed.

Our students experience a sense of meaning in the inquiry when invited to actively contribute to the learning. As we reframe our thinking to include students as co-designers, we foster a sense of ownership and agency and create space for learners to trust themselves and the decisions they make. Students reflect on their learning and playfully determine what evidence might be important to gather and what's no longer needed to support the learning. As inquiry educators, we remain active by modeling our thinking and lifting up critical concepts our learners might have overlooked.

Learning walls reflect a process of learning.

Learning is a process, not merely an end product. We design lessons to tap into background knowledge, gather artifacts that anchor these learning experiences to scaffold connections and deepen thinking, and mindfully pause this process to create opportunities for our students to reflect on their learning. As with any process, there's always a bit of a mess as the mind untangles big concepts and sorts through ideas. Learning walls are resources that are rooted in the work of meaning-making. They honor and celebrate this natural, messy process of learning.

Learning walls provide evidence and document learner voice.

A range of rich data and evidence informs our assessment practice and allows us to assess *with our students* instead of *to our students*. In *Inquiry Mindset: Assessment Edition*, Trevor MacKenzie outlines ways to rethink our assessment approach in the classroom and reframe our mindset and practices around assessment. With an inquiry mindset, assessment becomes a "we job" (teacher *and* students) instead of solely (and more traditionally experienced) a "me job" (teacher).

Learning walls allow us to lean further into this student-centered approach by calling on us to accumulate a variety of artifacts that demonstrate our students' growth and development. We may document learner voice by collecting wonderings jotted down on sticky notes at the start of a unit of inquiry and then mindfully moving those same wonderings around the wall while calling on learners to add new sticky notes as they draw connections. We may tack up large chart paper or student-generated posters that capture the co-constructed success criteria for an upcoming writing assignment or find small clusters of academic vocabulary notecards, worn with use, attached to the wall with pushpins. Regardless of whether the students are physically present, you can easily *see* the learners in that space.

Learning walls are accessible, equitable, and inclusive.

Putting our scholars at the center of learning means providing open-ended resources to support their different needs. Spaces that allow students to approach and comfortably interact with the learning help us meet those needs. It could be through tactile experiences, where they drag their fingers across taut strings that make the connections between content areas visible. Or by putting notecards and materials at learners' eye level, which not only makes content accessible but also reinforces the fact that it is designed especially for and by them. Or by choosing muted colors and a minimal display of artifacts that lessen the overwhelm and busyness school buildings can have while creating a sense of calming energy.

The inclusivity extends to the collection of evidence by ensuring that all our learners' voices are included and that different opinions and experiences are clearly honored. The diversity of artifacts placed on a learning wall can be expanded with Tug-of-War thinking routines, which highlight different perspectives around thought-provoking statements and stances. Using students' language to label the different areas of the learning as well as choosing an appropriate medium—digital or physical— helps make the space accessible to students.

Designing with students in mind and then asking them for feedback about this resource enables inquiry teachers to ensure that all learners' needs are consid-

> Tug-of-War is a thinking routine to provoke discussion, dialogue, or debate around a statement or option. To read more about thinking routines such as Tug-of-War, check out the suggestion reading section at the end of this book.

ered. By inviting them into the design and revision process, we are giving students the opportunity to reflect on who they are as learners and to communicate their needs.

Learning walls provide a rich sense of belonging.

Research on growth mindset from a variety of sources, including psychologist Carol Dweck, the Massachusetts Institute of Technology (MIT), and David Yeager's book *10 to 25: The Science of Motivating Young People*, tells us that when we, as humans, feel seen, heard, and valued, we experience a sense of connection. Building strong relationships and prioritizing collaboration fosters a growth mindset. Learners become more confident in taking risks when they feel supported by a connected community.

When we consider the different needs of our learners, we better understand just how learning walls help us authentically connect with our learners. The inclusive and collaborative nature of learning walls fosters that sense of belonging. These spaces show our students we value their thinking and ideas. When we ask them which artifacts might best document what we're exploring, we instill in them a sense of trust and independence that comes from having the opportunity to make important decisions. Being mindful of the ways students process information, we can use these spaces to make room for those who grasp concepts quickly but struggle to express their ideas in a way that clearly communicates understanding, as well as for those who are learning a second language and need more structured support to build on background knowledge and make connections.

When students have a prolonged absence, these spaces help lessen the anxiety of returning to the classroom or feeling disconnected. By displaying the evidence that scholars collected and building on existing knowledge, learning walls act as a starting point for sharing learning experiences and explaining how things are unfolding for the classroom community. Asking open-ended questions, we further encourage participation and reintegrate learners into the space.

In an era of AI and social media, we are constantly challenged by a lack of motivation and its negative impacts on emotional wellness. Although these tools are often meant to make work easier and nourish a sense of interconnectedness, they tend to do the opposite. Learning walls become an ecosystem in which a sense of belonging can thrive. When we add group reflections from a provocation sparked by their latest interests, track progress toward individual learning goals, or ask students to engage in collaborative feedback using key concepts from the unit of inquiry, we reinforce the power of planning, working, and learning together.

Learning walls reflect and capture the curiosity in the classroom.

Learning walls capture curiosity in a way that spans a larger learning narrative. By lifting up student questions and empowering scholars to shape the evidence being collected, the inquiry takes each classroom community in different directions. Even within a school, learning walls look different across grade levels and departments. Some may be rooted in a grouping of essential questions that provide a springboard for learning experiences, while others take on a timeline structure that highlights how the wonder and awe from each unit of inquiry builds on another. We hear and see evidence of what cognitive scientist and author Guy Claxton calls the "split-screen" approach to teaching and learning, equally homing in on how we ask questions and what we ask questions about.

Leveraging the walls of our offices, hallways, and classroom spaces is a powerful way to honor learning while working within the demands of time and the ever-changing needs of our learners. It's a practice that empowers us to step into a more dynamic role—one that moves beyond traditional methods to collecting evidence and documenting data. With this progressive approach, we can make things easier for ourselves while inviting and equipping our learners to become confident agents of their own learning without losing the depth and meaning that make learning transformational.

Pause and Reflect

Now that we've outlined some general characteristics of learning walls, it's time to take a look at your own four walls.

* Which qualities of learning walls stand out or appeal most to you? What makes you say that?

* How do we create the conditions for curiosity to thrive in the environments in which we lead?

* What stories do your walls currently tell? How do they align with what you value as an inquiry teacher?

Chapter 2

Tenets of Equitable Evidencing

Inquiry teachers know well what it's like to feel out of step with the traditional education system. The phrase *marching to a different beat* comes to mind. Even so, we must work within this system of requirements from our schools and districts. The tenets of learning walls help us maintain an inquiry mindset even when navigating these mandates. They are the building blocks of equitable evidencing and are best viewed through a lens of curiosity.

We strengthen our practice by revisiting these tenets often, reexamining them from a fresh perspective and an openness to approaching our role in different ways. The questions that follow invite you to reflect on your unique context. My hope is that they challenge your thinking as you construct your own understanding and provoke critical thought and discussions with colleagues. As you explore the tenets of a learning wall, visualize your classroom or learning space. Give yourself time to settle into a flow that allows you to be playfully curious and to make personal meaning.

Five Tenets of Equitable Evidencing

I. What's important to lift up in learning?

As facilitators of inquiry, we observe students interacting, and we tune in to their questions. We notice patterns of thinking or misconceptions that emerge. We also listen for the hum of engaged learners working independently.

Listening, observing, and trusting your expertise will help you determine what to lift up in the learning. With a mindset of reflection, you respond to the learning, using what you see and hear to plan your next steps:

- Do your learners need more time to build background knowledge? If so, do you need to scrap your lesson plans for the day and lean into that need?
- Are your learners asking questions filled with misunderstandings? How might you skillfully turn those questions into a provocation to launch new learning the next day?
- Have you noticed a lack of independent research skills? Do you need to scaffold experiences or provide more supportive resources, such as question stems or research mats, to build agency across the academic year?

 A research mat is a Google or PowerPoint slide with pre-selected links that guide and support research skills for students. From your favorite videos to links to articles that guide learners towards current events, I find that this scaffold is an essential strategy to have! Take a look at a play-based learning research mat I created for my first publication to get a sense of how you can create your own research mats too!

Reflection is often misunderstood. Often, we think of it as a solitary activity that requires an extended period of quiet in a place absent from distraction, when in fact, reflection comprises skills that we flex and strengthen through multiple experiences. One way we sharpen the skill of reflection is through listening. Relying on what we hear and on our experience, knowledge, research, and capabilities as educators enables us to determine what needs our focus.

The "Sharpening Skills of Reflection" sketchnote outlines the five skills of reflection. As you scan the graphic, notice the interconnectivity of the skills and the playful way they fuel one another. Take a moment, too, to consider how each one shows up in the process of inquiry to reinforce this essential skill of reflection.

When we treat our walls as a third teacher and build nontraditional displays of learning, we engage in a similar reflection process. We pause, reflect, and consider the story we want the learning to tell—and what is important to lift up.

- Is it a narrative rooted in a universal concept that can be identified in your curriculum and standards, such as perspective,
  conflict, or play?
- Is it an essential question sparked by student curiosity?
- Is it the opportunity for students to take risks with their
  learning and flex core competencies such as communication,
  friendship, or self-assessment habits?
- Is it a compelling or provocative statement that reflects what
  we value in the unit of inquiry or across a term?

Pause and ask yourself what you want from your learners. What
are you hoping they display in their thinking as you explore the curriculum together? Are there competencies nested in your standards that
sometimes get overlooked? How might you take stock of the social
and emotional needs of your learners and align movement and action
forward? *What is most important to lift up in the learning?*

If we want our learners to make transdisciplinary connections across subject areas, we create a space that brings together
co-constructed anchor charts from reading, academic definitions
from science, and the sticky notes and thinking routines we generate in
math. If we want our scholars to set meaningful goals, collect evidence,
and give reflective feedback to their peers, we curate an area with sentence stems to support collaboration. We showcase a flipchart of collected work—one that celebrates the process over the final product by
showing the many edits and revisions that shaped their thinking. And
if we want our students to apply the skills we have been teaching to
their final written compositions, we ensure they have access to success
criteria, sticky notes capturing class-generated questions from novel
discussions, and key themes that serve as inspiration for their writing.

When we slow down long enough to consider what's important to
lift up in the learning, we look at our walls with a refreshed perspective. The final and perfected drafts of student writing come down. We
no longer segregate learning into reading or math walls, and we stop
blindly tacking up essential agreements or group norms that no one

really remembers after the day they were created. We realize that data walls aren't enough. For the content of a learning wall to be relevant, it must be student-centered and meaningful to the learners themselves.

2. How do you build capacity for your students to make connections?

Inquiry requires us to engage in a deep learning process that asks the learner to identify and transfer skills, make connections across topics, and take the learning to a conceptual level. Diving deep into learning is hard work. It requires listening and skilled dialogue with our scholars, which means that it doesn't always stick to structured timetables or the never-ending swings in curriculum focus. This kind of deep, wonder-filled learning doesn't fit neatly into a static scope, which can make it difficult to document according to scripted standards.

Learning walls help us engage in deep work in a way that authentically builds meaning and personal understanding in real time. Students direct the process of planning and teaching as we navigate our constraints, finding a rhythm through collaboration. This process scaffolds toward their growth of knowledge and skills while ensuring the quality of the shared learning experience.

We can't just hope that our students will make connections to the skills and core content we're teaching. We must intentionally plan for it by creating spaces and structures that encourage student discourse, discovery, and deeper learning. Here are a few strategies for doing that.

Sentence Stems

I'm a big fan of sentence stems! I love the way they bring a purpose to planning for collaboration amongst learners. I love how they clarify the type of thinking we are scaffolding toward. I love how they gently invite all learners to contribute ideas and participate in the learning.

Sentence stems amplify the classic Turn-and-Talk structure by guiding the conversation. An Exit Ticket takes a more meaningful direction when we use sentence stems to prompt learners' personal reflections of the learning. This tool gives learners a sense of confidence by highlighting patterns and paving the way for deeper thinking and connection making. At the same time, sentence stems help us clarify what we want our students to understand while supporting the development of communication, collaboration, and thinking skills.

In Part Two, you'll read about how other educators are using sentence stems to build students' capacity for connections and invite conversations within the learning community through powerful language. In the meantime, jot down a few sentence stems you might use to nudge your learners toward making connections. What phrases do you already use or have you seen modeled that encourage learners to think and build understanding about the evidence they have before them?

Stringing Along

The brain constantly searches for patterns to organize information and make meaning. Neuroscience research reveals that the brain's neural network is strengthened by these connections. When designing instruction, we can honor the way the brain works by arranging our inquiry units and standards so they build on one another. Paying attention to the sequence and flow of skills and concepts, we can harness the brain's natural inclination to make sense of the world. Even if your context doesn't allow you to rearrange units and skills, you can approach your curriculum by searching for and using patterns in the curriculum.

Our students are constantly making connections, although many of them go unnoticed because they are a matter of routine. From the moment they step into our classrooms and find their seats, they settle into a learning mode that takes cues from the teacher as they recall yesterday's learning or launch into a new topic. Students' brains take in new data, classify, sort, organize, wonder, and build new and deeper understanding. We can more easily access this busy highway of connection making by embedding structures and learning routines in our practice and making them visible.

Source: Amy Osborn, First Grade Teacher, Spicewood Elementary, Austin, Texas

One way to bring students' attention to the connections is to use string or yarn to link the evidence or artifacts. This physical manifestation of connections can be added to the learning wall in a few different ways:

- They can be generated organically by the students themselves during a class reflection.
- The teacher might prompt learners with a question, such as, "What connections do you see within our learning?"
- The teacher can add the strings *after* students have left the classroom.

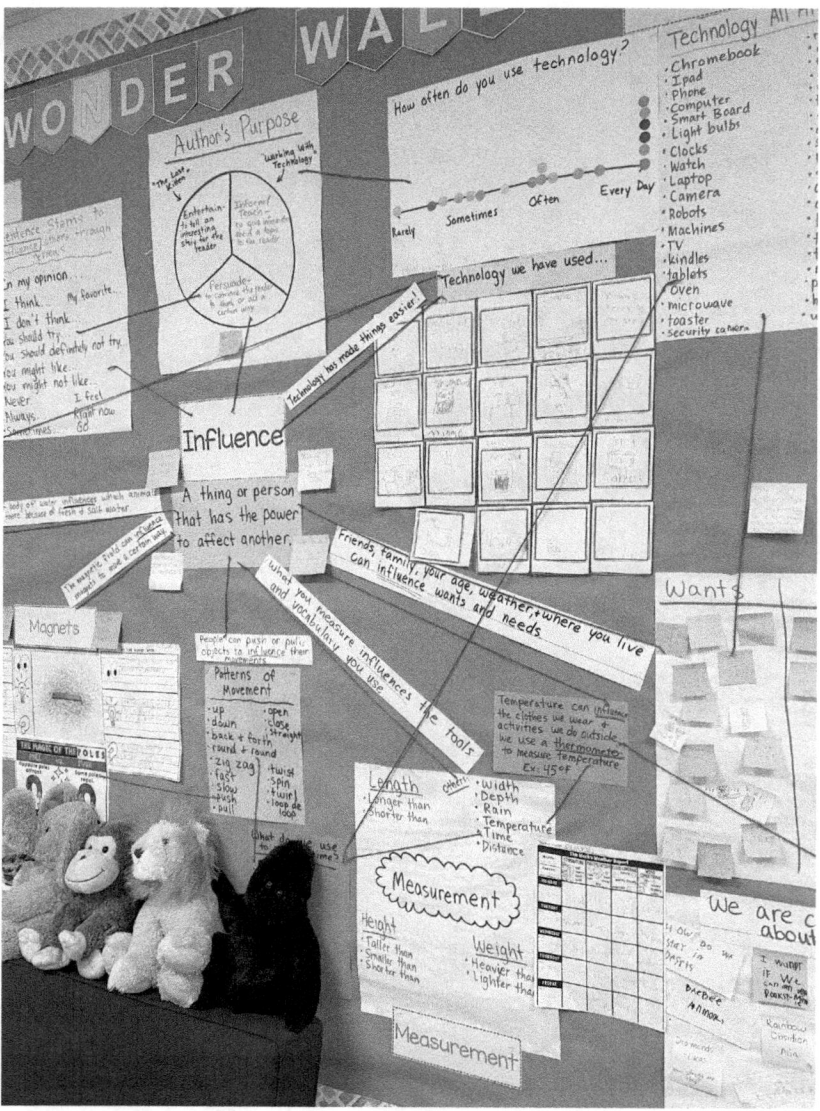

Source: Samantha Jorgans, First Grade Teacher, Laurel Mountain Elementary, Austin, Texas

Regardless of how the strings are added to the wall, what's important is to model how the ideas, topics, or questions within our units of inquiry are connected. We pull back the curtain by using clear language and essential vocabulary, approaching the learning wall and physically showing our learners the connections between artifacts we've chosen to display. Relying on intentional sentence stems, such as "I noticed a connection you made . . ." or "This also reminds me of . . ." while pointing to related artifacts reinforces the patterns and connections. With time, our learners replicate our language and movements and, in doing so, see their knowledge and understandings emerge.

This tactile approach engages more of the five senses and supports young learners and emergent bilingual students. Prompts, such as "Show me your thinking" or "I'm curious what links you are making with our learning," gently nudge students toward the learning wall. There, they engage in the cognitive process of explaining their thinking and finding patterns.

It's important to resist the urge to step in and interrupt them. Instead, listen for language and links to learning. Jot down misconceptions to address with a future provocation or small group instruction. Nod to affirm them in their sharing, and document evidence of their learning to be included in the marking or reporting process.

When combined with careful observation of student reflections and classroom discussions as well as the use of intentional questioning (such as "What makes you say that?"), this scaffold helps us confirm learners' understanding. The learning links made in the students' minds become visible as we see them make meaning and express the variety of connections they find in their learning. In time, the skill of making connections will become a routine part of learning conversations, and yarn or string may not always be necessary.

Time, context, and your learners all impact how you might use this strategy to make connections visible. Not every connection needs to be physically represented. Rely on your expertise about the curriculum and knowledge about your students and their needs to determine what's most important to lift up in the learning.

In the table that follows, you'll find a summary of different ways that I've seen inquiry teachers and leaders use Stringing Along as a strategy to make connections visible. I encourage you to play with at least one from each column. When you do, notice what it does to the landscape of learning.

- Consider where you are within your unit of inquiry and what you want to find out.
- Consider your learners' existing skills as well as those they need to flex.
- Consider what prompts (sentence stems, academic language, or vocabulary) or other scaffolds might support their learning.
- Consider how connection making might be most appropriate for your specific learners' developmental age, language level, skill development, etc.

During Active Learning	Outside of Active Learning
• Teacher uses the learning wall to model connections between learning artifacts. • Students gather around the learning wall and are asked to identify two connections they are making so far within the learning. • Strings are used to echo the connections students make. • Learning wall is used as a tool to summatively support student reflection and learning. Take a photo of learning wall and ask students to use a digital tool to draw and explain connections.	• Look at your anecdotal notes; stretch string between artifacts that reflect the connections students explicitly made during the lesson. • Considering the direction of your unit plan, add string between artifacts to provoke student thinking and scaffold connections. • Reflect on your spiderweb discussion chart to document a variety of connections learners made during the lesson. • Consider using the learning wall and connections as you report to parents about student learning.

Pull Up a Chair

As we shift toward a more playful and intentional practice, we develop new habits in our planning and in the way we collect evidence. Instead of sitting at our desk and moving through tabs of spreadsheets and folders of resources, we pull up a chair and sit with the learning *at the learning wall.* Positioning ourselves in this way gives us a new vantage point. Having an intentional wall space and collecting artifacts isn't enough. We must *use* that space by sitting at the wall at the end of the day, reading what's been said over the past few weeks, recollecting memories of where we've been, identifying what's recently unfolded, and looking ahead in our lesson plans to consider what's left to unpack with one another.

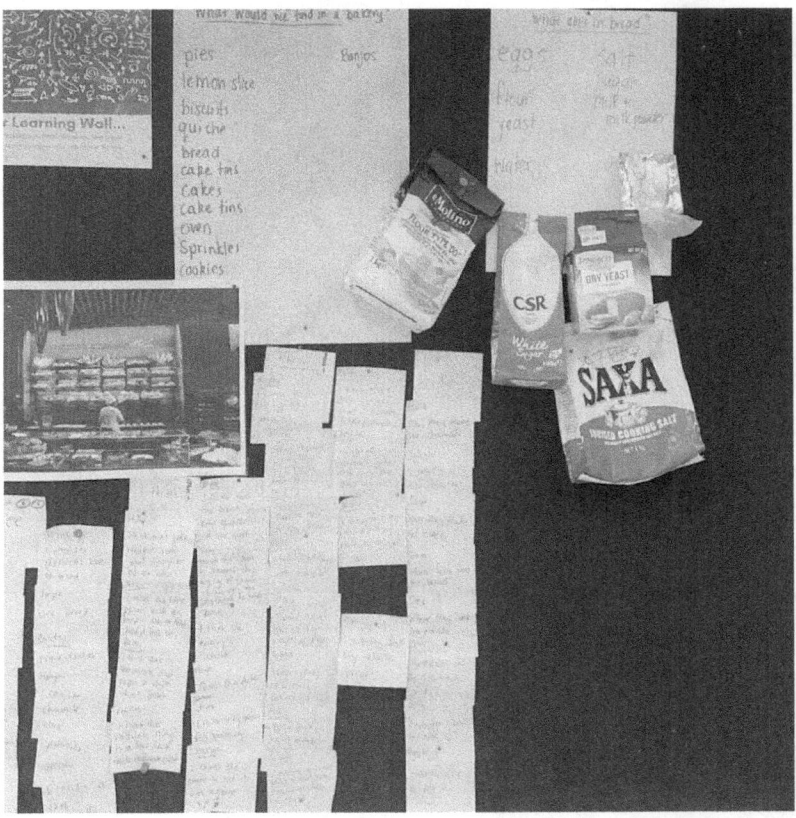

Source: Tania Steenholdt, Early Years Teacher, Glen Huon Primary School, Glen Huon, Tasmania, Australia

Just as we invite our learners to increase their capacity to make connections by interacting with the wall, we engage in a similar process to look over the learning to determine our next steps.

This practice of literally changing our perspective helps us balance our curriculum standards with the voices of our learners. Let's take a closer look at what one of these reflective sessions might look like. Tania Steenholdt, an early years educator at Glen Huon Primary School in Tasmania, generously shares her reflections on artifacts and learning experiences. She connects her initial plans and expectations to what the evidence is showing her to guide her in planning the next day's learning experiences. In reading her reflections, notice how she captures learners' questions and intentionally plans next steps and resources with those in mind.

> Reflecting this morning before work about how to help the children connect with the Learning Wall . . . added a visual prompt in terms of the pictures—the brain and neurons. I'm hoping this will give them something to talk with parents about. Have moved the board near the entrance so parents can look when they arrive.

The reflective practice of pulling up a chair to our learning walls helps us identify patterns to shake off the feelings of disconnection that the pace of education often creates. Authentically connected to the learning, we can respond to what we see and, in doing so, honor our learners and nurture a culture of deep engagement. By physically repositioning ourselves and taking in a wide range of examples, we are able to see the bigger picture and better understand what our learners need in the moment.

*Source: Tania Steenholdt, Early Years Teacher, Glen Huon Primary School,
Glen Huon, Tasmania, Australia*

Colorful Connections

As learning walls fill with artifacts, including student reflections, sticky
notes, and other paper mementos, they tell a vibrant story of learning.
The simplicity of building these walls is in the intentional and organic
gathering of evidence, but that also means they can become cluttered
and, over time, more challenging for our students to decipher. Making
materials accessible is essential, but we must also be both playful and
intentional about the resources we use to support our teaching.

Color is one way to craft learning walls for clarity. You might
choose one color for the background or essential questions, another

color sticky note on which students can jot down recent connections, and yet another color for thinking-routine templates where students can write their reflections and draw new conclusions. Just as a kaleidoscope uses mirrors and angles to sort loose bits of tiny glass parts to create new patterns with every turn, you can use color to support your learners as they zoom in and out of their learning and make critical connections.

Because of the predictability of colorful connections, those who teach several sections of the same subject or facilitate learning across different groups of learners particularly favor this method to support this stage of constructing knowledge. An added benefit is that when connections become obvious across subjects or classes, they pull learning communities closer by encouraging dialogue among colleagues or students who might otherwise feel disconnected from their peers.

Take a look at a few ways teachers have used colorful connections to visually assist and symbolize connections:

- Secondary science teachers build a collective learning wall to be used by all classes. Students attach sticky notes to selected artifacts, adding commentary and connections to further reinforce the importance of big concepts and ideas being explored.
- Elementary teaching duos individually build learning walls for the students they share while using colored index cards to illustrate connections across subject areas.
- Early years educators construct developmentally appropriate walls, using bright orange stars to highlight their learners' connections.

Regardless of whether these colorful connections are made during active teaching time or after students leave the space, they remind us of the power of constructing knowledge alongside our learners. Likewise, the practice orients us toward the interconnections and deeper learning opportunities we not only seek but also plan for.

3. How can you leave space for wonder?

Wonder walls are fantastic vessels that show that we value learner questions. However, as I mentioned earlier, they are only one note in the symphony of inquiry. That said, they can be a great start to planning with curiosity in mind. These tools help us balance our curriculum with student questions.

Mindfully adding artifacts that capture thinking and sorting ideas, we can revisit our learner questions to find alignment with our standards and attach their questions to the curriculum. With this practice, our students begin to see their questions as being directly tied to the learning narrative we are writing with one another. Each time we pull back the curtain and let them know that their questions have a voice in directing the learning, we build trust. Each time we step back and ask what new questions are emerging because of the learning, we build curiosity. And each time we remove or shift artifacts on our learning walls to create more physical space, we model thinking and build confident learners.

When you step into a classroom with an active and wonder-filled learning wall, the fingerprints of teachers and students are evident. Rich skill and competency development become clear when we see thinking routines that organize and synthesize ideas, sticky notes with students' handwriting that capture perspective-taking and diverse opinions, and evidence of student communication and collaboration. A well-designed space allows students to easily add artifacts and confidently step up to the wall and talk with peers about what they see.

Leaving space for wonder means recognizing the value of displaying all levels of knowledge—even misconceptions. This practice organically differentiates the ways our students may step into the learning. There's a sense of energy, wonder, and awe about where we may venture to next. Misconceptions can inspire our choice of provocations to provide a natural inclination toward curiosity, one of the skills of reflection. We too get curious about our learners' developing understanding and feel a sense of wonder as we view the evidence before us with curiosity and ask ourselves what we may be missing, where we might stay more open-minded, or how we might have to get off the path to reorient, find balance, and see the way more clearly.

4. How do you build capacity for personal meaning?

Personalized learning doesn't mean that we have twenty-three different worksheets or spend countless hours on the weekend curating resources touted by the latest social media trend. Personalized learning means establishing diverse structures and systems that support students as they self-assess and take ownership of their learning.

Learning walls help build capacity for personal meaning because they engage the learner, empowering their voice and choice through multiple entry points. Our students begin to see themselves in the learning and as essential contributors to the learning community. This may be a very different view from what previous schooling experiences have shown them.

We slowly build the capacity for students to find personal meaning through a collection of actions each time we step into the learning with one another. We may pause at the end of a lesson and ask our scholars what "work" might be important to take as evidence; we may call over cohorts of students to the learning wall and ask them to identify two things that are striking them so far with the learning; we may hand over the pen and a small stack of sticky notes and ask students to jot down their connections. We may even choose to mindfully add student names to each of the questions generated during a questioning protocol such as the Question Formulation Technique. Our scholars identify with the learning in a personal way because we *make it personal*.

5. What do you want your learners to retrieve?

The work of Jay McTighe and Grant Wiggins asks us to consider, "What's worth learning?" This question quiets the cacophony of standardized assessments, gives us a reason to pause to determine what we'll spend our time planning, and creates a space that allows us to be better attuned to the needs of our learners. When we determine what's worth learning, we're mindful about the artifacts we collect and the structures that house them. We carefully consider what best supports the different types of learners in our classrooms and the scope and sequence of skills they need to develop.

Asking what we want our learners to retrieve is a tenet of equitable evidencing that ensures clarity. It nudges us to plan for artifacts that help our students make generalizations, something that can't happen with a single example. It helps us see the bigger picture and plan for multiple entry points into the learning.

In Parts Two and Three of this book, you'll find many examples of learning walls, each displaying artifacts that are relevant and meaningful to the specific learning environment. They've been co-constructed by inquiry teachers and leaders who mindfully asked themselves reflective questions throughout the building process. As you pause to reflect on what you want your learners to retrieve, review these examples.

My hope is that these questions have stretched your thinking beyond facts and topics. The goal is to plan for learning opportunities that help your learners build understanding. To do that, you'll need to stay curious and be mindful of where your students and the learning are leading you.

As you build your learning wall and reflect on what's worth learning, here are a few more things to consider:

- What information is critical to the learning?
- What is the conceptual depth of the evidence revealed in your process?
- What's worth remembering?
- What might help your learners transfer understanding beyond this unit of inquiry?

- What do the connections tell you? What do they tell your learners?
- What student-generated examples or questions connect to the big ideas you are exploring?
- What graphic organizers or academic vocabulary are essential for understanding?

In addition to these powerful reflection prompts, take time to evaluate the evidence and notice patterns of thinking, potential misunderstandings, and other critical information that helps you create a plan of action. The artifacts and structures listed below can support the cognitive work that happens during retrieval:

- central idea or concept
- essential questions designed by the teacher
- learner questions generated during provocations or other questioning routines
- academic vocabulary written on sentence strips or index cards
- co-constructed anchor charts generated by both teachers and students

Planning, Designing, Revising, Growing

Effective learning walls don't just happen; they are carefully planned with these tenets in mind. Remember that these underpinnings aren't a formula, nor will they produce an outcome that is similar to any other. The examples and stories of learning represented in this book are expressive of the culture of learning and dialogue of thinking we continually strive for as inquiry leaders. They are meant to inspire you and provoke your thinking. They are meant to stretch you toward a deeper practice.

You will see evidence of these tenets in the many examples of learning walls you encounter in this book. Use the tenets, which are posed in the form of questions to spark curiosity, as you learn more about the nuanced ways these vertical learning spaces are constructed. Perhaps you have already noticed evidence of these principles in the learning walls you've made or other displays of learning in your space. Use the questions to take a reflective pause to consider what they reveal. Let's take our *own learning* off the page, shall we?

Below I've included a summary of the tenets in the form of a sketchnote. As you co-construct your own knowledge and personal understanding of learning walls, this sketch will be a guide I encourage you to return to. Print off a copy of this sketchnote and pin it up near your learning wall to help orient you toward these principles. Tuck one into your unit planner to encourage you to pause as you design your weekly lessons. Share it with your colleagues; use it during your next learning walk. My hope is that this sketchnote will be scribbled with your notes as you make personal meaning of these tenets. Let your connections guide you to experience all the ways these tenets come to life in inquiry spaces

Learning walks are essential in an organization whose aim is to nurture an environment where inquiry can thrive. The goal is not to evaluate individuals but to get a closer look at impactful teaching strategies being integrated into day-to-day routines, get firsthand experience of how values and vision are being executed, and encourage supportive collaborative conversations centered around pedagogy and teaching practices.

Want to learn more? Download this guide to Nurturing a Culture Inquiry with Learning Walks.

Tenets of
Equitable Evidencing

1-What's important to lift up in learning?

2-How do you build capacity for your students to make connections?

3-How can you leave space for wonder?

4-How do you build capacity for personal meaning?

5-What do you want your learners to retrieve?

Part 2

Building a Learning Wall

How did you do that?

Where do you start?

What do you do when there are too many artifacts?

How do you get your learners to use the wall?

Four questions. And only a fraction of the list I have collected during the past few years. These questions represent the dozens and dozens asked of me when I began to post about learning walls more frequently on social media. As I pulled back the curtain to show the process of documenting the campus-wide learning that was unfolding, I received direct messages from other educators and leaders around the world asking me to explain what I was building, how I determined what was important to add to this fluid space, and where to begin. Many educators who teach and lead within the International Baccalaureate (IB) reached out with piqued interest. They could see similarities to what's informally referred to as an *IB wall*. These educators wanted to know how to use this form of documentation in a way that rested more heavily in the hands of their learners.

The more questions I fielded, the more I was stretched to think about how I was using and facilitating learning through this vertical space. The more questions that were asked during workshops, the more I had to tune in to the creative and organically responsive process I easily fell into. The more one-on-one coaching I engaged in, the more I realized that just like the cycle that's commonly used to approach a design challenge, I too had followed a structure that ebbed and flowed with the cycle of inquiry learning.

These questions, along with the educators asking them, helped co-construct the framework for a sketchnote entitled "How to Build a Learning Wall." This illustration is a scaffolded structure that supports the process of building a learning wall. As a guide, it is flexible enough to allow for differentiation and meet the needs of any given context or type of learner. From whole-school implementation to small groups of educators diving deeper into their assessment practice to professional organizations outside of the educational landscape that are uniting teams of employees to work on department goals or projects, learning walls are for everyone because they are constructed with everyone in mind.

Let's take a closer look at the components necessary to build a learning wall. And just as questions guided the creation of this sketchnote, I'll leave you with several to ponder as we break down each section of the illustration.

Use the QR code to download the "How to Build a Learning Wall" sketchnote and keep this close as you are planning for artifacts, reflecting on structures and systems in your learning space, and making new meaning of this step-by-step process!

How to Build a Learning Wall

Find a Blank Space

Set an Intention

Retrieval

Are you teaching for the long term?

Co-Construct for Personal Meaning

Make Connections

Leave Space for Wonder

@jess_vanceedu #leadingwithinquiry

Chapter 3

Find a Blank Space

Your first task in building a learning wall is to find a blank space. Be creative with your thinking here! Perhaps you have a row of windows, a tired bulletin board that, begrudgingly, you haven't changed since the start of the school year, or a wall of storage cabinets that fade into the background. Or maybe it's a sheet of butcher paper pinned to a wall that turns a communal space, such as a library, mailroom, or conference room, into inspirational alcoves that document different learning journeys.

After visiting schools around the world and supporting inquiry teachers and leaders in building their learning walls over the past few years, I've seen a variety of traditional pin boards used as well as more creative and innovative spaces chosen to showcase the process of learning. There's not a perfect place to start building your learning wall. You simply need an awareness of where and how you'd like your learners to access their explorations on a vertical surface.

Here are a few ideas for blank spaces to get you started in your classroom, school building, or office!

- Teachers might collaborate and use the space between doorways in the halls.
- Primary teachers can use the space beneath the classroom whiteboard, which is at the perfect eye-level height for children in the early years.
- Grade levels or departments can use a common hallway bulletin board to collectively document student learning.
- Leaders might use the whiteboard in a principal's office or shared conference room in an office space.
- Foam boards or corkboards brought to an outdoor space such as a school garden or other community location can extend the learning beyond the four walls of the classroom.
- Butcher paper rolls can be stored in closets or large buckets and travel to different locations in an open-concept classroom.
- Classroom bulletin boards shared by dual-language programs can be learning walls that highlight academic vocabulary, wonderings, and skills developed across a unit.

I always prefer a physical space for making and keeping thinking visible, but sometimes our circumstances, shared spaces, or other limitations make a virtual space more feasible. The same creativity is required when determining which virtual space might best house the growth of thinking and unfolding of your learners' ideas over time. Consider what technology your learners have easy access to and what programs best suit their developmental needs. Think outside the box to extend the ways to mindfully make thinking visible.

Recognizing that the technology landscape is changing rapidly, I wanted to share a few apps and online platforms I've seen inquiry leaders and educators use for virtual learning walls. I'm sure you can add other creative applications to this list.

- Miro connects virtual learners across a semester as they gather artifacts and reflect on their learning weekly. Its open-ended space is ideal for older learners and has limitless ways of being reorganized and restructured. Take advantage of premade templates to focus attention or use shapes to confine artifacts into a central area.

- Padlet allows users to document research and learning in a timeline format so learners can see their growth from week to week. Try the Sandbox feature for Pages of Learning. It includes virtual renditions of tangible tools, such as sticky notes and drawing tools, that make it accessible to young learners on an iPad or interactive whiteboard.

- FigJam templates support the thinking and wonderings of several groups of students as they engage in book clubs or literature circles.

- The Freeform app is a fantastic choice for iPads or other Apple devices. Photos of physical evidence can be added to a virtual wall to enhance and encourage personal reflection and retrieval. This digital tool is also useful for brainstorming ideas and gathering research for a larger project.

- Google Slides can be used to collect learner questions, photos of co-constructed rubrics, evidence from classroom learning experiences, and links to big concepts and ideas. Slides can be added as the learning unfolds and rearranged as needed, and evidence can be cut and pasted across different slides as learners make connections and reflections.

Structuring Your Learning Wall

Determining how you will organize the thinking that your blank space—be it virtual or physical—will eventually showcase is another critical aspect of this step. Learning walls can be very structured or more open-ended collections of learning. Here are a few points to factor into this decision:

- your learners' current skills and those you want them to develop
- your personal teaching style
- the developmental age and capacity of your learners
- how you imagine your community will interact with this space
- available materials

Aside from those basics, consider the complexity you want to create and the type of thinking you want to lift up. You might choose to divide the space into the stages of the inquiry cycle or lean into a more playful, open-ended approach with no system other than an essential question. I find that experimenting with different types of structures is helpful. Each structure and strategy serves a different purpose as it works to ground the learning.

- Anchoring the space with a timeline can explicitly show the direction of learning.
- Using an already familiar graphic organizer, such as a spider-web or circle map, brings focus to the topic at hand.
- Color-coded symbols, icons, or sentence strips can create a sense of meaning in the organic messiness of learning and allow the eye to dance across the space.

From timelines to inquiry cycles to more free-form arrangements, I've used versions of each of these structures. The intentionality with which you use this blank space as a form of documentation is what makes it effective as a learning wall.

When I started experimenting with learning walls several years ago, I found the structure of the inquiry cycle helpful in organizing my thinking and planning for learning. A few weeks into our unit of inquiry, however, this space wasn't getting the traction that I had planned for. Rather than empowering my teaching practice, the sections of the cycle felt limiting. I got hung up on whether an artifact was in the *right* place. I was committed to this new approach to using space as a third teacher, but instead of sticking with the structure, I decided to explore what it might feel like to use something a bit more open ended. I pulled off the few artifacts I had tacked on the bulletin board and started with a blank space anchored only by the unit's central idea. The refreshed display was just what I needed to lean into a playful mindset where I felt more comfortable moving artifacts around. Pausing regularly to reflect on the evidence as I planned for the next week's lessons, I settled into a space that nudged me toward designing learning with a more intentional focus on skill development.

In sharing my practice, my goal is not to encourage you to completely abandon a structure or protocol that isn't working for you; in fact, that story is meant to illustrate the opposite. Inquiry is a responsive teaching practice. We try things on for size and notice how our learners respond. We consider the barriers and the impact of each of our moves as an action toward the development of a more capable person.

Inquiry is a responsive teaching practice.

We *listen* for curiosity.

We *observe* opportunities for skill development.

We *take action* with an equanimity or an opening toward something that better fits both the individual and learning community as a whole.

Sometimes, a clearer intention, a critical friend's reflective questions, or learner feedback can reveal perspectives we might have missed that lead us to structures that better suit the learning. Trevor MacKenzie, co-author of *Inquiry Mindset: Elementary Edition*, reminds us that inquiry teachers "step outside to come back in" to gain fresh insight and inspired action. I'm a big fan of visiting colleagues' classrooms to see how they might be approaching their learning spaces differently. Sometimes that's simply by scrolling other educators' posts on social media for inspiration. I encourage you to do the same as you find your blank space and determine the kind of structure you want to use for your learning wall.

Want some additional inspiration? Or do you want to share how you have been making and keeping thinking visible in your classroom? Jump on social media and use #learningwalls to join in the global conversation. Take screenshots and bookmark posts to revisit later. Don't forget to add to your own feed so others can learn and be inspired by your work too!

The rest of this chapter explores a variety of structures crafted by inquiry educators and leaders. Notice the differences, contemplate, and compare these with your learning wall. You might choose to replicate them in your classroom or take elements of a few of the structures and make something that uniquely fits your needs. Either way, with these ideas and your own creativity, I'm sure you'll find a structure to implement right away.

Structure: Central Idea or Concept

When working with curriculum planning or backward design, a central idea or overarching concept is a fantastic structure with which to start. Learning walls following this structure provide a clear focus while remaining open ended enough to mold to the direction of learning. Concept learning walls nudge learners to look at evidence with sharp attentiveness and invite multiple perspectives as they converse around connections across a broader concept.

Source: Amy Osborn, First Grade Teacher, Spicewood Elementary, Austin, Texas

There is not one *right way* to design this learning wall; however, the central idea should be clear and well defined for the learning community. Simple questions such as *How might this artifact connect to our overarching concept?* or *What do we now know about the central idea of our unit?* invite discussion. Ideas sparked from these questions can be used to create a mind map and give students opportunities to stack their learning experiences to create deeper conceptual knowledge.

Creativity, open-ended thinking, and perspective taking thrive when collective thinking is documented and grounded in a conceptual model. Personally, I appreciate the free form of the concept structure and love that it helps inquiry educators stay focused on the central idea while planning, teaching, and reflecting on the learning.

Structure: Virtual Learning Wall

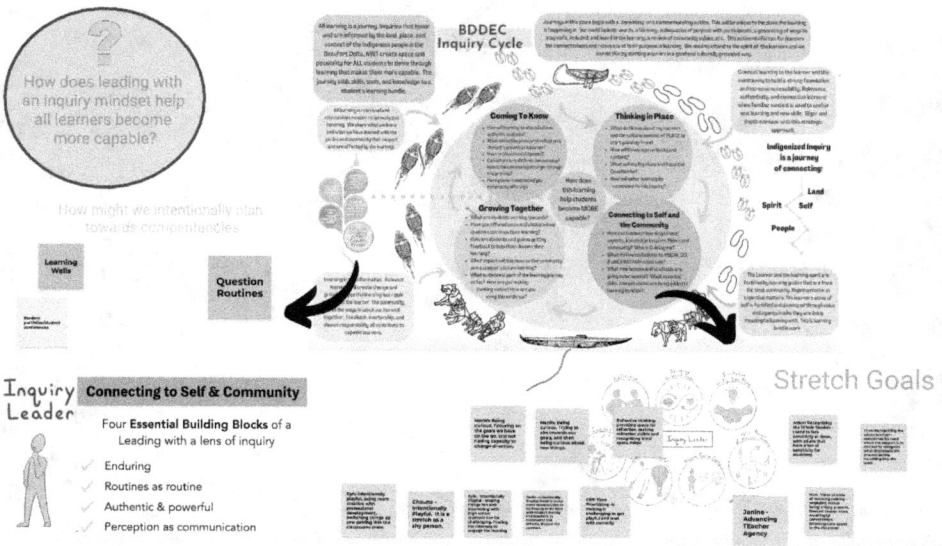

If you are short on wall space, your learners don't physically gather in the same location, or you share a teaching space with other groups, a virtual learning wall can be just as powerful as a physical one. Digital tools such as Padlet, Miro, or Google Slides capture authentic evidence of learning, providing a flexible alternative. Because virtual learning walls are not always visible in the physical space, it's necessary to create routines—keeping tabs open, building them into your lesson design, and employing consistent systems—to fully unlock their potential.

As with any virtual platform, it's essential to give yourself and your learners time to play with this digital tool. Consider how you will invite students to add artifacts and create opportunities for them to use evidence on this wall to directly support their reflections and new learning—and don't shy away from the undo button! As you explore different platforms and digital tools, be playful with the types of evidence you add to your learning wall. Grab screenshots of PowerPoint slides, use sticky notes features, add links to online resources and books, set up color-coded systems, and organize ideas with icons. The tenets of building a learning wall apply equally to these virtual spaces.

In Part Three of this book, you'll take a closer look at two different virtual learning walls and how they have empowered their learning communities. I encourage you to notice their process, choice of platform, purpose, and structure. I have learned so much from watching these learning walls evolve, and I am confident you will too!

Structure: Timeline

Timelines naturally encourage forward momentum because they highlight the process of learning and how thinking changes over time. This structure is a great choice if you are creating documentation in a shared space, such as a hallway, or if you are unsure about how to organize artifacts and documentation of learning. It's especially helpful for educators who are new to the practice of *artifacting* and evidencing with learning walls, who want to encourage collaboration and conversations amongst learners, or who teach several sections of the same subject.

As a school leader, I use a timeline to track schoolwide goals over large spans of time. Sometimes I'll start a learning wall with this structure as a means to sort thinking and help me identify cause-and-effect patterns. It is an easy one to get started with!

Structure: Essential Question(s)

Source: Lindsey Hofheins, Early Years, Laurel Mountain Elementary, Austin, Texas

As inquiry educators, we collect tons of questions, so I love using an essential question as the foundation of a learning wall! Learning walls structured on essential questions root us in wonder and curiosity. At the same time, the question(s) provide focus and help us stay clear on our purpose.

To find a worthy question, simply open your curriculum's scope and sequence and choose a question that lifts up wonders already generated from your learners during provocation or independent reflection (or a few that align conceptually). Or reflect on last year's unit plans for reminders of questions that were worth exploring.

The early year learning wall picture here uses an essential question as its starting point in a numbered sequence that shows how the learning story unfolds. Later in this book, you'll see other learning walls that use an essential question structure. As you look at these other walls, notice the placement of the question(s), examine the curation of artifacts, and ask what this might look like in your context.

Structure: Inquiry Cycle

Source: Amy Ing, Grade 5 Teacher, East Three Elementary, Inuvik, NWT, Canada

Not surprisingly, an inquiry cycle based on the work and research of Kath Murdoch (*Getting Personal with Inquiry Learning*, 2022) is a popular structure used in many schools and classrooms that embrace a mindset of inquiry. It's the same structure inquiry educators use when planning and reflecting on units, so we are accustomed to its flow and purpose. Through mindful practice, and having already embraced the language of each of the stages of inquiry, it is simple to introduce this structure and its purpose to scholars. The learning wall shown here reflects the cycle in its circular form. Pushpins and sticky notes are used to attach ideas to graphic organizers, student worksheets, essential questions, photos, and big ideas, making it easy to move notes to different locations on the wall to reflect new learning and connections.

If you choose to structure your wall using the inquiry cycle, I encourage you to think outside the box (or circle in this example). The labels for each of the stages of the cycle can take on any shape, really! An alternative to a circle could be a linear structure with horizontal columns that provide enough space to add evidence and artifacts of learning. Or consider organically clustering artifacts first, then adding labels of the cycle to help anchor what's visible.

Inquiry educators have used the inquiry cycle in so many creative ways. Jump on social media for inspiration. I'm confident you'll find many that you can make work in your own unique context or space. Don't forget to share yours with our professional learning network too: #learningwalls!

I've outlined five structures to prompt your thinking, but there are many other ways to organize these learning spaces. As your context and learners evolve, your blank spaces should too! Remaining playful and open is essential when planning, teaching, and learning with an inquiry mindset. If a structure is not working for you or your learners, don't be afraid to make changes, reorganize, or even remove artifacts. Get feedback from your learners and make notes about what you might do differently next time.

 Need another nudge or critical friend in helping you find and reflect on your blank space? Take a look at this chat with Anne van Dam, hosted by Becky Carlzon and Learning Pioneers.

Pause and Reflect

The reflection questions below have helped me plan—and revise—countless learning walls in a variety of spaces. Use them to help you approach this process with curiosity and wonder. In the coming weeks, pay attention to the different structures of the learning walls you see, not just in the pages that follow but also in your school and in photos posted by colleagues online. Refer to the notes you've jotted down in the margins of this chapter and your answers to the questions below to determine which structures might work best for you and your learners:

* How will your learners access and use the learning wall?

* How permanent will this space need to be?

* How might you rethink the usage of some of the walls in your space?

* What tech tools are your learners already familiar with? How might you leverage and build skills using these tools?

* How might you get feedback from your learners as you begin designing this virtual or in-person space?

* What structure best supports the structure you are considering for your learning wall (timeline, freeform, web, etc.)?

Chapter 4

Set an Intention

Rules can be guidelines for awakened action.
—Michael Stone

Teaching, leading, and learning with an inquiry mindset requires us to be present, mindful, and fully engaged. It necessitates that we regularly pause and reflect on our practice with a willingness to ask questions that begin with *why* before those that start with *how*. We must be clear about the purpose of our lessons and provocations, just as we must be aware of why we're asking our learners to share their wonderings.

Each decision creates a ripple effect. Understanding this reality, inquiry educators commonly engage in the practice of setting intentions. What's interesting is that neuroscience reveals the habit of setting intentions for ourselves changes the structure of the brain, allowing us to focus while remaining detached from a specific outcome. This unattachment to a goal allows us to attend to the moments that fill our day differently. We begin to hear our learners' questions with curiosity; we are able to slow down in the cycle of learning yet seem to accomplish more. Less concerned with failure, we are free to focus on the direction we've mapped out without having to know the specific details of every future step. Our focus on intention also brings a keen awareness to the impact language has on our mindset and well-being.

 Create a moment to set intention for yourself. Download this resource for helpful sentence stems, playful language, and structures that remind you to make this a weekly habit.

Set an Intention for the Learning Wall

The practice of setting intentions for ourselves is not dissimilar to the mindfulness we bring to setting intentions for our learning spaces, and it begins with knowing what we want to lift up in the learning and why. Having that clarity of focus frees us to ask other questions:

How long will the learning narrative be?

What different timelines will be necessary to support the various learning journeys we engage in across the academic year?

What competencies do we want learners to develop? How can we encourage them to be more mindful of these concepts across a semester?

The focus of the learning may be a broad concept that unites standards over a handful of weeks, a multi-year plan for a series of district goals to drive campus improvement, a project to scaffold skills needed for the final outcome, or essential vocabulary or phonological awareness that supports beginning readers in their journey toward making meaning of sounds and words.

No matter the intention, *it's intentional.*

I've seen learning walls come and go within a two-week window and others stay up for months. I've seen intentions for learning walls change once the learning got going. I've even seen some displays of learning removed entirely when the teacher noticed the scholars were not using the learning wall to support their process of meaning-making in the way they had originally planned. We name these spaces *learning walls* to call attention to a skill, question, or bigger idea worth exploring. Whether designed for a long- or short-term unit or to be temporary or permanent, learning walls, like all other inquiry moves, require us to maintain a habit of awareness regarding their effectiveness and the impact our actions have on the intended learning.

I often get asked what the best way is to determine what's worth documenting on a learning wall. Honestly, there's much overthinking about the *perfect* question or concept, and the uncertainty about what's *right* goes along with this question. My reply is quick and simple:

Reflect on what your learners need the most support in.

or

Identify your current unit of inquiry.

Begin from there. In the examples included in Part Three, you'll see a variety of intentions for building learning walls. For now, consider using one of the following intentions to help you get started:

- **overarching essential question** pulled from your curriculum or generated by your students
- transdisciplinary **theme** or **central idea** from an IB unit of inquiry
- campus-wide **professional learning** that spans an academic school year
- **concepts** identified at the center of your units of inquiry, such as organization, systems, identity, community, perspective, change, or patterns
- **skill** and **competency development** such as research, goal setting, reflection, collaboration, research, self-assessment, or communication

Intention: Perspective and Collaboration

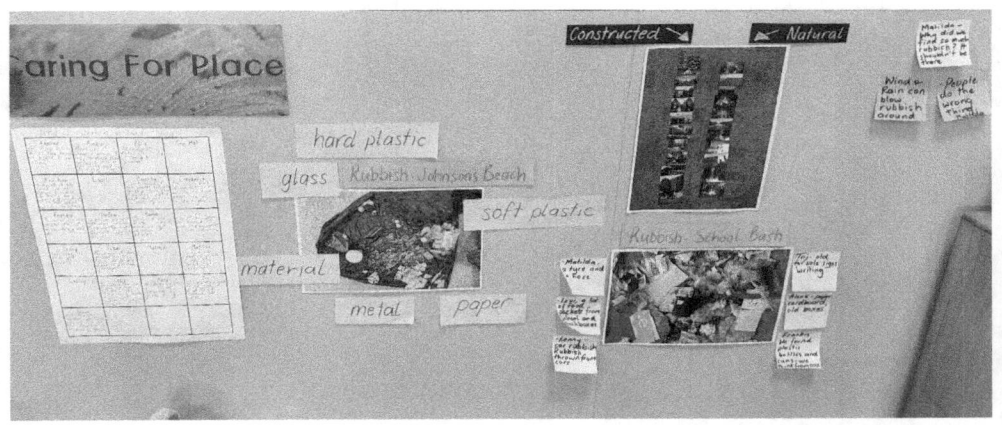

Intention: Connection with Places in Local Community

Intention: Research Skills

Intention: Concept of Circles

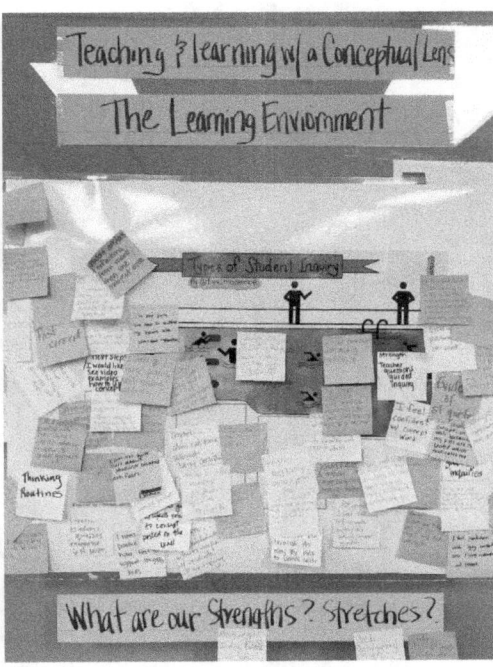

Intention: Building the Skill of Reflection and Nurturing a School-Wide Culture of Feedback

Intention: Connection, Curiosity, and Retrieval of Content and Skills

Use the questions that follow to set an intention for your learning wall, the focus, and what documentation it should include:

- Who is the learning wall for?
- What is important to lift up in learning?
- What skills would your scholars benefit from most?
- How long is the learning journey?
- Are there ways to get feedback or input from your learners to help you determine what's best?
- How might this documentation differ from more traditional displays of learning you have done in the past?

Set an Intention for Your Learners— and Yourself

It's as important to be clear about your intention for the focus of your learning wall as it is to have a plan for introducing your learners to this visual resource. A learning wall can quickly become just another Pinterest-worthy display if learners aren't an active part of the process of constructing it.

Once you've set your intention, the next step is to introduce your learners to the space. Share the essential question with them. Explain the structure of this collaborative space where, together, you'll take the thinking and learning off the page and make it visible. Let your learners know that *their* thinking, *their* wonderings, *their* evidence, and *their* needs will shape how this resource evolves. And then prove it by starting to use the learning wall *right away*.

Invite your learners to congregate around the wall and take a closer look at the questions you're using to kick off the day—questions they've generated previously. Grab evidence from a provocation or the chart paper that documented a reflective conversation, and add it to the learning wall. If you posted evidence to the wall while your scholars were away, point it out and allow for the time and discussions to make connections to the ideas you are exploring together. Be authentic but keep a playful mindset as you think of the ways that you use the wall. Think outside the box by asking yourself, *I wonder what would happen if . . . ?* and make a quick list of different ways you might get started with a wall. Here are a few ideas to get you started!

- Motivate your youngest learners by having them track and gather new words, vocabulary, or other foundational reading skills.
- Connect subject departments and other teams of teachers around professional goals.
- Enhance a self-study or other evaluation system with a learning wall demonstrating how standards and frameworks have come to life for your campus.
- Support the growth and development of grade-level leads and other inquiry leaders by documenting impactful skills such as listening, having crucial conversations, and collaboration.

Thinking about how you'll use this resource to support your teaching in the classroom is just as essential as considering the ways you will invite your learners to interact with this space. Here are examples of encouraging language that brings this routine into your practice:

> Until this practice becomes a habit, you may need to include reminders in your daily lesson plans. You might, for example, put a prompt in your slide deck to nudge you to pause mid-lesson and add thinking to the learning wall. Or gather weekly with your teaching team in front of a collaborative wall to ensure mindful planning and focus.

- Let's take your thinking off the page and add it to our learning wall.
- Help me gather artifacts.
- Can you help me add some documentation to our inquiry cycle?

- Is this evidence that we might want to remember later?
- What do you notice? What does this make you wonder now?
- Pause and reflect with your partner and share what's standing out to you.
- I'm curious: what have you noticed about our learning lately?
- Where do you see our learning story going next?

Encouraging students to interact with the learning wall is important regardless of their age, but it becomes even more critical with those in upper grades. Setting an intention for, introducing, and modeling its use is an action you may need to repeat multiple times with older learners, who likely have experienced education void of agency. Many have become complacent and developed transactional habits of learning. They tend to be deficient in skills required for taking ownership of their learning. When asked to use a structure that requires them to do more of the heavy lifting of learning, their initial response may be disengagement, disinterest, and incompetence. I've observed this to be the unfortunate case in many classroom cultures. Blame for this reality is easily placed on technology and social media trends or the common complaint that "these kids are different." It is because of these very challenges, however, that the intentionality of learning walls causes seismic shifts in the foundation of learning cultures.

No matter how old your learners are, the process is the same: Introduce, frequently model, revisit, revise, and wrap your teaching around purposeful collections of evidence and artifacts of learning. These intentional actions are the intentional ways we model the value of learning walls and show our scholars how they enhance and support their learning. I've observed success and seen sizable shifts in classroom cultures in both primary and secondary spaces when teachers commit to the following actions within their practice. I've included examples for each.

Task your learners with assignments that bring them to the wall.

Routinely incorporating the learning wall into your classroom work solidifies its importance.

- Ask groups or pairs of students to generate questions from a selection of text and add them to the wall to drive inquiry.
- Call on learners to jot down academic vocabulary or other important language on notecards and pin them to a tiered vocabulary learning wall.
- Have students post their math strategies to the T-chart you've been co-constructing as a class.

Physically point to artifacts tacked to the wall.

Research tells us that gestures are almost like a second language, adding information that might be absent from our words. The visual impact of pointing to and physically interacting with the wall invites learners to move toward taking action and thinking more deeply. This mindfully powerful move can be used with the whole class in one-on-one interactions:

- Engage with the artifacts during class conversations or while reflecting on connections.
- Point to and post artifacts while facilitating a direct instruction lesson.
- When you're working one-on-one with students, consider calling them to the wall to guide them toward resources to help them complete an independent assignment.
- Pull up a pair of desks to the wall and take a seat beside your scholar directly in front of artifacts to help them focus on the task at hand.

Notice the impact of proximity. How might you leverage gestures and movement to best meet the diverse needs of your students?

Make connections.

Demonstrate the value of the artifacts by talking about how they support the development of thinking and learning.

- Call on students to help you identify evidence on the learning wall as they share connections of meaning-making.
- Before students start a project or longer assignment, draw their attention to the success criteria you co-constructed to establish a sense of confidence and remind them of the scaffolded action.
- Revisit the essential agreements outlined at the start of the term and connect them to a session on goal setting. Help students retrieve ideas and knowledge by having them pause to review organized evidence before drawing new conclusions and connections.

Act with Intention

Now that you are clearer on your intentions for your learning wall, I encourage you to revisit the examples I've included from other educators in this section. Notice the structures that anchor their walls, and note which you would like to put into practice. Remember: There's not one right way, and later in this book you'll see even more examples.

Being intentional in both your approach and reflection will maximize the impact of your plans for learning. As you set an intention for the focus and structure of your learning wall, consider how it will function.

* How do you already use documentation with your learners? What differences can you identify between what's been proposed here and your current practice? What's one small shift you can take right away?

* How might you use the tenets of a learning wall to help you set an intention for this vertical space? Which of those could give you the start you need?

* What motivates your learners? How can you leverage this motivation to help you intentionally plan for usage?

* What structure (timeline, split screen, free-form, inquiry cycle, etc.) best supports the intention you've set for the learning narrative? How can this structure best support how you and your learners interact with this space?

* How do you intend to capture learning in your classroom as it's unfolding?

Chapter 5

Retrieval (Part I)
What's Worth Knowing?

Between the scripted curriculum maps we need to get through before the week's end and the pressures of assessments and deadlines, our daily and weekly lesson plans rapidly fill with a long list of things to do. Weighed down by standards and mandates and confined by schedules dictated by others, at times, agency and *extra* time both seem nonexistent. Creating checks for understanding for our scholars would be nice, but who has time?

These systems. These structures. These patterns. These habits of mind keep us stuck. We take one step forward—and many more backward in frustration. We see students who are disengaged, educators leaving the profession in droves, and an imbalance in the curriculum between content and skills.

With the constant input of our modern world, how do we slow down enough to catch our breath and ensure that the time we spend planning learning experiences is truly beneficial for all of our scholars? How can we be sure that all the effort and time we invest in the classroom have the impact we hope? How do we give ourselves space to pause and determine what's truly worth learning amidst the ever-changing list of standards?

We cut through that cacophony of demanding deadlines, shifting curricula, and looming assessments to find the answers to the challenge of supporting our scholars by asking the simple question: ***What do we want our learners to retrieve and be able to take with them in the long term?***

Whether I am sorting through student-generated questions after a powerful provocation, reflecting with a school leader about a professional development plan, or huddled around a conference table with a team of teachers designing a unit of inquiry, I always return to this question to stay grounded in purpose, intentionality, and focus. Though simple, it causes me to pause and reflect, and at the same time, guides my forward action.

When co-constructing learning walls, this question guides decisions about the evidence we collect and what artifacts best document thinking. Knowing what we want our learners to be able to retrieve points us to the connections and interactions our scholars need to have with this vertical space. In Chapter Two, I introduced this question as one of the five tenets of equitable evidencing and provided a few suggestions for questions and artifacts to guide your thinking. (See page 40.) In the pages that follow, we'll use this question to explore *how* we can transform passive learning into a dynamic, collective process that nurtures critical skills and promotes deeply connected learning while reinforcing the inquiry cycle.

Everything Can't Be Most Important

When my skills with learning walls were novice at best, the corkboard space I claimed was overloaded: laminated sentence strips, *every* essential element of the PYP for the current unit of inquiry, Sharing the Planet, a bare KWHLAQ template I had been meaning to use, and a generous but untouched collection of student wonderings gathered weekly earlier after the unit's provocation. Next to this display was a large whiteboard where I projected videos and other digital teaching resources, a short list of questions outlining learning intentions for the day, and the scribbling of scholar handwriting. The remaining walls were plastered with anchor charts, made with a feeble attempt at co-construction but heavily influenced by my choice of cutesy fonts and the perfect title written with my favorite marker, Mr. Sketch.

In those early days, I assumed that *everything* worth knowing needed to be visible at all times. I didn't question whether there was a better way to display the learning targets required by the district. Nor did I think twice about how packed my IB board was with *my* handwriting, *stagnant* anchor charts, and *perfected* headings—or that my learners didn't take a second glance at all those careful details, despite the hours I'd put into them. Riddled with misconceptions and influenced by the classrooms I had spent countless hours in as a student, the way I displayed the learning was doing *everything but* lifting up what mattered most.

As you reflect on what's worth knowing, I want to equip you with two additional tools to support your planning process: *provocations* and *edit to retrieve*. Using them will help you build routines and habits that simplify planning and invite reflection. The wealth of resources, depth of research from experts in the field, and mental models ahead are sure to inspire and influence your approach!

Provocations

Every inquiry educator's practice includes a variety of provocations. Some are thoughtfully designed before a unit of inquiry begins. Ideas for others surface in response to learners' questions and misunderstandings, or simply to stretch their thinking.

Provocations are an essential inquiry move. The research and work of Jay McTighe and Grant Wiggins reminds us that deeper learning occurs when the brain is able to find patterns and make meaningful connections that bridge and transfer knowledge. Provocations (which act like conceptual Velcro) are from the *anticipatory set* in a traditional seven-step lesson plan or the *engage* stage of the 5E Model. Provocations root the learning in curiosity and invite scholars to a collaborative learning space in a connected way that differs from other learning structures. The longer shelf life of provocations allows us to plan toward possible misconceptions that provide a natural way of inciting wonder while maintaining a lens that allows scholars to see big ideas as they develop necessary skills.

 How do we move toward deeper learning? This short article co-authored by Jay McTighe and Harvey Silver highlights two essential instructional shifts of big ideas and making meaning to pave the way.

The novice learning wall I described earlier was full of "all the things," which had muddied any intention toward function and purpose. Since that time, my approach to planning provocations and the artifacts that support retrieval have shifted dramatically. Now, when I review the curriculum to plan next steps in the learning or pull up a chair to reflect on the artifacts on our learning wall, I ask, *How can this make the learning sticky?* This reflective question guides me back to my intention for the learning. As long as I am clearly grounded in the larger concepts and transferable skills within my scope and sequence (both underpinning principles of Wiggins and McTighe's *Understanding by Design*), this simple question helps quiet the noise of that impossibly long list of things to know, do, and assess. It moves my practice toward more meaningful and curious learning.

Whether it's a provocation carousel with a series of eye-catching photos, an excursion to a local nature preserve, or an open-ended question such as *What is a community?*, we design provocations with intention. We consider the experience, evidence, and larger purpose behind each one. By weaving big ideas across the curriculum, we can teach toward the long term and focus on what's worth knowing *and* understanding rather than a string of unrelated facts and information that learners struggle to attach to prior knowledge.

I love a well-planned provocation carousel and find countless ways to differentiate this to meet the needs of any learning context! A provocation carousel is a curated series of photos or gifs intentionally placed on a slide deck in a scaffolded order. The carousel can be facilitated with the whole group or shared with students so they can collaborate on it with one another. "Ask this photo a question," or "What does this image make you wonder?" are simple prompts that get your learners talking about and sharing their thinking.

I am also a big fan of thinking routines, such as See, Think, Wonder or Looking: Ten Times Two, to structure group discussions and class conversations. If you are not familiar with these routines, I encourage you to visit Project Zero's website for a step by step guide!

Editing to Retrieve

The artifacts we collect from provocations and display on our learning walls also support the retrieval process. Editing to retrieve helps us gain clarity about what's needed to support our scholars. It is also quite helpful in editing a learning wall. This step is a habit we establish to ensure we enter the learning space with curious confidence about what's most important to lift up. When you are sifting through student evidence or are taking a quiet moment to reflect on the day's learning, the following questions can guide your thinking and the process of editing for retrieval. As you work through them, you may decide to remove or replace items—or keep the artifacts just as they are. Use the questions to build this habit or for the next time your learning wall feels overwhelming. As with any habit, repetition and time will make this practice a natural pattern. Until then, mark this page or jot some questions on sticky notes for easy access.

- What does this artifact say about the learning?
- Where are we now in the learning? Is this relevant to all learners?
- What evidence do I have that supports this assumption or claim about the learning?

- What's worth lifting up? What supports teaching toward the long term?

The table below outlines some ways we plan and reflect with retrieval in mind. There are many ways to use the evidence we collect to revisit the first steps in learning. The examples shared with you below are just some ideas to get you started, and you'll see more in action in Part Three of this book. Review these examples with your mind open to what they could look like and how they might work with your community of learners.

Evidence	Purpose
Questions generated from learners	Pin next to select artifacts to model the purpose of asking questions as a means to drive learning.
What? So What? Now What? thinking routine	Thinking routine used as a structure to facilitate low-stakes retrieval for scholars. Once placed on the wall, teacher connects some ideas shared to other artifacts with string.
Chart paper displaying a T-chart that shows a sorting of student thinking about *wants vs. needs.*	Throughout the unit of inquiry, the teacher directs scholar attention to T-chart as new learning is uncovered. Students move and add sticky notes as appropriate.
Graphic organizer displaying student prior knowledge and wonderings gathered before a field trip	Intention and purpose for the field trip was clearly defined. Graphic organizer used as an artifact to support reflection after excursion.
Looking: Ten Times Two thinking routine next to a small collection of photographs	Academic and nonacademic language generated during the routine used as a pre-assessment.

After reading the examples above, I encourage you to thumb through the other pages of this book and take a closer look at the artifacts displayed on the different learning walls I've shared with you. Zoom in. Pause and reflect on how an artifact might support a big idea or central concept. How does the displayed evidence support and make the learning sticky? Mark pages, circle, or highlight examples you want revisit. Jot down your thoughts as you construct your knowledge and understanding about building a learning wall that supports retrieval and deepens learning with your scholars.

> **Tip!** While an artifact might strike the interest of one group of learners and support their process of retrieval, the same artifact, from year to year, might connect differently. Be sure to take note of learner responses and be willing to rethink and revise your approach.

Purpose in Equity

I was at the end of a two-year professional learning journey facilitated by The Holdsworth Center, an organization committed to fostering changes within the educational system across the state by supporting and developing educational leaders. Throughout those two years, the program tasked us (the participants) with taking a critical and curious look at ourselves as leaders diving deeper into our practice of empowering campus staff through a shared leadership stance. As a cohort, we spent endless hours developing and applying the skills necessary to create and maintain change within ourselves as school leaders. We were tasked to identify a "Problem of Practice" that pushed us to see familiar challenges from different perspectives. Through honest and vulnerable reflection, we considered how small actions and decisions we made as leaders could contribute to meaningful, systemic change.

The experience changed me as a leader. What I learned drove me toward innovative and collaborative decisions at the campus where I served in a formal leadership role. It also better equipped me to write

Leading with a Lens of Inquiry. I learned different ways to communicate and engage school community with a collective vision. We practiced a variety of equitable talk structures and reflective protocols. I also experienced an extended inquiry alongside my colleagues that truly put us in a learners' mindset, navigating mistakes, missteps, and uncertainty as we deepened our understanding around barriers that impacted our most vulnerable students. After all that learning, it came as no surprise that, even amongst the summative and celebratory atmosphere, I learned something new: *the Doorway Effect.*

Learning about the research and study of human memory from the University of Notre Dame, we were asked to, one final time, reflect on our experiences over the past few years. It was impossible to ignore the connection between the study that the professor referenced and equity through the lens of retrieval. Pausing, I couldn't help but think about the stones we had overturned that lifted up blind spots in our practice as leaders: 1) how to use feedback protocols to ensure equitable contribution by all team members; 2) how to use the structures and systems of documentation of learning in which The Holdsworth Center had asked us to actively engage; and 3) how those habits and tools had opened us up to new perspectives and stances of knowing.

At the same time, I couldn't help but make broader connections to the teaching and learning happening on campus with our students. I thought about the things we put on our walls and how they support our learners. I considered the many transitions our students are exposed to in a given day and what impact those transitions have on the way students experience school, and how the science and research on how the brain functions impacts how we plan for the diverse needs of the learners we support. And it made me think about my own biases and misconceptions and forced me to ask whether I was doing enough to support and nurture a culture in which excellent and equitable outcomes for each student occurred.

The Doorway Effect

The Doorway Effect is a natural event that occurs in the brain and functions to support memory. This event model suggests that as we exit and enter different rooms, our brain gets signaled to purge information to make space for the new data that it's about to receive. When we are focused on a task and get interrupted by a message on our phone or walk into room only to forget why we are there, we are experiencing the impact of this system of memory. Simply put, our brains are continually sorting, moving, and retrieving information to make connections that establish meaning and understanding for what we are experiencing in the moment. The brain naturally assumes that what is in front of us is more relevant than what we experienced even a moment earlier.

Now, bring one of your students to mind. Mentally walk with that student through their day. From the front door of their home to the main entrance of your school building, across thresholds of classrooms and corridors, how many doors do they enter and exit? That number is a fraction of the number of times their memory system is put to the test as they are asked to retrieve critical information to build on new ideas or recall facts for both formative and summative assessment purposes. How does the way our school days are designed put unnecessary barriers in place for our students? How does retrieval ensure that we are reaching and supporting all students? In what ways might knowing about the retrieval process give us all a greater purpose toward creating spaces and learning opportunities that allow for greater equitable access to learning in the classroom? When we plan and teach with retrieval in mind, we achieve equitable learning environments that are balanced, invite the learner, and most importantly, usher in connection.

With students constantly in and out of our classrooms for personal or health reasons, support services, or intervention groups receiving the most intensive support, the process of planning for and keeping up with all of their varied needs can feel frustrating, even impossible, to manage on our own. The practice of having an active learning wall *and* planning for retrieval means we don't have to do it all alone. We rely on and trust the wisdom in the room to collaborate and make connections to level the playing field of learning while lifting up what's most important. We leverage and lean into this knowledge in several ways. The examples that follow are reminders that we don't have to be the sole facilitators of learning. I encourage you to be playful and open minded with your thinking as you integrate these habits into your practice.

Student to Student

Structures that allow space for students to do the heavy lifting are essential to any inquiry classroom. It's common for elementary educators to give their students jobs each week to ensure that the classroom stays tidy. In the same way, I love to task students with the role of inviting their peers back to the learning. When we view students as a vital asset to telling the stories of learning, we can purposefully time moments of sharing to work within the constraints of schedules.

Whether you assign a formal title for this role, such as "Storyteller of the Week," or simply task students with this job as you see fit throughout your lessons, look for ways to fit this routine into your daily schedule and lesson plan. Where are opportunities for students to interact, add, edit, and use this co-constructed space? How might you leverage a collaborative structure that's deeply embedded in your practice by asking pairs of students to use the wall to support their collective conversations?

When we plan and create opportunities for how our learners will use the learning wall as a tool, our students begin to experience scaffolded independence. The simple act of planning time for students to engage with the learning wall is the first step. The examples that follow offer prompts for retrieval that invite students to interact and collaborate. Consider adapting these invitations for your purposes as you plan for learning:

- Identify an artifact on our learning wall that helps you share your thinking with your group. As you listen to your peers share, use a question to help them explain in more detail.
- Pull up a chair to the learning wall and share a connection you are making so far in our learning.
- Before getting started, take a tour of our learning wall and discuss what's standing out to you now.
- What's one question you might ask about our learning?
- After a student has been absent, call on another student to be the "Tour Guide" of learning. Ask the "Tour Guide" to highlight one thing on the learning wall and ask the student returning to class to make a connection with the evidence of learning that they are seeing and what they already know.

Educational Assistants

Educational assistants play a crucial role in our learning settings. Their flexible positions allow teachers to differentiate and deliver lessons. Students can access material through additional scaffolds and other prompts while the learning community comes together, emphasizing the importance of collaboration and collective thinking. More often than not, however, the role of these educational assistants requires them to shift between a variety of teaching styles or classroom environments at a moment's notice. They may be asked to flex and attune to the varied needs of learners and personalities of homeroom teachers, and they have a caseload that may change from one day to the next.

The challenges noted above are real, and yet they don't have to limit what we are able to achieve when we use structures and routines to keep everyone up to speed on the learning. Time might always be a limiting factor in education, and even more so with the relationship between teachers and educational assistants, but a few powerful habits can have a positive impact on the overall classroom culture by bringing clarity and purpose to the roles of everyone who enters and exits the learning space.

Habit #1: Educational assistants stop to pause and retrieve first.

With the many transitions required for the role of educational assistant, it's critical to create routines that allow them to take stock of the space and the learners who compose it. While this moment of pause is brief and doesn't require overthinking, it's a time to ask, *Who are the learners in the room?* and *How are the learners responding to the learning so far?* This is the time for the educational assistant to take note of the learning wall and how it might have changed since they were last in the room. Reflecting on the vertical space, they can quickly refresh their memory of the learning has been occurring and bring to mind what they know about the topics and concepts being explored.

Habit #2: Educational assistants use artifacts and documentation as a provocation for retrieval.

It is the responsibility of the classroom teacher to model strategies, point out supportive artifacts, and ensure equitable access and contribution to the learning. Educational assistants skillfully observe these actions, listening for language and mimicking moves that drive the learner to retrieve essential knowledge and skills. Because of the fluidity of the role, they are not always present for the direct instruction of the lesson, which means they must leverage documentation and artifacts attached to learning walls. As they work with groups of students, educational assistants can task learners to gather select artifacts from the learning wall to support the table's discussion. They may choose to pull up a few chairs to the vertical space to anchor a reflection between pairs of students. Or they may simply point to academic vocabulary cards or a collection of sticky notes to stir thinking when working with a student one-on-one.

If an educational assistant is unsure about the content being explored or is jumping into supporting scholars in the middle of a unit of inquiry, using simple prompts such as "Tell me more about . . . " and "I'm curious what connections you're making with . . . " are helpful in directing students toward using artifacts as a means to share their thinking, retrieve facts, and recall vocabulary needed to make connections with the learning.

With retrieval in mind, language such as "When I look at this artifact, it reminds me of . . ." or "Two things that stand out to me about our documentation are . . ." models what it means to lift up big ideas and make meaning.

Habit #3: Educational assistants scaffold questions to co-design and extend.

Educational assistants' roles are designed for timed and targeted support, making the pressure to perform an inherent challenge. Attending to the work might seem like the most important part of the job, but that focus comes at the risk of neglecting the important step of retrieval and connection making in the process of learning.

Instead of jumping into the busyness of completing a product or submitting to the pressure to have all of the answers, leave space for educational assistants to ask questions and ease into the learning community. Questions create an opportunity for scholars to think more deeply about their thinking, and it's in their sharing that educators hear potential connections, insights, and misconceptions. This process allows teachers and educational assistants to co-design additional scaffolds that may be needed to support next steps.

We can let go of the need to be the expert and do *all the things* when we allow others to provide support and pair questions with documentation to further engage in retrieval. The questions below are some that I've collected after several decades of observing and closely working with many educational assistants. They provide easy entry points into the learning and classroom community. Encourage your educational assistant to ask several and note where it takes the thinking:

- What can you tell me about your learning so far?
- I'm curious: what are you working on?
- What else can you tell me about that?

- What might be helpful to use as a resource now?
- Hmm, what does this make you think next?
- Where might it be helpful for us to start?
- What's standing out to you now?
- Can you think of something that this reminds you of?

 The questions above will get you started. You also might find it helpful to download my Question Badge and keep it handy. I used these tried-and-true questions every day with learners!

By partnering with our educational supports, we collectively teach and scaffold skills in real time, unbound by time restraints, lack of collaborative planning opportunities, or the unavailability of professional learning. We continue to dismiss thoughts of what's lacking and rethink this as an opportunity to engage in learning and meaning-making together. As classroom teachers, we commit to leveraging these roles in our learning communities and are mindful about the way we invite and share this space with others. We pause to greet our student supports with a nod as they enter the room, then give students an independent task to create space for a quick connection. In those moments, we honor their expertise, invite them into the conversation with an open-ended question, and create room for them to share their thinking, support retrieval, and ease into the collaborative learning space.

Instructional Leaders and Coaches

More often than not, when I talk with teachers about their experience with administration and instructional coaches in their classrooms, I notice a few common themes. Many have shared that they feel uncomfortable having anyone other than their students in their space. Others have told me that the way administrators engage in conversations about student learning feel more like an evaluation laced with quiet judgment than productive dialogue. On the whole, the energy of these interactions isn't overly positive, nor are they viewed as a valuable use of time.

I get it. I've been there too. I know what it feels like to be acutely aware of *all the things* that went wrong during the ten minutes my principal visited my classroom while students were engaged in not-so-quiet math stations. I can still recall feedback from administrators who seemed more focused on their personal preference and style of teaching than in sharing expertise to improve my practice. And I, like many educators, regularly wrestle with feelings of perfectionism.

The Doorway Effect reminds us about the role retrieval plays in learning for our students. But what about us? What strategies can we use to bring ourselves back to the big ideas in our units of inquiry after we've followed scholars' questions to see where they lead? How do we design meaningful reflections to summarize key takeaways after an action-based project? Or sift through evidence from a provocation to plan the next steps?

We also need routines. And we have the power to rewrite the role of administrators and instructional leaders in our practice. By shifting our perspective, we can choose to view these leaders as partners who are nudging us to reflect on our practice, recall what matters most, and look for new ways to lift up the learning.

In *Leading with a Lens of Inquiry*, I wrote about the seven essential dispositions of an inquiry leader and the foundational roles they play in nurturing relationships and school cultures of inquiry. In that book, I call on leaders to consider how they extend an invitation to try new things. I ask them to shift their thinking about the traditional ways they coach teachers and how campus-wide professional development is planned and facilitated. Shared leadership and being attuned to the learning community are required of this disposition of inquiry leaders and nudge them to think deeply about and implement these strategies.

At the beginning of this section, I asked *you* to reassess how you invite others into the planning and process of retrieval. Regardless of title or position, calling on critical thought partners is a habit in which inquiry educators regularly engage. It's typically easiest to connect with colleagues in our department or grade level and to develop relationships with peers who are in similar roles. Collaboration most often occurs laterally because of proximity, common content and curriculum, titles, and system constraints. These commonalities, however, also narrow our perspectives about other possibilities that may lie outside our patterns.

What would happen if we reimagined the way we partner and view varied perspectives and roles as assets toward our own retrieval? How might we pause to notice and retrieve, then playfully invite reflection to help us better co-plan and co-design next steps?

A lack of experience or the invisible power dynamic may make starting these conversations uncomfortable when you are building and reflecting on your learning wall. You may have a coach or administrator—or be a coach or administrator—who is unfamiliar with engaging in these reflective conversations. I have included prompts to help you begin these conversations. Be bold! Invite others to help you take a closer look at the physical evidence and artifacts displayed on your learning wall and ensure that there's purpose in planning equitable learning for all scholars.

Questions Inquiry Teachers Ask

- I'd love to hear your thoughts about . . .
- Let me show you something that surprised me in the learning!
- This documentation of learning is making me wonder about . . . I'm curious what you think?
- What connections do you see?
- What do you suggest our next steps might be?
- Can I show you something that really excites me?

Questions Instructional Leaders Ask to Promote Inquiry

- Can you give me a short tour of your learning wall?
- What are some of the artifacts telling you about some possible next steps?
- What would you like me to see? What evidence are you excited about?
- Tell me more about . . .
- What might this particular evidence reveal about your learners?
- What's something you're excited to share about the learning journey here?

Chapter 6

Retrieval (Part II)
Me vs. We

I f we know that multiple, meaningful, and varied experiences are necessary for learning to transfer, we lean into documenting learning and use our vertical spaces differently. No matter where or when students are entering our classrooms, they have equitable access to co-constructed rubrics, thinking routines, research resources, essential academic vocabulary, and sentence stems that give them a place to begin. As we plan for learning, we pay attention to our outliers and think about how we can create spaces with multiple access points. Learning is better, richer, and more meaningful because it's done together.

One of the benefits of learning walls is that they house a collection of everyone's ideas, encouraging collaboration and the co-constructing of knowledge over time. They further establish the importance of shared contributions to the learning space and nudge us toward considering how the learners will begin to shape where we will journey to next. As we move through different types of inquiry, we also shift the weight of control in the learning. We intentionally step forward to provide direct instruction and scaffolds to ensure our scholars have a foundation of knowledge and skills. We then step back to create space for them to flex agency and autonomy over their learning.

With experience, we become adept at knowing whether the task at hand is a *me* job or a *we* job. Likewise, as we build learning walls with one another, we move along a similar spectrum of control. Below are a few loose structures to consider as you engage in the process of building a learning wall.

Take Stock

Having a plan for learning is essential. We consider timetables and opportunities for learning, and we have a projected vision for the direction of our units of inquiry. As we position ourselves in the ongoing process of retrieval, we take stock of the evidence and artifacts before us. We pull up a chair to our learning walls and take a curious look at the evidence we have gathered, asking ourselves what it's telling us about the direction we've planned for, how it aligns with the needs of our learners, and whether the evidence is no longer necessary in supporting the learners on their journey. As we take stock, we might decide to pull down a few artifacts to quiet the visual noise, move artifacts to a different location on the wall to better direct attention toward critical vocabulary and resources, or simply pause to take in all the evidence before us to help reorient ourselves in the process of learning. Simply put, taking stock is a quiet and intentional action we engage in to make sense and meaning of learning. Depending on how much evidence we have collected and where we are in the cycle of inquiry, taking stock might be a brief moment of pause or require us to schedule a longer block of time.

During this stage, I might walk over to the wonder wall and sort through learner questions that have collected over time. I revisit their reflections to evaluate what connections they're making. I sift through evidence I've set aside but haven't tacked to the wall yet. Sometimes, I'll call on a critical thought partner to sit alongside me to offer a fresh perspective to the evidence before me. Here are some questions you might find helpful as you take stock:

- Are my learners retrieving the knowledge and big ideas I've planned for?
- What evidence is displayed that supports their process of retrieval of what's most important in the learning?
- What evidence might I display to support retrieval for my learners?
- How is this structure of the learning wall working for learners?
- What experiences do I not want my learners to forget?
- Feedback from learners

Inquiry teachers carefully observe actions, lean in, and listen to conversations. They thoughtfully take in the landscape of the room around them. These essential yet informal data points can be used to track the learning, revise lesson plans, and drive the reflection process. Being curious about what's unfolding and pausing to sort through indirect feedback is critical, but it isn't something you have to do alone.

Whenever I am unsure about the evidence tacked to the learning wall or even overthinking lesson plans for next steps, I often pause and instead go straight to the source—the learners. Gathering feedback from our learners can be simple, and in less than ten minutes we have an experience that builds competencies along with a new collection of data that we can instantly use. One way to do so takes only a sticky note and an intention to be open to what emerges from this feedback.

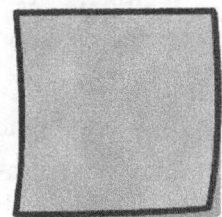

To open, I tell our scholars that we need their feedback to plan for next steps. I am explicit with my sharing during this step to reinforce the value of learner agency and to promote the exchange of ideas as an essential part of the learning in our space. Next, I give a sticky note to each of our scholars and direct them to the wall while asking them to consider which of the artifacts before them represents the knowledge that's most important to them. I often find it helpful to provide sentence frames such as "I used to think . . . now I think . . . because I learned . . ." or "When I think about . . . the most important thing to remember is . . . " or even "I learned . . . It makes me wonder . . . ?" to scaffold students' deeper thinking and support the retrieval process.

After students have engaged in a few moments of quiet reflection, I couple this retrieval technique with a Turn and Talk or the Give One, Get One collaborative routine to further reinforce big ideas and lift up the wisdom in the room. Finally, I call on our scholars to attach their feedback to the learning wall. I might call on individuals to share what they notice or simply leave the evidence for a later date. Either way, the sticky notes attached to artifacts create a colorful reminder for us to return to when we take stock of the learning, evaluate evidence, and determine what actions might best serve the good of the group.

We also must consider the process of gathering learner feedback as an opportunity for our scholars to reflect on who they are as learners, taking stock and tuning in to how they best make meaning for themselves. When we pause and ask our students to consider what resources they have found most helpful, what they might need to take independent action, or how they best learn, we nurture spaces in which confidence, risk-taking, and curiosity can thrive.

We turn to the valuable resource of learner feedback to guide us when faced with uncertainty about the effectiveness of artifacts displayed on our learning walls or when we sense our scholars could use a little nudge toward more interaction with these vertical spaces. With a small pinch of sticky notes (my preference is the smallest size of sticky notes for this), we ask our students to "vote" on which artifacts they find most helpful to support their learning. As students place their sticky notes on the wall, notice trends and patterns, take note of assumptions around which evidence we think is most important, model aloud our thinking as we see collections of squares gathered on particular artifacts, and call on individuals to explain more of their reasoning about the placement of their sticky note. I find this interaction to be one that promotes agency for our learners as we empower them to decide what's worth keeping and hanging onto as we dive into a new unit of inquiry. This engagement can be helpful if you find your learning wall a bit too filled with anchor charts and other resources. It is also useful if you are still tinkering with the types of evidence you plan to display or if you want to identify and evaluate the big ideas and skills that are having an impact on your learners.

Pause to Connect

The power of the pause. From wait times allotted to patiently giving space for an answer to emerge after posing a question to moments we give ourselves before responding to a dysregulated student, taking a moment to pause can completely change the landscape of the experience.

When we pause to connect, we link ideas, nudge thinking toward deeper meaning, and celebrate the constructing phase of knowledge building. Pause to Connect might begin with the teacher modeling the process. From the youngest learners to those engaged in studies at the university level, I've witnessed the artful way teachers point to artifacts on their learning walls and unpin select pieces of documentation to highlight the ways that they connect and build on greater knowledge and understanding. They are intentional with the artifacts they single out, mindfully choosing language that models and encourages the type of thinking and connection making in which they hope learners will learn to independently engage. Let's take a look at some of the sentence stems that frame the process of retrieval:

- When I look at these two pieces of evidence, it makes me think . . .
- A connection I am making is . . .
- This reminds me of . . . because . . .
- I see a connection between . . . and . . . because . . .
- I used to think . . . but now I think . . . because . . .
- These two artifacts are important because . . .

As you read through these stems, notice how they provide a clear structure of the direction of meaning-making yet maintain an openness to a variety of ways one might connect to the learning. When you plan for retrieval, it's essential to also plan for the language you know will empower independent scholars. Consider academic vocabulary content specific and related to the unit at hand as well as vocabulary words that connect ideas and transcend the subject area. You might even find it helpful to revisit the tenets of equitable evidencing in Chapter Two as you begin to make these plans. In that chapter, I shared several different ways to model connection making for your scholars. Each of these helps promote the elements necessary for students to transfer and apply knowledge in new contexts and situations, expanding learning from rote memorization and superficial recall to organizing sets of ideas, allowing students to make deeper connections between the topics and concepts we facilitate learning around.

Over time, Pause to Connect will also include student-to-student interactions, encouraging collaborative, low-stakes retrieval opportunities that provide learners with the frequent feedback needed to help improve retention and enhance the transfer of learning. Students learning English as a second language benefit from this protocol because this peer-to-peer connection relies heavily on visual evidence from the learning wall to support conversation and application of language skills, fostering a more immersive and equitably engaging learning experience.

When asking learners to Pause to Connect, one of my favorite protocols to plan for the retrieval process, help structure thinking, and get my learners collaborating with one another is called Two Things. I love the flexibility of this protocol. (I'll share some ways to differentiate this structure below!) It requires little to no prep, and it can occur at any point within your unit of inquiry. When launching Two Things, you simply display your virtual learning wall or invite your scholars over to the physical learning wall you have established in your classroom and ask them to identify two things about a specific prompt. For example,

> Retrieval practices and strategies come from the work of cognitive scientist Pooja Agarwal and educator and author Patrice Bain. In their book, *Powerful Teaching: Unleash the Science of Learning*, they outline the research and benefits of retrieval practice and how we use it in our classrooms. I've shared some strategies and question prompts from their publication in this chapter and encourage you to check out their body of work!

- What two things have you learned today?
- What are two things you learned this week?
- What are two things you'd like to learn more about?
- What are two things that you're still wondering about?
- What are two things that connect on our learning wall?

The key here is that students have to support their thinking by identifying some evidence on the learning wall to help illustrate their "two things." It's worth noting that whenever we plan for retrieval, we first plan for "think time," giving the brain space to pause, recall information, and make connections. Again, we continue to be mindful of how we nurture spaces that are soft for our learners to step into and build a trusting confidence that they have the capacity to do so if given the appropriate structure, time, and differentiation to meet their various developmental needs and abilities.

After a contemplative pause, we may ask our scholars to jot down their two things.

Students can simply flip open the notebooks they already have on their desks or be provided a sticky note or a scrap of recycled paper. The longevity of the artifact is not what we are after here, so don't overthink preparedness. Jotting down ideas helps support the psychological safety of our scholars as we ask them to Turn and Talk, sharing their thinking with a partner or group.

Of course, as partners share with one another, we are dutifully moving about the room to witness the construction of knowledge that unfolds. We may sidle up to scholars who might need a bit more confidence building and choose to be an additional partner in a pairing. We can stop between pairs of students to lean in and listen to the types of connections students are making, or we might choose a location in the room that allows us to survey the busy murmur, tuning into key language we hear bubbling up in this timed collaborative sharing. We resist the urge to step in and correct in the moment, choosing instead to take notes for next steps in planning for learning or perhaps lift up a small handful of conversations and takeaways we overheard before moving on to the next activity. As with all of Agarwal and Bain's retrieval strategies, we don't need to allot too much time for this learning strategy. We flip the act of recalling information into a positive experience, reducing anxiety, empowering agency, and stretching learners toward a balanced cognitive friction.

This protocol can easily be adapted to meet the differentiated needs of each of our students. The ideas below are also great alternative scaffolds to consider throughout a term or academic year. It's important to remember that we don't have to jump in the deep end of the inquiry pool to get started with retrieval. Meet your learners where they are and respond as needed!

- **Start with one thing.** Use a structure similar to the one described above. Consider how you might ask a few questions or provide feedback (in the words of Ron Berger, "kind, specific, helpful") to your learners to further learning and boosting the impact of the retrieval process.

Watch this short video to hear from Ron Berger himself. He outlines these tenets and walks you through a short example that is sure to give you the language you need to use with your learners too!

- **Short on time or materials? Have learners who aren't ready to put pen to paper?** Use Two Things as a verbal exchange of ideas instead! While the same consideration of wait time, collaboration, and usage of the learning wall applies, this collaborative and playful strategy nudges students to do the heavy lifting of sharing ideas.

- **Want to get your students exploring new perspectives and self-assessing along the way?** Pooja generously offers a collaborative alternative to the Two Things by adding One More Thing. After your scholars have generated their Two Things, prompt them to pass their paper to a peer. Each person adds one thing to their classmate's list before returning the paper. This version of Two Things is particularly successful when promoting communication and collaboration skills. Invitations that encourage the exchange of ideas might sound like *What's one more thing you can add to your peer's paper?* or *How might you connect your thinking to one of the ideas generated by your partner?* We nurture collaborative learning communities and remind scholars of the value of connecting with and stretching one another when we provide opportunities for low-stakes retrieval and sharing.

- **Save it for later.** You already know I am a big fan of collecting artifacts as a means of supporting the skill of reflection. Before turning the page on this learning strategy, ask your scholars to tuck their sticky notes into their inquiry journals or anchor them on another vertical space in your classroom. Plan on revisiting this collection of thinking later to see how learning has evolved or perhaps as a provocation to drive further reflection and synthesis of learning.

Nurturing the Capable Person

Capable person is a term I learned while working with a group of school leaders and educators in the Beaufort Delta Divisional Education Council (BDDEC) in the Northwest Territories of Canada. Its origin comes from the indigenous people on whose land the school district resides. The term grounds the work happening in schools across the district as it continues to decolonize curriculum and mindfully work to honor traditional ways of being and becoming a capable person.

The strengths-based approach that drives the teaching and learning throughout the district means that the "gifts, talents, and strengths" of students are an essential part of the planning for learning. As the region further develops curriculum, they use cultural calendars to ensure that land-based learning opportunities are rooted in their practice. Elders and community members are invited to impart their expertise with students to ensure that traditional knowledge and ways of being in the community are shared, and they use learning walls as a tool for reciprocity, encouraging students to share back their learning with their peers, simultaneously giving gratitude to the learning guides from the community.

Just as the BDDEC plans and documents learning with the capable person in mind, as inquiry educators, we must consider the way learning walls capture our scholars' gifts, and we must have a clear understanding of the impact they have on our learning community. Skill development is not unique to this district, of course. Walk into any school and you'll likely find evidence of a Portrait of a Graduate displayed at the entrance, hear district leaders approving funds for special programs, or see leadership redesigning traditional conferences to include a student-led approach. Schools allocate budgets for science, technology, engineering, and math (STEM) and other exploratory and enrichment programming. With innovative, open scheduling, students practice self-management skills.

These value-driven efforts are even more powerful when competencies and attributes are intentionally lifted up, authentically documented, and reflected on as an essential part of becoming *more capable*. Instead of simply hoping these skills emerge in response to the experiences themselves, we use learning walls to make them visible. These intentional spaces create opportunities for our scholars to retrieve, recall, and share what they are learning about themselves as a learner.

In *Hidden Potential: The Science of Achieving Greater Things*, Adam Grant emphasizes the importance of intentionally developing competencies and skills. He notes that the impact of an achievement is greater when the focus is on improving rather than on earning a "gold star." Instead, he defines achievement as the growth nurtured when we have opportunities to explore doubts, embrace imperfection, and feel supported in the process.

Grant's research reinforces the need to focus on developing a range of skills alongside our learners. Three frames of thinking to consider include *integration for impact, building a community of learners,* and *accountability toward agency.* I'll show you several different strategies within the frames. The subtitles anchoring the strategies below are excellent prompts in themselves to help you think about how you currently put planning for these "soft skills" at the forefront during student-to-student engagements, student self-assessment, and overall responses to learning.

Integrate for Impact

If teaching and planning with skills feels more like an afterthought than intentional, take a closer look at your standards to identify what skills are already part of your curriculum. If you teach several courses or subject areas, start with just one, and scan the standards. Jot down the skills you see listed. Some will be easy to spot, such as *discuss, write,* or *explain* (communication skills) and *ask and answer* (collaboration and critical thinking skills). Other skills, such as *analyze or develop* (reflection and self-management skills) and *represent and reason* (research and thinking skills) might require a bit more time to identify.

When you have a list of skills, pause and reflect by considering what skills your learners need *most*. Do you find your scholars unable to sustain productivity when working with their peers in pairs or on group assignments? When tasked with something more open ended, do your learners struggle to self-manage and organize first steps forward? Or do you notice a lack of deeper thinking and rich reflection when asking students to self-evaluate and make connections with their learning?

Whatever skills you notice that your learners need most are the ones to integrate for impact. Let's take a look at a few classrooms and how they integrate skills development into their learning walls.

Skills: Communication, Collaboration, and Relationship Building

The learning wall you see here belongs to a classroom of early years students and their teacher, Ms. Hofheins. After many weeks of observation, during both structured and unstructured learning time, the teacher identified that students needed some support and intentional practice building communication and collaboration skills with their peers. Using part of her classroom whiteboard, she started her learning wall with a simple brainstorming structure. The familiar form of documentation anchored a collection of class conversations that generated the questions you see posted here.

Notice that student questions are sorted into *like* categories (sharing, characteristics, process, etc.). This allowed Ms. Hofheins to easily identify question trends and direct the conversation toward specific skills.

A modeled wondering from the teacher, such as "I'm curious what it means to share?" creates a ripple of related questions and invites even the most introverted or reluctant learners to contribute. Ms. Hofheins then weaves threads from the collection of wonderings into her lessons in the different subject areas. She can use them to launch conversations of reflection at the end of unstructured playtime as students debrief experiences with their peers. Their responses provide evidence of the current thinking in this early years classroom.

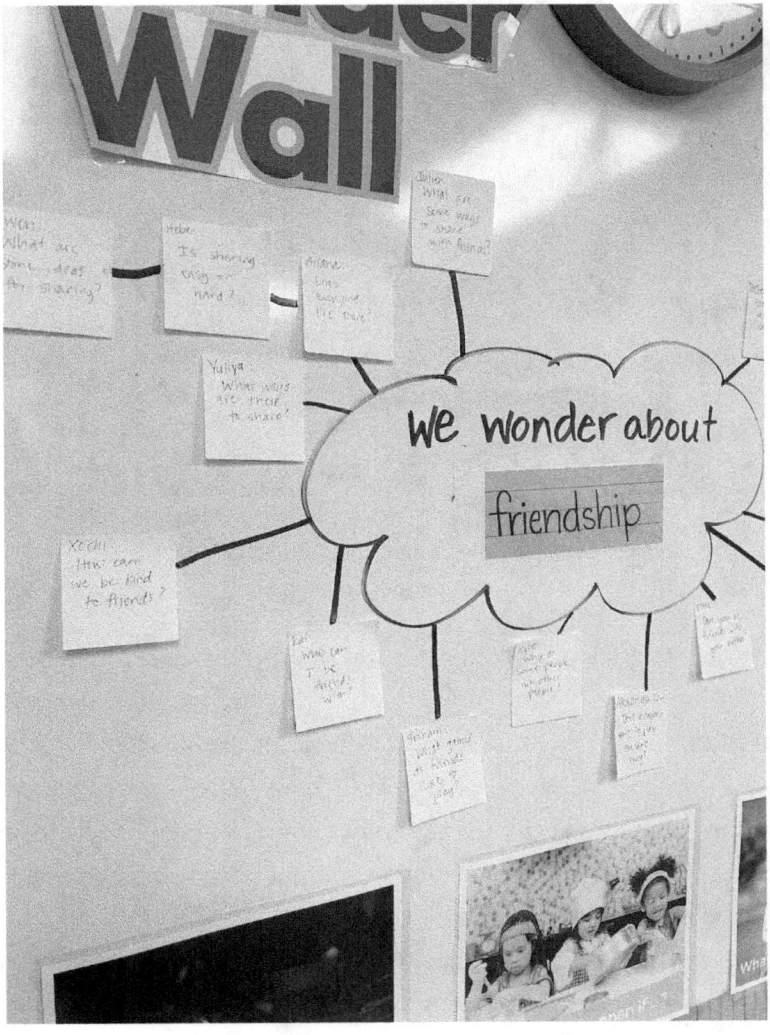

Source: Lindsey Hofheins, Early Years Teacher, Laurel Mountain Elementary, Austin, Texas

Skills: Research and Communication
Using resources to support conclusions and connections

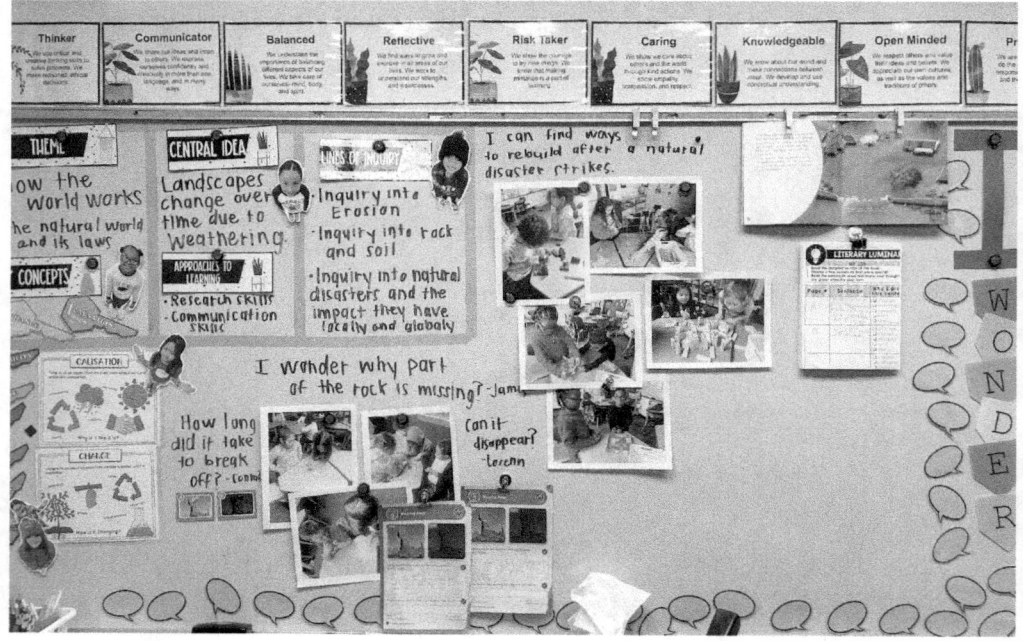

Source: Amanda Carroll, Natomas Unified School District,
Sacramento, California

Now, let's take a look at a different wall, a different set of learners, and some similar skills with an alternative structure for documentation. The wall you see here belongs to Amanda Carroll, a second grade IB PYP teacher at Natomas Unified School District in Sacramento, California. Before beginning the six-week unit of inquiry, she identified research and communication as the skills her learners needed to flex and practice.

Using Guy Claxton's Notice and Name strategy, Amanda documented several examples, using photographs as evidence of students practicing these skills together. She later referenced these learning experiences to help scholars retrieve and recall while co-constructing new learning intentions with her class at the onset of a collaborative activity.

Invitations to retrieve and identify particular skills may sound like *Today we're going to flex our communication skills as we work within our groups. I want you to set an intention for what productive communication looks and sounds like.* Or, while pointing to select photographs on the learning wall, *Remember when we were building and rebuilding different structures with our thought partners? What was helpful in collaborating with our peers when things didn't go as planned?*

Other artifacts on the learning wall include workbook pages torn from district-mandated curriculum resources and questions Amanda overheard students asking while researching and working with their tablemates. Additionally, she clipped a book open to a page about the impact of floods. The selected page shows a photograph with labels and a caption, key nonfiction features her scholars need to be able to identify as indicators of research resources.

Artifacts are mobile and attached to the wall with magnetic clips and pins, making it easy for her scholars to take down resources and bring them back to their desks or to move the items to different locations on the wall. Amanda intentionally displayed artifacts she believed to be valuable tools that would support her scholars. She demonstrated how to use each one during whole-class direct instruction as well as during small-group work sessions.

Mindful moves, such as using sentences that start with *I noticed that when we were reading our nonfiction text yesterday . . .* and *How might we use some of the information we've already collected on our learning wall to support our thinking about . . .* invite, encourage, and empower competent and capable scholars.

Integrating Reflection and Retrieval

Your school may have already adopted or be in the process of embedding Guy Claxton's Learning Power Approach and the attributes of the Learner Profile into your curriculum. Perhaps your campus prioritizes Habits of Mind, the work of Art Costa and Bena Kallick, in every interaction with students and colleagues.

Schools prefer a language that does not belong to a particular country but to the culture of their community. Their students and teachers share this language and speak it in their classrooms, halls, and conference rooms. It shapes the culture and empowers capable learners.

If this describes your school, you experience these benefits and know the mindful work that goes into nurturing the whole child. Your challenge is different from those who are on the earlier part of this inquiry journey. Your challenge lies in the maintenance and resistance of complacency. Schools are ever-evolving organizations. There's a constant ebb and flow of the student body. Classroom teachers move from one subject area or grade level to another based on interest and campus need. School leaders come and go, bringing varied experiences, values, and visions to their role. With the constant changes, *integrated* and *ongoing* reflection must also be part of the school culture. Open-ended, yet provoking questions, such as *What got us here? What may keep us here?* and *How do we integrate and onboard new staff?* create reflective opportunities of retrieval.

Nurture the culture you've worked to cultivate by ensuring that current perceptions of students, staff, and other community members align with the intended impact. Collect data as authentic evidence by surveying students and staff. Invite people from outside your organization to bring in different perspectives and ideas.

Building Community to Boost Retrieval

Taking risks, exchanging ideas, working with peers and partners, sharing experiences, identifying commonalities, and respecting differences are all elements that foster a community of learners. Open-ended questions and low-stakes opportunities for scholars to contribute to the collective thinking create a sense of psychological safety and early stages of trust.

Building a community means connecting with one another. In the inquiry landscape, that includes co-constructing thinking and building on ideas to make meaning together. Building community in an inquiry classroom also means co-designing language and other indicators that permeate the physical spaces and interactions between learners. The intentional effort put behind community building boosts effort, scaffolds toward more equitable learning spaces, and reinforces a skill our learners take well beyond the four walls of our classrooms.

One way to build community is by asking learners for input. This might look like using student feedback to refine lesson plans, encouraging self-reflection, or asking questions to gauge understanding.

In Ms. Cera's fourth grade classroom, building a community of learners meant focusing on skills that she noticed her students lacked. When she decided to add a learning wall to her teaching practice, she did so with the intention of using her district's SEL curriculum and employing strategies to help students develop their collaboration and communication skills. Virtual schooling and COVID safety precautions had significantly impacted her students' opportunities to interact and partner with peers. Ms. Cera committed to planning learning experiences and lessons with the skills of collaboration and communication at their core. This included highlighting key strategies for students to reference when conflicts arose, co-constructing a contract of class commitments, and including key phrases and other evidence from SEL lessons the school counselor conducted (see Inner Critic vs. Inner Coach, on the following page).

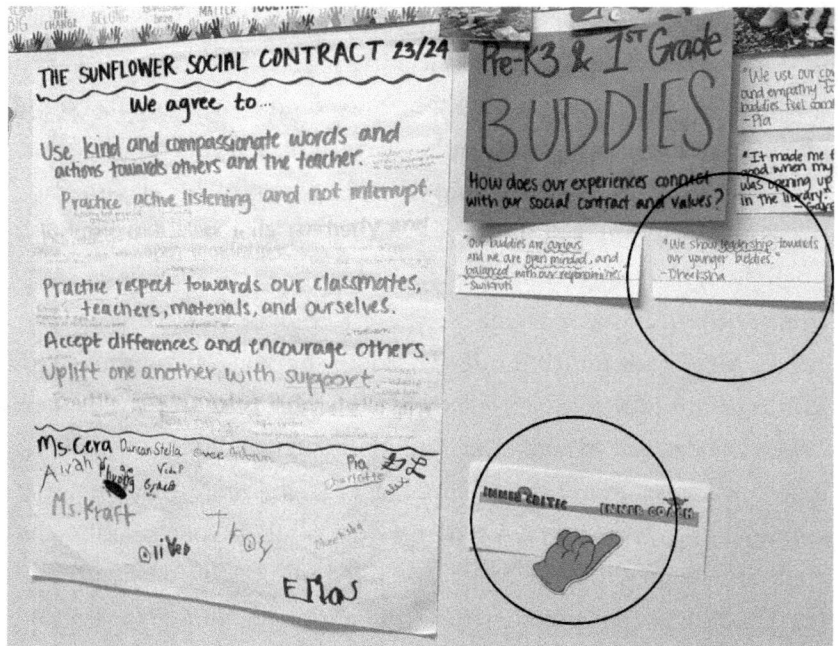

Source: Megan Cera, Fourth Grade Teacher, Laurel Mountain Elementary, Austin, Texas

Here's another example of co-designing with community in mind. Anticipating the students' need for collaboration for an upcoming project, this third grade teacher posted a few questions on vertical surfaces (whiteboards, posters, and sticky pads) around the classroom. Students were divided into small groups and invited to discuss the questions. Keeping the groups small promoted personal connections and helped to ensure that everyone had an opportunity to share.

Students considered and documented their responses to questions such as *Where in life are you a good collaborator and teammate outside of class?* and *In a team, how can we all contribute to a shared goal? What might we do when it's not working out?*

A timer kept the students moving around the room. As students rotated to the next question, they read the responses recorded by the previous groups and stretched themselves to add something new to the list. The teacher walked around the room, listening to discussions

Source: Trevor MacKenzie and San Jacinto Elementary

and noticing that even the more hesitant students were participating. Keeping the conversations going, the teacher gently dropped additional questions and prompts, such as *What might have been helpful in that experience if you had to do it all over again?* And, *Tell us more about how that felt.* Adding new responses to the questions became increasingly challenging as students rotated, and the provocation nudged scholars to think outside the box. They had to think back to previous experiences of teamwork and collaboration and recall the positive and negative feelings related to them. The sharing led to rich discussions and an invaluable list of strategies, ideas, and the retrieval of knowledge that they could build on. The lesson culminated in a whole-class reflection during which the artifacts from this session became the focal point for their learning wall. The flexed skills and their authentic documentation supported the learning that followed in the coming weeks.

Whether you use prescribed curriculum as a guide or create something on your own, keep one thought in mind: Building community and focusing on content is not an either–or proposition. It is always *both!*

Accountability toward Agency

Kindergarten and early years teachers are masters of routine. They know how to break down an activity into scaffolded steps that support their younger students. These steps create and maintain routines while balancing the needs of an environment rich in exploration, open-ended materials, and choice. Each time I step into one of these classrooms, I learn so much about the fluidity of movement, the listening that goes well beyond simply hearing scholars' comments and questions, and the kind of guidance that envelops each step without smothering it. These intentional micro moves come through practice—from playfully taking risks and holding firmly to the capability of even younger children.

Agency for Children in the Early Years

A few years ago, I was coaching Samantha Jorgans, a first grade teacher who was inching herself toward these goals of instilling agency and promoting capability in her learners. Having spent time in other teachers' classrooms, she had seen some examples of learning walls in primary settings. She had a few thinking routines, provocations, and question protocols in mind to try with her learners. As the semester progressed, we met every other week to co-plan lessons based on district timelines while mindfully balancing learner interests and curiosities. Between our sessions, I'd drop off books in her mailbox, email resources, and share examples I knew would support the work she was doing with her students. In time, she noticed that her learners were gaining an independence that she wasn't used to seeing so early in the academic year. She also noticed that her mindset had shifted from *students can't . . . because they are only in first grade* to *my students can . . . when I . . . .*

With an increased confidence that her five- and six-year-olds could "do inquiry," she excitedly shared about a whole-class research project they were wrapping up. As we talked, she wondered aloud whether the same energy, ownership, and inquisitiveness they had experienced through the inquiry unit was possible when teaching skills or foundational curriculum such as phonics and vocabulary that typically required direct instruction. She pointedly asked, "Is an inquiry approach even possible?"

Embracing the challenge, I asked the teacher which of the things in her plans for the upcoming week felt like a roadblock to an inquiry approach. After some pondering, she told me she was grappling with her tiered vocabulary instruction. Although understanding its importance for reading readiness and meeting the needs of her emergent bilingual students, the instruction felt lifeless and disconnected from the learning experiences that promoted agency and engagement.

I followed up with another question—the same one that opened this chapter: "What do you want your learners to retrieve and be able to take with them in the long term?"

Her goal, she explained, was for students to feel a sense of ownership and agency with personal language development and goal setting. She wanted them to be able to refer to past knowledge and understanding when they were working on independent writing and reading tasks and make connections to the rich learning that was happening in other subject areas. With those goals clearly defined, we found a blank space beside her whiteboard and got to work. We designed a vertical space and a teaching plan that drew on the research-based curriculum she was using *and* her inquiry mindset.

That very afternoon, she introduced her students to the vocabulary learning wall, showing them the space where the words they explored would go. Starting with a small stack of basic words on notecards and two words plucked from their research learning wall, the class discussed and categorized the terms accordingly. She called students to the wall to help place the terms, infusing an early sense of ownership and establishing new routines for using and playing with words. Whenever it was time to introduce a new list of sight words or unpack academic vocabulary during a reading, or when a term in a video sparked student interest, she *and her students* would return to this small learning wall to add, edit, organize, sort, and make new connections.

The value of this resource didn't end with the lesson. Students were held accountable to use these words when they engaged in the editing step of their writing. They knew they had an open invitation to unpin a notecard from one of the sections and use it as a resource while they self-checked their work. The teacher also created reflection routines. After reading together, for example, she called on the scholars to pause and share a word that surprised them with their elbow partner (these words were discussed, and partners would agree on what might be interesting to add to the wall). During phonics instruction, they analyzed and reorganized words based on the new vowel patterns they were learning. They would also highlight letter pairs or add small illustrations and symbols to show a deepening of understanding and thinking.

Notice the features on the vocabulary learning wall pictured here that support agency while keeping students engaged in the co-constructed process. Using pushpins instead of staples and placing notecards and sticky notes lower on the learning wall invite scholars to add, remove, and use the vocabulary terms with ease. In front of this wall is a small table stocked with sticky notes, markers, index cards, and pins. The accessibility of these tools suits the intended accountability and supports the habits and systems that organically integrated the use of the learning wall into classroom routines.

Pay attention to the overall structure of this wall. On this open-ended space, there are no dividing lines or sections. This encourages flexible word placement. The headline *What Words We Are Curious About* also motivates students to add words they come across as they are reading or when engaging in conversations with peers. Simple yet powerful, moves like these take our vertical spaces to the next level, influence a sense of student ownership, and demonstrate that inquiry can flourish within all modes of curriculum and instruction.

Ms. Jorgans and her first graders co-constructed a few learning walls throughout the academic year. The growth of her students' research, self-management, and independence skills was noticeable.

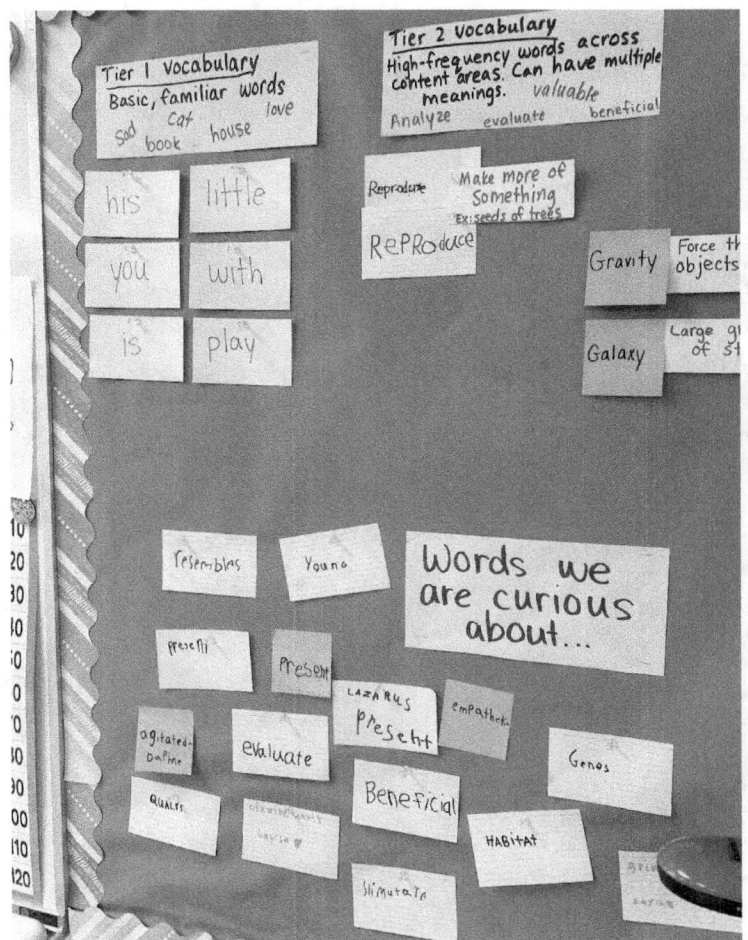

Source: Samantha Jorgans, First Grade Teacher, Laurel Mountain Elementary, Austin, Texas

Overseeing and maintaining more than one space might feel overwhelming, unnecessary, or unattainable for some educators. We still promote the agentic nature of ownership and self-reflection through noticing and naming skills in connection with the learning harboring routines that keep and maintain accountability in all students.

Agency in Assessment and Reflection

The learning wall you see below is full of co-designed anchor charts, student reflections, helpful sentence stems, teacher questions, and a variety of other artifacts that document the learning around a central concept: *organization*. As learners construct knowledge and make connections with the learning, they can add to the wall, using small attribute squares or magnets. These become a tool for formative assessment and layered reflection.

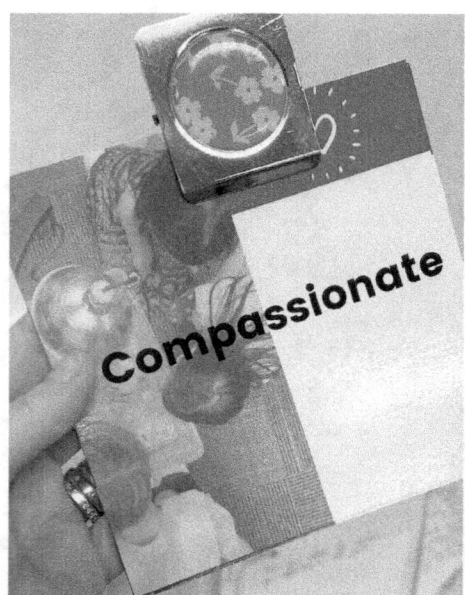 

We let the walls do the talking and hold our learners accountable by tasking them with exercises that encourage them to use the artifacts as evidence to support their thinking, reflections, and other connection making. One way we can do this is by asking them to select an attribute card to pin on the classroom learning wall and share their reasoning with a peer during a collaborative structure, like the Texas Two Step, that maintains engagement and a playful exchange of ideas and perspectives. Conversely, we can attach attribute magnets to artifacts before our learners enter the space, creating a provocation that launches more classroom discussions and opportunities for them to stop and jot and illustrate how they are making personal meaning of the learning that is unfolding. Flexible resources such as these magnets help us establish routines that drive us back to reflection and competency development.

They are simple tools that remind us to reconnect with what we know builds confident, capable, and connected learners.

Texas Two Step is a fun, interactive way to get students up and out of their seats practicing perspective-taking within set time limits for recall and retrieval. Use this QR code for step-by-step instructions, ways to differentiate, and tips for managing student behavior.

The examples shared throughout this book are the result of a mindset and culture of learning grounded in the belief of the benefits of planning, teaching, and reflecting with the whole child in mind. The educators who have shared their stories and pictures get distracted, just like you and me, by external forces and deadlines. Regardless of those circumstances, however, they remain steadfast in their commitment to innovating their practice and gaining an ever-broadening understanding of how to best nurture a culture that tunes in to learners and meets their needs.

In the Retrieval chapters, I shared three overarching frames—What's Worth Knowing, Me vs. We, and Nurturing the Capable Person. I urge you to reflect on the question, *What's essential for my learners to retrieve and to be able to take with them long term?* As you do, use these frames call you to hold steadfast to your values and remain relentless in your mission to bring something different to your practice and, in turn, your learners. Revisit these frames when you come to your learning wall. Let them guide you as you determine what's most important to give time and space to in the learning.

* How do you currently plan for retrieval and recall? What are two things you'll put into practice right away?

* What potential benefits and challenges do you anticipate you'll need to plan and scaffold for?

* How does knowing more about the purpose of artifacts shift your thinking about experiences, evidence, and purpose?

* Curious as to what makes a "good provocation" or wanting a bit of inspiration to help you plan your next invitation for learning? I encourage you to take a look at Trevor MacKenzie's Provocation Design Reflection Tool!

Chapter 7

Make Connections

I feel fortunate to spend most of my days engaged in the school setting—leading campus-wide professional development programs, greeting students in the morning, visiting classrooms during active learning times, and coaching teachers. As a teacher or school leader, you probably aren't surprised by the varied activities of my day. Educators wear countless hats that extend beyond our official titles. We pick up extra duties and tasks when substitutes don't show up or colleagues call in sick. We remain flexible, knowing that schedules can change at the last minute or that a student who is dysregulated may need a longer break and some additional support.

I step into school buildings with an inner awareness that my work is not just about the duties I've been assigned. Each action and interaction accumulates experience that allows me to build trusting relationships with colleagues and make meaningful connections with students. Collectively, this experience enables me to understand the needs of an ever-evolving community of learners.

As a school leader, I've found that being in classrooms is one of the most impactful ways to create sustainable changes and nurture a community of continuous and balanced learning. There are many commonalities between facilitating learning for adults and for students, but the length of time between allocated professional learning days dramatically limits the opportunity to confer and coach, reinforce or redirect, and accurately assess knowledge and understanding of pedagogical concepts and strategies put into practice in the classroom. To maintain a pulse on the learning, I encourage prioritizing weekly learning walks. Doing so gives you a broad sense of the learning in the building and allows you to authentically experience the application of strategies and approaches to teaching and learning.

No matter your role—school leader or classroom teacher—learning walks offer insights into how micro and macro decisions impact school systems and the people within them.

Learning Walk or Walk Through?

There are subtle but distinct differences between a learning walk  and a walk through. Each one has a unique purpose and value, and both should be part of your culture of learning.

Watch this Edutopia video to see a walk through in action.

When you have a learning wall, you can engage in a similar kind of "learning walk" without leaving your room. As you walk up to the learning wall, you can view the collection of artifacts with a curious mindset and the intention to make relevant and meaningful links within the learning. Walking the wall with your learners invites discourse. As you use retrieval strategies to lift up the learning and remind learners of where they've been, you set the course for taking action in new ways. Authenticity, open minds, and curious hearts are what make both kinds of learning walks so powerful.

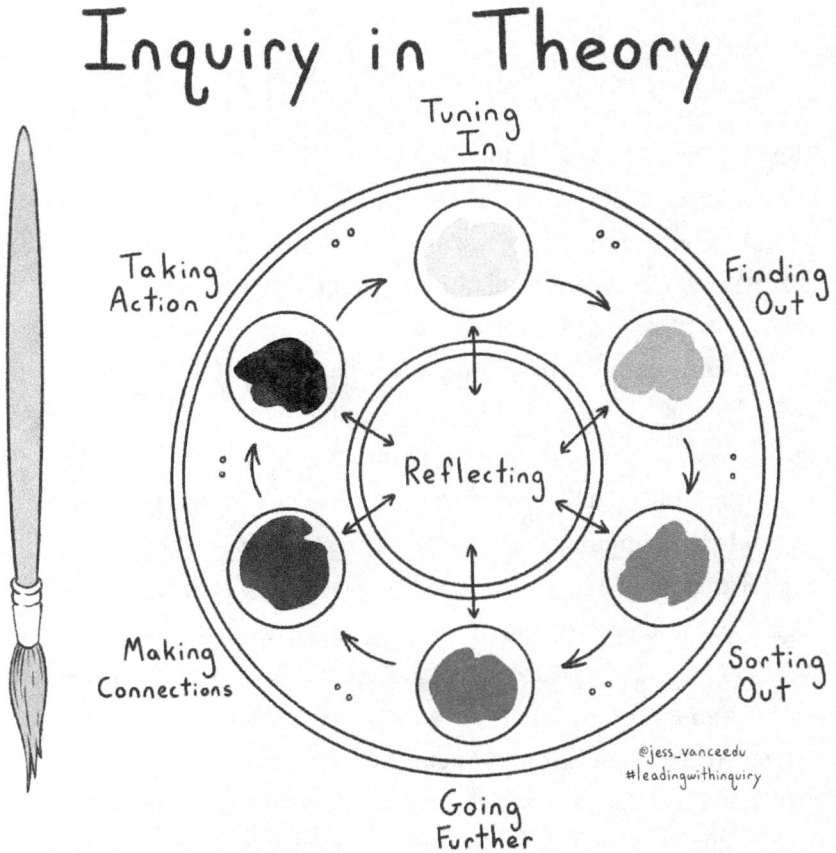

The cycle of inquiry reminds us to take part in continuous reflection. The latter stages of the cycle, however, specifically empower us to make sense and extend our learning by drawing conclusions and linking to prior knowledge. Throughout this book, I've shared many examples and strategies that help you build learning walls with an underlying theme of connection. With that theme in mind, this chapter highlights eight ways you can make connections using a learning wall. As with all inquiry teaching and learning, there is not a one-size-fits-all approach; however, the approaches that follow are aspirations toward which we should all strive. As you read through this chapter, think about how these connections are currently in your practice, which are a bit outside of a perspective you've considered before, and which ones you are immediately drawn to and inspired to put into practice right away.

1. Taking Action with Learning

This step near the end of the inquiry cycle is sometimes overlooked, but it is vital. It is where we call on our learners to make connections with, to, and through their learning. Doing this in collaboration with their learning community as they share their new knowledge impacts collective thinking. This stage drives an inquiry unit's summative assessment, synthesizing the big ideas being explored. We hope and even plan for this stage in the cycle, but all too often, timelines seem to shrink, deadlines loom, and the "action step" *evaporates*.

Could it be that our mindset and the habit of tucking this stage at the end of the inquiry cycle are what create the seemingly inevitable barrier to action? If so, what would happen if we planned *and looked* for action differently? What impact might there be, for example, if we were to view the purpose of action as a provocation for learning rather than a summative experience of what we've learned?

Jay McTighe and Grant Wiggins's Understanding by Design model offers an innovative and helpful backwards-planning frame that allows us to rethink our traditional approach toward action while reinforcing the underpinning pedagogy of the inquiry cycle. As you read about the different ways action can be implemented in the cycle of learning, keep in mind the three stages of backwards design: *identify desired results, determine acceptable evidence,* and *plan learning experiences and instruction.* Notice the evidence, the structure chosen for the learning wall, and how the planning and documentation support connection making in the process of learning. The examples in this chapter come from both leadership and classroom perspectives, but the viewpoints and process transcend any role or learning space. As you review these learning walls, circle elements that stand out to you. Make notes about how those things make you rethink connection making and action in your classroom.

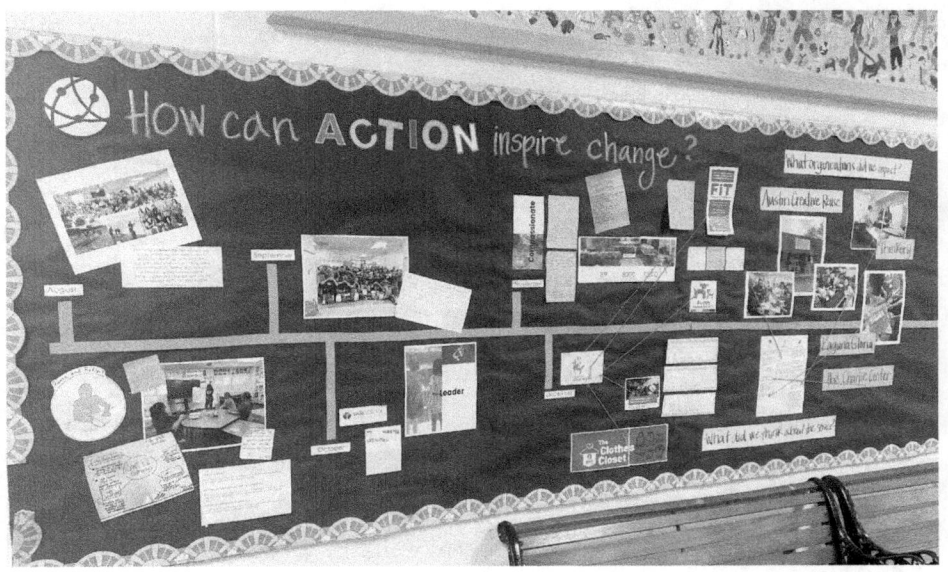

Source: Laurel Mountain Elementary, Austin, Texas

The example above is of a schoolwide learning wall our school leadership and staff built collaboratively with the intention of inspiring educators to consider how taking action provides authentic connections to community. Seeking to make connections to action, community, and learning, we used the backward-design model to build a learning wall that encouraged us all to plan, think, and *look* with action in mind while capturing evidence throughout a school year. Starting with our academic calendar, we identified district professional development days as opportunities to lead learning with this value of action at the core. We also identified the United Nations International

Volunteer Day as an ideal avenue to provoke new ways of thinking and engage in a schoolwide learning experience that would extend across the academic year. With that intentional but loose frame in mind, the rest, we hoped, would be driven by teachers and students as they experienced the immediate benefits of moving learning beyond the four walls of the classroom.

The school year began, and the learning around service and action took shape. As leaders, we tracked the big questions and themes that emerged from classrooms, collecting evidence through photographs, lists of nonprofit organizations, student and teacher reflections, and data that measured the impact action and service were having on our community. During our weekly planning meetings with teachers, we reviewed and shared picture books as provocations, introduced local nonprofits that connected to the curriculum, and posed questions to guide action-oriented planning.

We leveraged our Wednesday afternoon staff meetings to provide teachers space to pause and reflect with colleagues. We discussed how the focus on action nurtured learner attributes and contributed to social and emotional wellness, as well as how these experiences connected to our overall intentions with implementation. We soon found that the action prompted by the co-constructed wall extended beyond the individuals and organizations we served as a learning community. It promoted new attention toward action as a means of learning, mirrored the types of documentation we saw in classrooms, and created ongoing conversations around purpose, skills, and agency. This year-long span of inquiry created a systemized approach to empowering all learners and planted seeds for school change.

The learning wall in Amy Osborn's fourth grade class shows a collection of learning around a handful of the United Nations Sustainable Development Goals. This space innovatively leveraged the *lack* of time left in the semester to challenge students to take action in a different way.

Source: Amy Osborn, Fourth Grade Teacher, Laurel Mountain Elementary, Austin, Texas

Amy Osborn is an educator who doesn't shy away from asking herself or her students how things can be done differently. She often reflects on what's needed to nurture confident and independent learners, and she carefully scaffolds skills that support self-management and research across the year. Having worked closely with Amy over the past decade, I've noticed that our conversations often begin with *I wonder how we might . . .* and end with a map of sticky notes, open-ended question stems, and a clearly defined list of teacher and student responsibilities.

Amy believes that all of her students *can*. She routinely pulls from her toolbox of inquiry moves that empower them to do more. We sat down one Monday afternoon to review an upcoming unit of inquiry centered on some of the UN's Sustainable Development Goals and noticed that the time she thought she would have for an in-depth, independent research project was running short. As usual, we paused and asked, *I wonder how we might . . .*

After a quick ping-pong of ideas across her horseshoe-shaped table, we cleared the air of the stale energy of time limitations and instead leveraged a learning wall and a collection of research mats to nurture the student agency that an independent research project typically evokes. Having co-constructed their classroom learning wall throughout the year, the students were familiar with the process of collecting artifacts and evidence to adorn the space. Amy tasked her fourth graders with building a new learning wall as a demonstration of action *and* learning.

Constructed of simple resources found in most classrooms, the students structured the learning wall around the essential questions that they had generated in small groups after a provocation around the UN goals. The collective project reflected their research with artifacts. They evidenced their connection-making skills through diagrams, illustrations, and persuasive headlines. All of which synthesized the learning with *action*.

As the learning wall took shape, students noticed patterns and trends in the research collected by other groups. These findings sparked the learners to organize and rearrange artifacts to better reflect relationships and connections found throughout the collaborative structure. It was a powerful summative assessment of student knowledge, connection making, and learning!

- Notice how structures in the learning walls in these examples support and encourage action. What might be a way you can organize your learning wall to encourage action too?
- How do you currently plan with action in mind? What do the examples here inspire you to consider next?

How might you use Understanding by Design to guide your learning in making connections? Download Jay McTighe's UbD template (version 2.0) to use as you plan learning experiences and brainstorm ideas for your action-centered learning wall.

2. Feedback and Assessment

Nurturing agency within our assessment practice requires that we continue the traditional scales of who gives feedback toward the learners. This starts when we model what good feedback looks and sounds like and by co-constructing indicators to empower our learners. Having equipped them, we then call on them to use elements from our learning walls to level up their feedback to their peers while supporting reflection and self-assessment of learning.

Reviewing the feedback our scholars give and receive allows us to assess their knowledge and the connections they've made. The screenshot above shows how a virtual learning wall can be used as a supportive assessment tool—and reminds us that assessment is *part of the learning*.

Using the digital platform Seesaw, Ms. Lough's first grade students submitted their projects for peer feedback. The learners gave

Kendall Lough
@lough_pyp

First Graders are using technology to make their community better by commenting responsibly. They give their peers specific feedback on their work on Seesaw. #digitalcitizenship @tech4fun @ibjvancepyp @TeyanPageRRISD

Matthew

Emilio, Makayla, Vir

Matthew I am proud of my spelling
Noah I like your steps
Vir I like your ending

and received ideas, suggested edits, and made revisions before submitting their final drafts. What's worth noting here is the *kind*, *specific*, and *helpful* feedback this student received from his peers. In addition to being proud of his spelling, the student goes on to make explicit connections to the big ideas, vocabulary, and concepts explored in the six-week unit of inquiry.

Feedback itself can become an artifact that documents knowledge growth and skill development, as well as the learners' ability to give and receive feedback. One way to use these artifacts is to save them and lift them up later in the school year as a provocation toward extending this skill of assessment.

This virtual platform shows us the endless ways to use learner-generated evidence and artifacts to authentically connect ideas, stretch their thinking, and assess knowledge and understanding. And this strategy and format are not limited to young learners. In Part Three of this book, you'll step inside a postsecondary classroom that leveraged a virtual platform to encourage discourse, feedback, and self-assessment.

- What does this example make you think about when you look at the artifacts on your learning wall?
- How might you choose artifacts that support assessment in your classroom and encourage your learners to use them as formative and summative assessments?
- As you consider your scope and sequence, what kinds of artifacts might you save for future learning?
- How might these steps help you plan and engage in a richer and less stress-inducing assessment cycle in your classroom?

3. Curricular Standards

For decades, schools have focused on teaching specific literacy skills under the assumption that the more clear and thorough our strategies (e.g., identifying captions, main ideas, and details), the better able students will be to tackle reading and independently create meaningful connections. The latest research and cognitive science of reading, however, shows that this approach to teaching foundational skills ignores the separate but interwoven skills necessary for language comprehension and word recognition. It forgoes other knowledge-building components of learning that are found in other academic disciplines such as social studies and science.

Hyper-targeted instruction leaves unintentional gaps in the experiential learning students need to build rich vocabulary and background knowledge that can be recalled, retrieved, and transferred across disciplines. Simply put, the "rabbit holes" we allow—STEM and STEAM (science, technology, engineering, arts, and math) experiences, the mini-inquiries into kingdoms and castles, the field trips, guest experts, and intentional time for discussing, reflecting on, and connecting ideas—*all* matter.

What's critical here is to pause, get curious about the artifacts and our learners' patterns, and consider how we can best use our expertise to support contextual understanding of our curricular standards. With this mindset, learning walls aren't just "nice to have"—they are essential tools that help us build background knowledge, stoke curiosity, and invite new learning. They help us untangle the fascinating web of thinking that develops when we prioritize making connections to a wide range of experiences.

As you consider learning walls throughout this book, slow down and notice how different educators use these documentation tools to integrate varied skills, disciplines, and curriculum.

- What connections can you make to your content?
- How do the artifacts on your learning wall reflect the curriculum?
- How might some of the artifacts enhance or differentiate knowledge so that students think critically about the concepts and ideas being expressed?

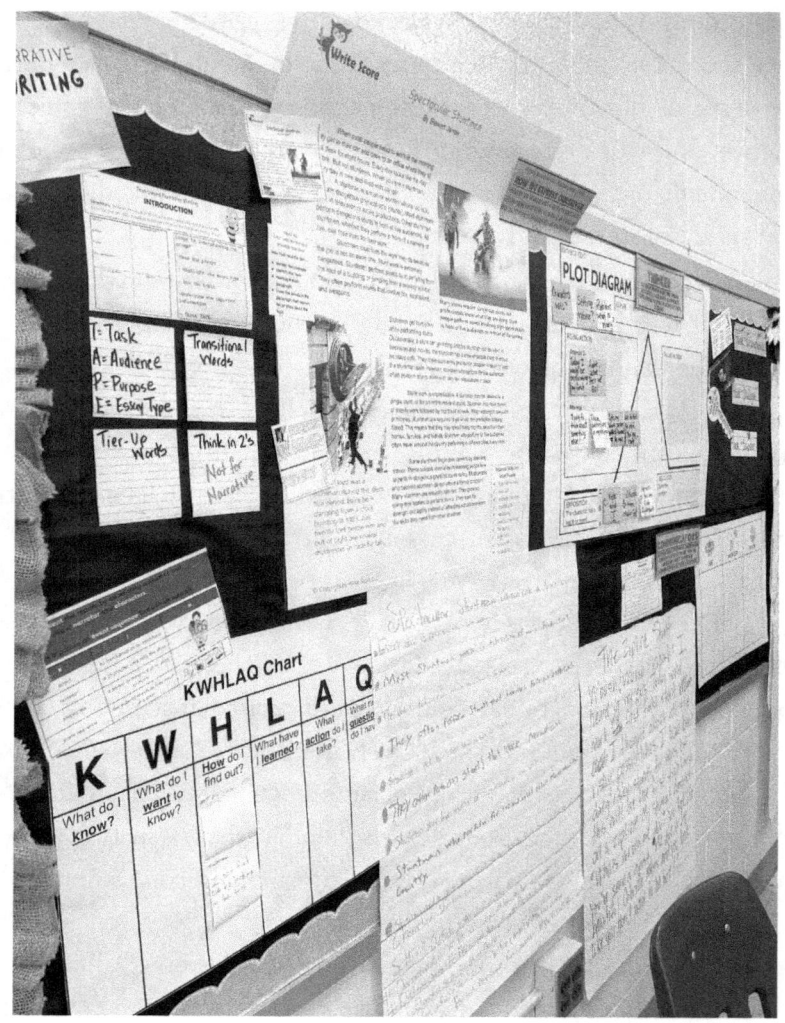

Source: Continental Colony Elementary School, Atlanta, Georgia

4. Nurturing School Vision and a Culture of Learning

Before my job included planning and leading schoolwide professional development, I experienced a variety of quality learning opportunities that really stretched my practice. I also sat through my share of lackluster training sessions that either didn't apply to my role or lacked the thoughtful differentiation needed to meet the various levels of experience and expertise represented by the teachers in the room. Now that I'm in a leadership role, I have a better understanding that there are a number of reasons that some programs are effective while others simply aren't. One of those reasons is that the constant demands on leaders' time and attention impact everything, including how focused they are on curating connected and meaningful professional development. Fortunately, this is one thing we control by being intentional about how we cultivate a culture of learning.

In *Leading with a Lens of Inquiry*, I asked readers to reflect on the essential question that continues to surface in my work with school and organizational leaders: *How do we cultivate our garden so it flourishes?*

How do we cultivate our garden so it flourishes?

@jess_vanceedu
#leadingwithinquiry

Learning walls help us *see* the culture we are nurturing. Offering visible cues for dialogue amongst colleagues, they bring focus by reinforcing three facets of *how we lead* with a lens of inquiry:

- Commitment to consistency
- Allowing space for agency
- Modeling the model

These facets don't exist in a silo; they are intertwined. Although they manifest organically and differently in each community, they cultivate the conditions in which learning can thrive—at every level in every culture.

I've included three different leader-instigated learning walls as models to consider as we explore each of these facets of leading with a lens of inquiry. Notice the unique ways each wall invites connection making, upholds the principles of constructivism, and fosters opportunities to align our actions with the visionary goals we set for ourselves and for our schools. Note also that although these ideas are presented with school leaders in mind, they apply to the way all educators lead their learning communities.

Commitment to Consistency

A commitment to consistency calls leaders to plan, design, and facilitate professional learning with the school vision as the constant guide. These values not only direct improvement but also keep us grounded when challenges arise. When navigating district mandates or delivering information to staff, we align each action with our year's learning focus, ensuring it connects to the vision and larger goals we're striving to reach.

The learning wall pictured here reflects the initiatives of our elementary campus. It is littered with artifacts that illustrate our focus on the attributes of a learner, making thinking visible, and provocations. Our staff meetings routinely generated new artifacts to add to the wall. We mindfully co-constructed and regularly added to a list of thinking routines that pointed learners to the toolbox of resources and strategies that could be used in the classroom.

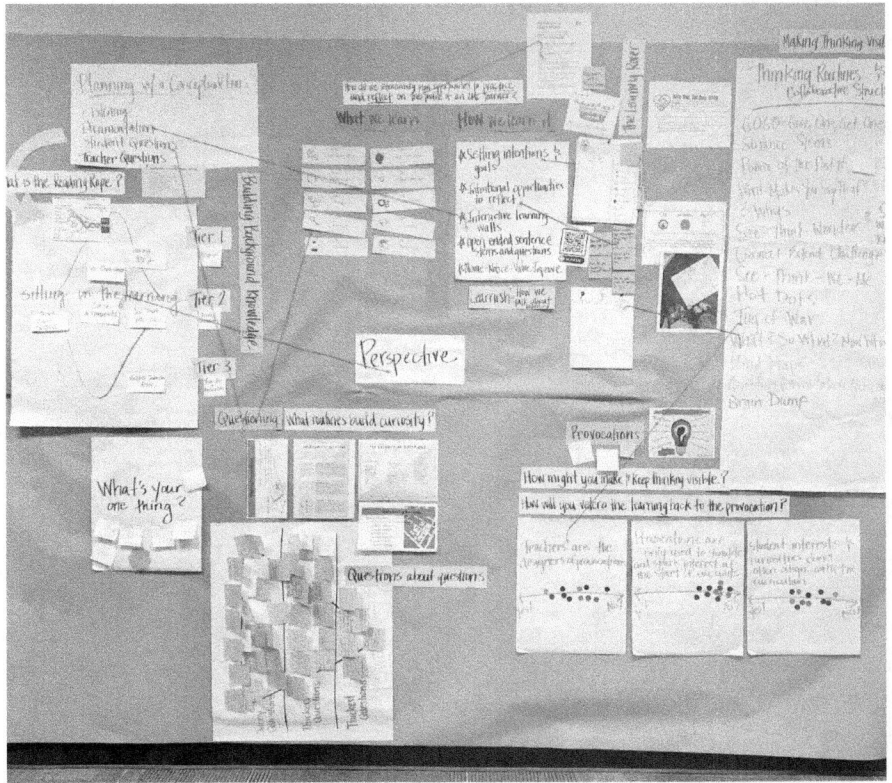

Source: Laurel Mountain Elementary, Austin, Texas

The year that we designed this wall, our leadership was tasked with implementing a new curriculum and asked to support different data-based initiatives. Returning to this wall to make connections to our vision and values helped us filter those changes and integrate them into our school culture and transformed how we leveraged learning around these new ideas through provocation. We approached these tasks with a sense of wonder and curiosity influenced by the practice we encouraged our teaching staff to employ. The routine connections we had made to this vertical space throughout the year became pivotal when deadlines loomed and factors outside our control impacted timelines or challenged our approach toward teaching and learning. Each time, what we had created and revisited kept us focused and moving together toward our unified vision.

When we commit to consistency and routines become *routine*, our capacity grows. It gives us the bandwidth to take mindful actions that, even if they are small, move us toward sustainable and manageable change in our schools, programs, and organizations.

Space for Agency

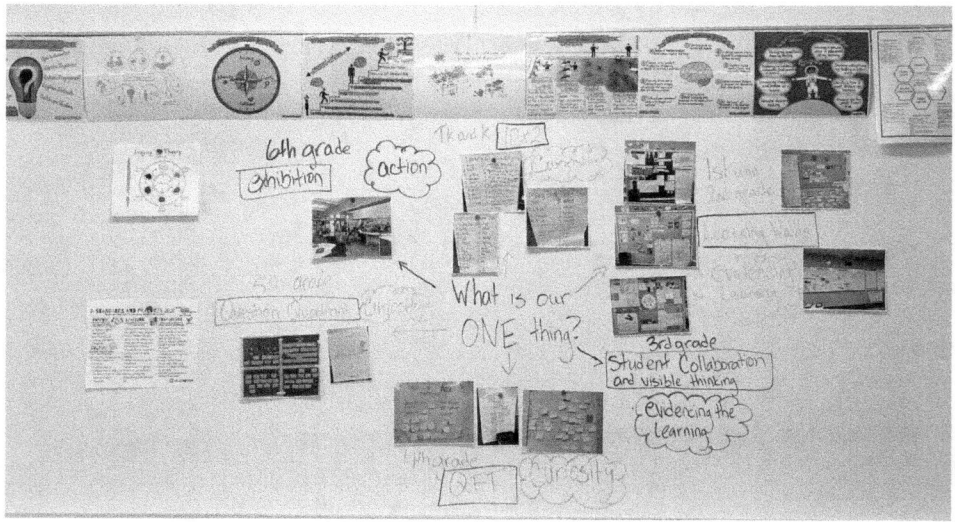

Source: Mary Rimbey, Natomas Unified School District, Sacramento, California

Learners gain independence when the systems and structures balance support with an exploratory undercurrent. This is as true in our classrooms with students as it is for adult learners. With that in mind, our job, as leaders, is to create space for our teachers to exercise voice—something that curriculum frameworks and scope and sequence tend to diminish. When we document professional goals, carefully design our professional development calendars, and adjust daily schedules to reflect the interests and needs of our adult learners, we communicate that we trust and value the agency, growth, and development of *all* learners in our buildings.

Professional learning communities (PLCs) are one way to ignite and move energy toward a school culture that values agency. Program coordinator Mary Rimbey used PLCs and the whiteboard above to document each grade level's "one thing" for the semester. The learning wall lifted up what was important to each group of learners who added big ideas and, over time, evidence to this space.

Pictures were captured during learning walks and taped to the wall, as were graphic organizers and other printed resources. Teachers proudly brought evidence from their practice to this growing space. With the groups all having a unique focus, each applied their learning at their own pace. The process of collective documentation nudged everyone to think about their personal goals in relation to the broader landscape of professional learning occurring across the campus. The agentic nature of this structure led to greater collaboration across grade levels and connections between personal goals and the learning community's focus. The result was meaningful professional learning that aligned with the school's vision.

Model the Model

Inquiry lives in all spaces. It's within our approach to building relationships, it lives in the way we embrace questions as the roadmap for what's important to give our attention to, it shows up in the dispositions we embody as leaders, and it is evidenced in the values we instill in the school cultures we help build. "Model the model" is a facet of leading with inquiry that reminds us to express this pedagogy in all of our decisions, initiatives, and coaching conversations.

Inquiry leaders, like school principal Kristen Horton, do not shy away from modeling the model. Horton sees this approach to leadership as an invitation to deepen professional practices, even when involved in tasks such as data collection and management (see image on left side, wall of school-wide data collection). The collaborative

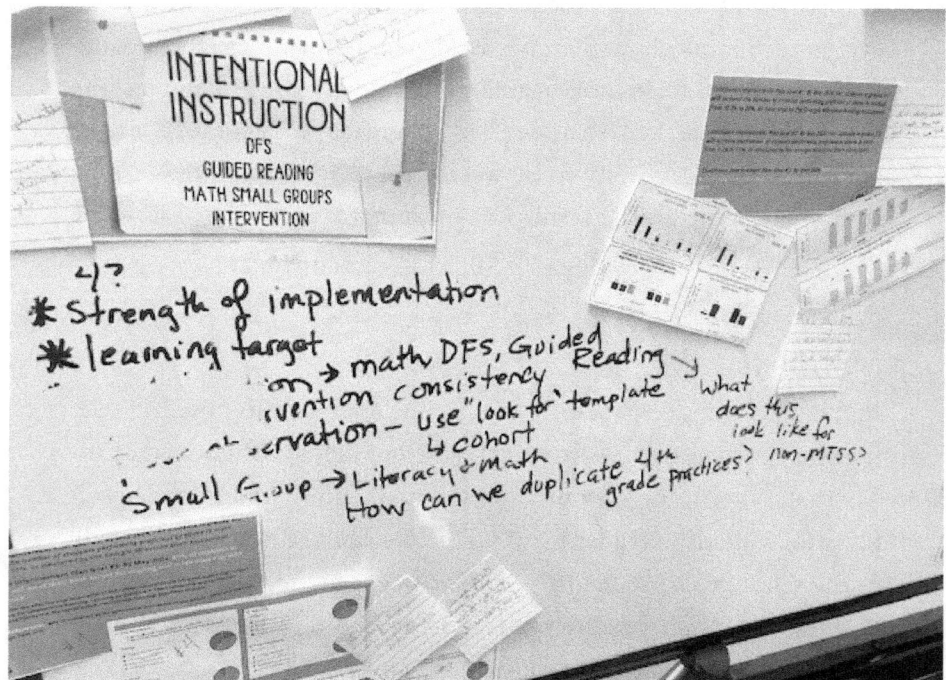

Source: Kristen Horton, Principal, Continental Colony Elementary, Atlanta, Georgia

meeting space you see here houses a campus-wide learning wall. The intentional and ongoing use of the space to collect documentation supports Horton and her instructional leadership team. They refer to the wall for short-term planning meetings and to review the goals and strategies from the school's continuous improvement plan. During formal meetings, the team pinned literacy and numeracy assessment data, sorted big ideas, made connections to strategies, and grounded each of these sessions with a brain dump of wonderings (on yellow sticky notes) that became the provocation for action steps moving forward.

Rather than settling into a rote system of data collection and analysis, as inquiry leaders, we can choose actions that support meaning-making for our adult leaders. With consistency, allowing space for agency, and modeling the skills we hope to see in our classrooms, we help promote a continuous cycle of learning. Practicing the skills of questioning, authentic documentation, creating flexible learning spaces, ongoing reflection, and collaborative thinking drive a culture of learning. Leaders intentionally plan for and model these practices, demonstrating their value to every level of learner in the school. These actions help shift our focus toward what matters most when we analyze data to refine our practice.

- Kristen Horton carefully balances the managerial tasks within her role while leaning into an inquiry mindset. Her approach to her role illustrates what it could look and sound like to "model the model" for learners. How are you "modeling the model" for your learners? What might be something that you could do with more intention?
- Mary Rimbey helps her adult learners set goals and remain focused through the busyness of their days. How might you help your learners set and monitor goals too?

5. Research Skills

Research is a skill that takes time. It's often messy because it is, in fact, a collection of skills that requires higher-order thinking and self-management. When we multiply the complexity of research by the number of scholars in the room, it can easily feel overwhelming, underplanned, and exhausting before we even get halfway started!

Learning walls are a tool we can use to help scholars track the process of their research and see the connections take shape between the big ideas and the information they gather. With the visibility and flexibility of the artifacts and with resources such as graphic organizers, learners can revise ideas and plan next steps.

The two classroom learning walls described below use different structures, but both empower their scholars to flex their research skills. Let's *walk their walls* together now.

Using a timeline structure, Colleen Ruplinger adds artifacts from left to right as the students engage in personal inquiries. Knowing that organizing materials is an area of growth for her primary learners (Grade 2), she has pinned graphic organizers to the learning wall and stored research materials in bins below the wall. The lower placement of the learning wall and the materials chosen to construct it allow students to access books checked out from the school library, easily reference co-constructed anchor charts, and take down note cards of research held by binder clips.

The learning wall naturally differentiates for scholars at every stage of the research process. Its flexibility supports the varying needs of individuals, allowing Colleen to conference with students and provide feedback, using the wall as an instructional support. As students approach different parts of the wall for resources, Colleen informally assesses where students are in their research. She takes inventory of students' progress so she can revise her plans and timeline for research accordingly.

Consider how an approach like Colleen's research learning wall might support your learners in their next research project.

- What materials would be helpful to have at the ready?
- What space (virtual or physical) best organizes thinking, resources, and the scaffolding of skills you are working on to help your learners develop?

- How might you include physical movement across the wall to reinforce the process of uncovering information as a way to make meaningful connections in learning?

Source: Colleen Ruplinger, Second Grade Teacher, Laurel Mountain Elementary, Austin, Texas

Let's take a look at another learning wall that considers research skills and experts as an essential part of making meaningful connections to the community and *coming to know*. Reinforcing the place-based inquiry cycle adopted by her northwestern Canadian school, Paige Driscoll used one section of her learning wall to organize research resources.

Pulling from her previous teaching experience and accounting for grade-level standards, Paige collected a range of resources for her students to reference throughout the unit. Over time, the wall filled with reputable websites, industry experts, teacher-selected maps and tables, and other resources provided by the school district. Then, with the intentional decision to lift up her Grade 4 students' voices, she paused and asked them for feedback. Together, they co-constructed the remaining section of the wall (see the right triangle portion of the learning wall).

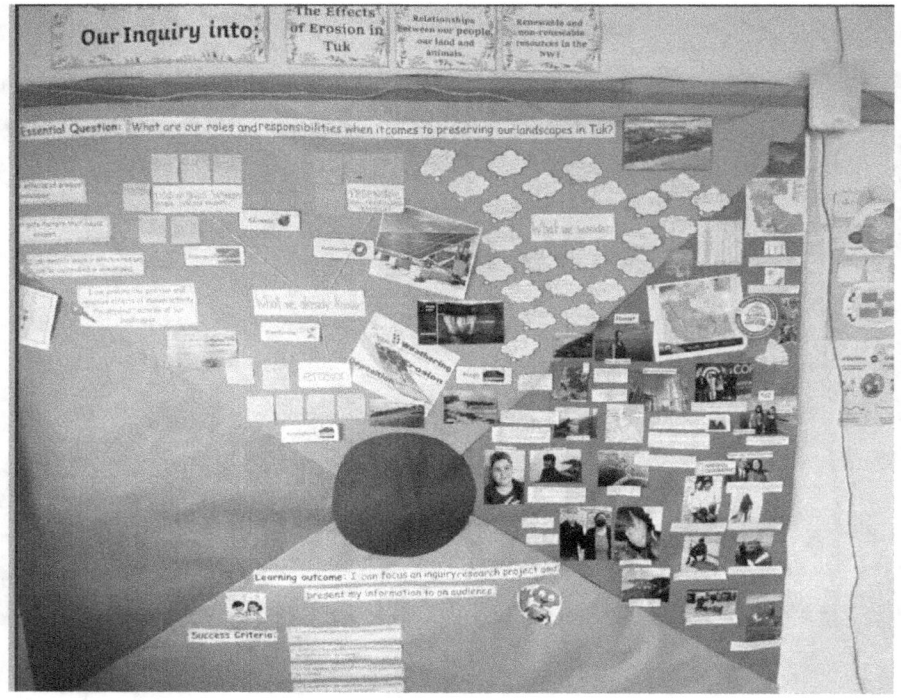

Source: Paige Driscoll, Mangilaluk School, Tuktoyaktuk, NWT, Canada

Paige asked her students who they knew personally who might be willing to help the class learn about the Tuktoyaktuk community in which they reside. The initial list was sparse and included the voices of only a handful of students. In response to the data before her, she asked targeted yet open-ended questions. At her encouragement, students began sharing the names of family members and neighbors who were knowledgeable about the topic. Some identified elders whose deep wisdom and history in the region offered an authentic perspective regarding change over time. More photos were added to document these experts, and these *new* resources became a co-constructed space that expanded her students' thinking about *how* to research. The exercise reinforced understanding of the vital knowledge base that resides within our communities.

How often do you plan for opportunities that prompt students to pause and look within first, deciding who or what might be a good place to start with research *before* jumping to Google for an answer? As we look at Paige's classroom wall, Project Zero's thinking routine called Think, Puzzle, Explore comes to mind. It is another powerful tool that encourages learners to *think*

Place-based learning is an approach to teaching and learning that immerses students in local heritage, culture, landscapes, and community opportunities to enhance meaningful curriculum connections. This pedagogical approach is known to increase student belonging and sense of self, narrow equity gaps, and foster a sense of academic persistence and resiliency.

about their thinking and decide on avenues and resources that might help them find the answers they seek. By planning for skills that foster independence, we take a place-based approach, creating supportive structures that activate prior knowledge and prompt collaboration and human connection. In doing so, we design immersive experiences that bring inquiry to life.

- How might you start and co-construct a learning wall to support the development of research skills for your learners? Is there a structure or other organizational system that you can leverage to scaffold skill development over time?
- It's essential that asking and listening to the voices of our learners be a part of our inquiry practice. What would happen if you took inventory with your learners first, before starting to build your learning wall, to get their ideas and feedback about what could be helpful for them across their research?

6. Building Collaborative Communities

A community thrives when psychological safety and trust are at its core. Learners see themselves as a connected group, not as competitors. They rely on their peers to challenge and stretch their thinking, and the classroom becomes a harmonious community of thought partners. We make connections to build community and recognize that space acts as the third teacher in these collaborative communities.

Becky Carlzon is an educator, author, and co-creator of Learning Pioneers, an online professional learning community. She has cultivated a space that embodies this idea. I invite you to use the QR code to take a virtual peek inside her primary classroom to get a sense of the intentionality she brings to learning walls. Pay attention to the way Becky prioritizes strategic, cognitive, emotional, and social skills to empower students to support one another in their learning.

 Have a look at Becky's classroom now! This interactive resource allows you to virtually walk through this dynamic space and take a closer look at the start of some fantastic learning. As you explore these spaces, consider the tenets of a learning wall and note what connections and applications you see in your classroom and practice.

Each time I return to Becky's classroom, she gets me thinking about the connection learning walls have to collaborative communities. I'm sure you'll find her generous resource quite helpful as you work with your group of learners and leverage your learning wall as an essential tool for relationship building. There are, however, three particular spaces in the 360° classroom I'll bring to your attention now:

Get Unstuck Wall

The title of this wall says it all and reminds the learners in the room about the process that ensues with rich and deep learning, highlighting this co-designed space as an asset for problem-solving and maintaining a growth mindset when the work feels particularly challenging. I've seen many classrooms leverage similar spaces for conflict resolution, self-management, or any of the other core skills of social and emotional learning. These walls house sentence stems, calm-down strategies, student goals, photos, and other artifacts that aid in taking action forward. What type of "Get Unstuck" wall might be supportive for your classroom to keep taking care of the relationships in your learning space?

Teachers as Learners

This section, tucked into the corner of this classroom, is such a beautiful example of how tinkering with our own learning in a visible way impacts the energy and mindset of the classroom. Teacher learning walls become a personal playground of inquiry and reflect our own sense of wonder as we seek support from the learners in our classrooms, our colleagues, and other critical thought partners and friends. Becky's learning wall models notetaking and artifact collecting and shares her current interests. She leaves space for wonder and may even reference the artifacts on this wall as the class co-constructs others in this space.

Reflection Wheel

I love the mainstay of a reflection wheel and similar resources in the classroom. If you watched the little learner in Becky's classroom speak about feedback, you'll be convinced of its value too! The reflection wheel is based on the reflection tool called Balance that was developed by Tom Wallace. It reminds us of the impact that clear systems have on purpose, community, and connection making. I can only imagine the different artifacts and resources that could be added to this wall as learners get used to giving and getting feedback. A range of exemplars, co-designed rubrics, sentence frames to support collaborative conversations, and key vocabulary are just a handful of artifacts Becky added to this space to support learner independence and reflection. As the year unfolds, these artifacts could easily be exchanged to stretch, scaffold, and align with new skills and topics.

Asking what may help us *learn together* and pausing to think about the bigger systems we have in our classrooms is a critical step in building learning walls and fostering student-to-student relationships. They gift us the potential to do great things *together,* to be great people *together,* to have meaningful and connected experiences *together,* and to create a space in which we fail, grow, stretch, reflect, and think *together.*

- Which of the three elements I have highlighted from Becky's classroom most speak to you, your context and group of learners? How could you implement something right away?
- Take another peek at Becky's classroom. What other qualities or characteristics stand out to you? Is there something you could adapt to best meet your group of learners?

7. Writing Reports and School Action Plans

Writing reports and report card comments can feel like a daunting and never-ending task. We begin this job by looking at the columns of markings in our gradebook. Knowing those marks tell only part of the story, we flip through our notes and review evidence to identify patterns that illustrate strengths and stretches. We reference our standards and compare them to the skills our learners have been practicing or mastering.

A similar process ensues as school leaders revisit goals and strategies outlined at the onset of a school year to monitor progress. We analyze campus reports and data, reference slide decks from staff meetings and campus-wide professional development days, and may even review data entry systems used for formal and informal walk-throughs.

Although valuable, our due diligence to track progress requires an impossible amount of time. The sifting. The sorting. The overwhelming amount of data that muddies the task.

But what would happen if we used our learning walls to aid in this process? How might the co-constructed data wall we have before us give us a clearer and more unified approach to the way to align our assessment of progress? How does engaging with the data in this way help us see connections more quickly than we have before?

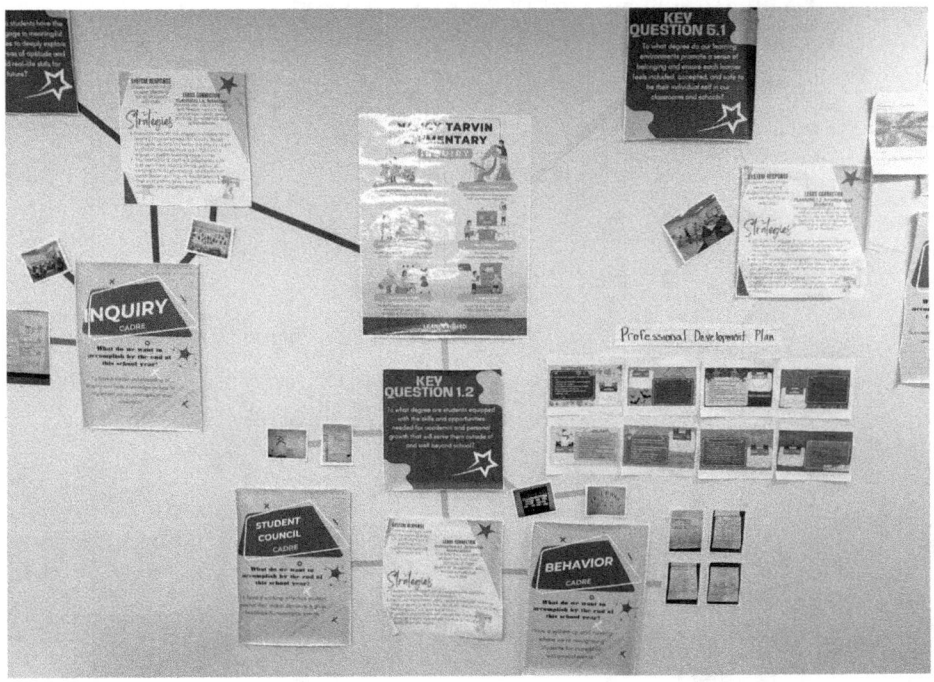

Source: Tarvin Elementary, Leander, Texas

The learning wall pictured here tracked a schoolwide continuous improvement plan across an academic year. Leaders added evidence after PLC learning walks, attached data that connected to school goals, and relied on the wall to aid in reflections and measure progress over time. At weekly team meetings, they updated data as required by the district, then referenced the wall as well as site visits from district leaders to enhance conversations. From there they dug into the specific strategies that contributed to student and campus growth. Although this is *one way* to use a learning wall, it's *not the only way* to use these spaces to support assessment, data collection, and reporting.

Working closely with school leaders, classroom teachers, and district superintendents during the past few years, I've collected a series of reflective questions for sorting through formative evidence to aid in reporting. With your learning wall front and center, use these questions as you annotate learner progress on reports, update your campus improvement plan, or prepare presentations for district board and council members. Use colored tape or yarn to visually represent the connections between the goals and evidence that has been collected. If needed, move artifacts and documentation to support the meaning-making that occurs at this stage.

Questions for Reflection

- What were our goals? What does the evidence tell us about our goals?
- How might the evidence reflect our progress toward these goals?
- What did we learn about ourselves (and/or our students) through this process?
- How do the data reveal our next steps?
- Where are there continued stretches? What are areas of strength?

After you have walked through these prompts, ask yourself what's missing in your assessment practice. What additional data would be helpful in your report-writing process? Is there space for you to include photos of the evidence on your learning wall to further enhance your narrative report card comments? How might there be ways to include your learners in this process or report writing to lean toward a more learner-centered approach?

Create a routine for yourself using these five questions. Use them frequently and introduce them to a critical thought partner or friend as a way to help you gain new perspectives!

8. Student-led Conferences

Pairing student-led conferences and learning walls presents many opportunities. On the individual level, there is an opportunity to reinforce reflection across a longer span of time. Challenges and unexpected learning experiences sharpen students' skills. They acknowledge their growth and celebrate their commitment to a process that's about more than perfection.

On a community level, there's an opportunity to invite parents and guardians to be partners in learning. Student-led conferences and learning walls shift parents' perception about the point of school by putting their attention on the experience of learning. The rich conversations that result focus on nurturing the whole child.

On the school or organizational level, there's an opportunity to reinforce the value of scholar voice, choice, and ownership. Pairing student-led conferences and learning walls expresses a learning community that's committed to learning—*not just* grades, standardized assessments, or quantitative data—and to keeping learners at the center.

Student-led conferences and learning walls don't just happen, of course, and as you reflect on how to use learning walls in conjunction with student-led conferences, we consider three parts that help bring intentional purpose and connection-making to these agentic celebrations of learning: *before, during,* and *after.*

If your school community already has a well-established routine for student-led conferences, consider how you might refine your approach and invite new voices and perspectives to these conversations about learning walls. If this student-led approach is a newer practice for you, the structure that follows is a perfect frame to scaffold you and your learners into this process. I'm curious how these lists support your reflection and movement forward!

Before: Preparing for Conferences

Ensuring that our learners feel empowered to engage in student-led conferences doesn't mean that we need to stop all other learning to prepare for this event. We start by considering the ways we have already modeled using a learning wall for our learners and then engage in conversations with students about how they have engaged with the artifacts and partnered with one another for discussions. Ask them what questions, prompts, and provocations have sparked conversations. In short, get them to reflect on these vertical resources and how they've used them.

From those conversations, curate a list of keywords, helpful phrases, and sentence stems that learners can refer to when they are preparing what they would like to share with their families and caregivers. It may be necessary to add language to support learners' growing communication skills and equip them with the prompts they need to authentically reflect on, connect, and share their learning. Here are a few prompts to consider:

- I'm really proud of the way that I . . .
- I used to think . . . now I know . . .
- At the beginning of the year/term I . . . now I am . . .
- A strength for me is . . .
- A stretch for me still is . . .
- One thing I was surprised by was . . .
- One thing I'd love to show you is . . .

Call on students to practice with a peer. Move around the room to lean in and listen to conversations and encourage learners to use artifacts that support their sharing. If needed, provide kind, specific, and helpful feedback. This preparatory learning experience supports

the attributes we are already building with students and may even
provide the ideal opportunity for
you to formatively assess progress
made toward these skills.

If this process is new to your
learners, generate a list of words,
ideas, indicators, and other language that students could draw
upon. I've also seen teachers partner to co-teach this exercise to
model sharing and to explore dif-
ferent ways of expression. Be playful with new ways students rehearse
and celebrate learning with one another.

During: Engaging In

During conferences, step back and let your students shine as they share
the connections they've made to the learning. To support the adults in
the room, I find it helpful to provide prompts that encourage curiously
reflective conversations and model the tenets of feedback that our
learners are used to experiencing in the classroom. A simple list on the
board, a half sheet of paper with sentence stems, and gentle invitations
from the teacher are low-prep and uncomplicated ways to connect,
build relationships, and communicate what's most valued during these
interactions. Empower parents and caregivers by creating a word bank
that allows them to use academic language within your programs. The
approaches to learning in the IB, attributes from your district's portrait
of a graduate, and school values are all great places to look for language
to add to the vocabulary of the learning community at large. Here are
some prompts to get you started!

- I notice that . . . can you tell me more?
- I'm really proud of how you . . .
- I'm curious to know about your learning about . . . ?

- Tell me about what this artifact represents. What makes you say that?
- What does your learning make you wonder about now?

Remember that the adults in the room are learners too! Decide how to scaffold for their success as well. A simple email that outlines the intention for the day and includes the short list of prompts, a quick video recording created by the students that explains the purpose and structure of these student-led conferences, or providing stations and cues for them in your room are a few possibilities for nurturing a space that is infused with trust, connection making, and the celebration of progress and growth over time.

After: Reflecting on Action

To make the most of the energy after a student-led conference, I jump right into reflection. I've noticed that the closer we place the reflection to the conference, the more specific and authentic the experience. Facilitate a Give One, Get One, ask your learners to do a gallery walk, or use another collaborative structure to reflect and draw new conclusions from this process. Ask them to discuss what went well, what changes might be helpful next time, and what they learned about their learning from leading the conference. Dutifully attend to the feedback and reflections, make connections with the broader goals by referencing your learning wall, document thinking, make it visible, and organize it using Plus/Delta/Wonder or Compass Points. Reflect, connect, and plan your way forward alongside your learners!

As you draw conclusions and make connections with artifacts and evidence, I hope you will create routines that unleash deeper and more meaningful learning in your learning environment. Keep the eight frames presented to you here as possibilities to help you develop consistency in your routines and recognize new patterns and relationships within the learning. The pause and reflect questions that follow are an additional nudge to stretch you toward action and synthesis of this step in building a learning wall.

Pause and Reflect

* If you are a school exploring or deepening your practice around learning walls and documentation of learning, perhaps you and your staff co-construct an index or catalog of examples on your site. How might the resource you create together be one that unites you in your journey as an inquiry school?

* By now, you've probably already identified strategies to add to your toolbox of inquiry moves. What's *one thing* you're most keen to put into practice? Choose this one thing and go take action right away, then create a plan for yourself to assess impact and modify your approach as necessary. I know our learning community would love to see and learn from your process, too, so consider sharing on social media, using #learningwalls.

* Student-led conferences and similar celebrations of learning are common practice on many school campuses. What are the elements of these events that could use some refining or could be encouraged to go a bit deeper? How might you backwards plan and create a list of the opportunities and experiences that students will need to feel confident and comfortable before these events? In what ways might this influence the culture you are nurturing as a school community?

Chapter 8

Leave Space for Wonder

Leaving space for wonder seems like an obvious element of any unit of inquiry. We design provocations with learner curiosity in mind. We anticipate the kinds of questions we might overhear and the thinking that may surface. We also prepare our mindset with clear intentions, using language like, *Today I intend to remain open-minded and curious*, or *I intend to listen and pause before jumping in right away*. We remind ourselves to ask open-ended questions such as, *Tell me more. . .* or *I'm curious, how do you know. . . ?*—questions that invite our learners to pause and think just a moment longer about their thinking.

And just as the small figures in the sketch that welcomed you into this chapter illustrate, there's not always one clear path to getting "there." As inquiry educators, we know the potential that questions have to help us engage learners in meaningful and purposeful learning. As artificial intelligence becomes part of our everyday lives, we are increasingly conscious of the need to know how to ask and answer the "right questions."

The physical and cognitive actions of building a learning wall are two ways we leave space for wonder. This balanced approach to managing our curriculum calls us to identify space where our learners' voices drive personal meaning. Leaving space for wonder is the piqued curiosity we *allow ourselves* to dawdle in because we deserve to honor ourselves as learners too.

Before you continue reading, take note of how you currently leave space for questions, wonder, and awe in your practice. What protocols or systems do you routinely revisit to ensure that curiosity is at the forefront of your practice? Jot down a short list now to use as an artifact of reflection after you finish reading this chapter. I'm curious what new insights you'll have, the small shifts you'll decide to implement right away, and how you will integrate this step of documentation further into your mindset and overall way of being.

Wonder Walls

When I was introduced to the idea of an inquiry classroom, it included desks arranged in small groupings, a bulletin board dedicated to the current unit of inquiry, and a small display of photos that celebrated the ways the students had been inspired by their learning and had taken action in their school and neighboring communities. And, of course, it included a wonder wall. As I walked through several other classrooms that had so generously left things intact after saying goodbye to their students so that I, and a few other newly hired teachers, could get a sense of the different types of learning environments we would be teaching in, I immediately noticed that each of these classrooms had a space dedicated to a wonder wall. These open-ended spaces housed collections of sticky notes penned by both students and teachers that reflected the myriad interests of the scholars who had once occupied the room. I was still unclear about exactly what planning, teaching, and facilitating inquiry looked and sounded like, but a wonder wall seemed like an easy enough entry point. So that was the first thing I found a home for in my fifth grade classroom. A tangible space to collect questions was a great start to recentering my practice but was only a small piece of the puzzle. *What I did* with the questions was what really mattered!

If you are reading this book, this artifact of learner curiosity is something you are most likely familiar with in your practice and may even be the very thing that you started with in your classroom too. Wonder walls are not a requirement of a flourishing culture of inquiry. They do, however, remind us to keep learner curiosity at the forefront when planning. They implicitly tell our students that we welcome and value their voices—and that they have a say in where our learning journeys take us. Wonder walls can be a permanent fixture in your physical space or something a bit more fleeting, like the virtual Padlet sandbox below or an exit ticket you ask learners to place on the door before they transition to their next class.

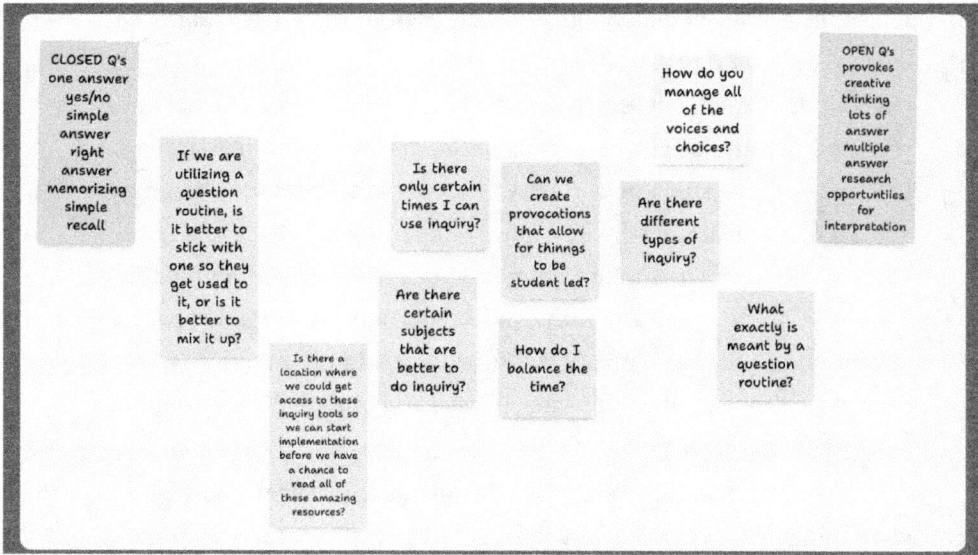

I love the creative and thoughtful spaces that educators choose to place wonder walls in their classrooms. Backs of doors, underneath whiteboards, the fronts of storage closets, windows that lead to communal teaching and spaces, and virtual walls using popular platforms such as Padlet, Google Slides, FigJam, or Mentimeter are playful ways to infuse our physical and virtual spaces with our students' wonderings. I've been fortunate to visit and co-teach in many different classrooms around the world and am always intrigued with the innovative ways teachers and leaders rework and rethink ways to structure and organize learner questions. If you've been using wonder walls for a while and are looking to stretch your practice or have barriers within your physical space, I encourage you to consider one of the following whimsical walls.

Lingering Questions

Source: Rachel Kothmann, Forth Grade Teacher, Laurel Mountain Elementary, Austin, Texas

One dilemma teachers face is what to do with all the questions scholars ask. From off-topic questions to those that we simply run out of time for, there will always be questions left unanswered. The first misconception is that we need to answer all the questions. For those you want to save for later, consider creating a space for *lingering questions*. The photo here from an elementary teacher shows some of the unanswered questions her students had about resources and water.

Easily stored on a single sheet of construction paper, this flexible artifact is something you could return to when planning future inquiry units or pull from to reinforce students' research skills. Alternatively, students can review the lingering question during opportunities for free inquiry. The collection also can be used as a reference for students as they generate questions using the stems, language, and structure as a launchpad for future inquiry units. When we think beyond the perpetual question-and-answer opportunities for co-constructing a deeper understanding around the role of questions, they flourish!

The point of lingering questions is not to keep all questions but to create a sustainable system that shows learners we value process over product and affirms the fact that their curiosities hold deep meaning in our practice.

Take Note

Source: Nicole Levitan, Second Grade Teacher, Laurel Mountain Elementary, Austin, Texas

Several years ago, I was working with a teacher who was new to learning walls. Curious to give it a try but unsure of what value they would hold for her students, she decided to start small by blocking off a section of the whiteboard she frequently used at the front of her classroom. Not long afterward, the teacher facilitated a provocation that generated piles of questions. She analyzed the questions, looking for patterns in wonderings that had emerged. She sorted the sticky notes into groups and attached them to the whiteboard, creating an artifact of current thinking in the room.

Each day, the questions served as the launch pad for lesson planning and classroom conversations as the short unit unfolded. The teacher added notes, definitions, and examples to the space to support and scaffold the knowledge and new thinking about the math concept *around* the student questions.

Take Note is a small but powerful shift in an approach to leverage curiosity in our classrooms. We model how to jot down key takeaways, lift up big ideas from conversations, and capture important ideas or examples for later use. At the same time, we model an interest in our learners' questions. If an active and functional wonder wall is something you have been seeking in your practice, I encourage you to Take Note. Consider giving your learners the power to add to this flexible space. Using a pen and sticky notes, ask them to reflect on their growing knowledge and evolution of thinking. A good question to ask is, *How does this collective note-taking device create equitable access to the learning?*

Question Frameworks

You may find that you and your learners need more scaffolding and structure at different times across an academic year than an open-ended wonder wall might typically have. A question protocol or routine transforms wonder walls into spaces that classify and organize students' questions while sending the message that learner voices give purpose to where we go next. Although most question routines can be the start of a wonder wall, I'll share three examples that are flexible enough for any context and space. Let's take a look at those now.

A Continuum of Questions

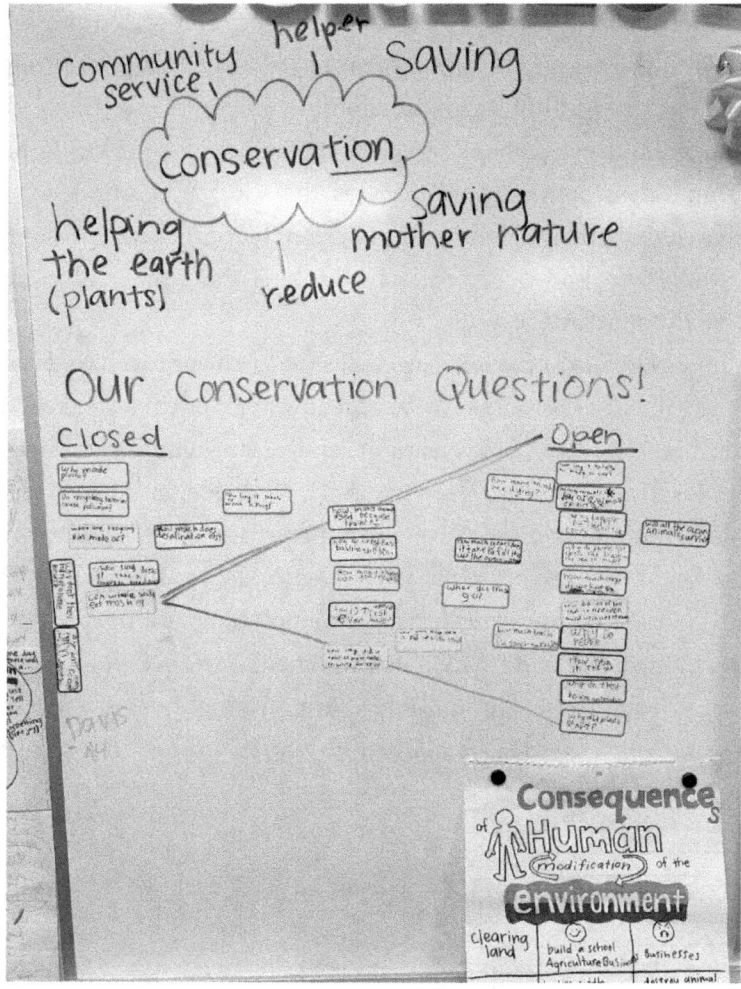

Source: Audrey Davis, Second Grade Teacher, Laurel Mountain Elementary, Austin, Texas

Anchored on a whiteboard and flanking one of the classroom walls in this elementary classroom, a question continuum is used as a vehicle for student curiosity. Learners write their questions on wipeable magnets, then sort them along the continuum from open ended to closed ended. The space is accessible to the students, so they can add to it easily. But the class has agreed that only the owner of the question or the teacher may shift or remove a question or move it to another place on the learning wall.

A whiteboard provides a versatile surface for a wonder wall. On top of the question structure, you can see the beginnings of a graphic organizer that displays a brainstorming activity around the central concept, conservation, and includes language that some of the students have clearly used as they generated their questions. Move your focus to the column of open questions on the right side of the continuum and you'll find another artifact that the class has started to co-construct with their teacher in their effort to begin to unpack the related concept of consequences. The placement of artifacts, materials chosen to construct the wonder wall (e.g., whiteboard, magnets), and ease of access all reflect the notion of student agency and ownership of the learning that is documented on this vertical space.

The Question Quadrant

The Question Quadrant calls on learners to evaluate the significance and depth of questions. This protocol can be used in tandem or in place of a wonder wall, and it can be used in a professional development setting as easily as it can be used in a classroom. It is a great protocol to introduce to get you using the wonder wall more actively. I want to share two different scenarios of how this flexible protocol can be used.

Several years ago, I was co-facilitating a half-day session of learning with grade-level teams of teachers at our school. They wanted to learn more about the skill of questioning for both themselves and their students, so I anchored the session's curiosities in the Question Quadrant.

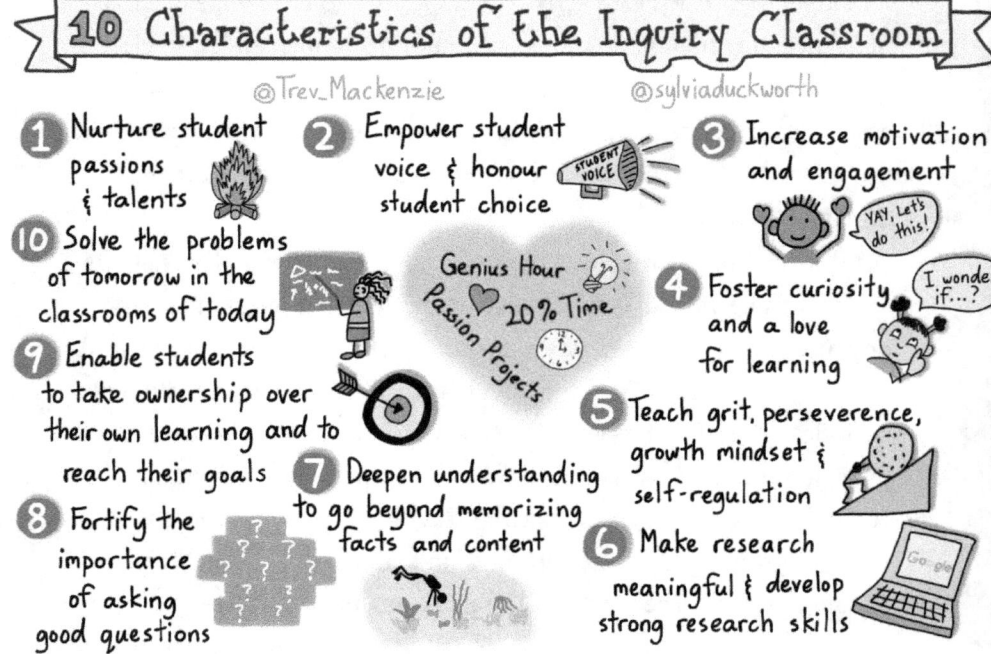

10 Characteristics of the Inquiry Classroom

@Trev_Mackenzie @sylviaduckworth

1 Nurture student passions & talents

2 Empower student voice & honour student choice

3 Increase motivation and engagement

YAY, Let's do this!

Genius Hour
Passion Projects
20% Time

4 Foster curiosity and a love for learning

I wonder if...?

10 Solve the problems of tomorrow in the classrooms of today

9 Enable students to take ownership over their own learning and to reach their goals

5 Teach grit, perseverence, growth mindset & self-regulation

8 Fortify the importance of asking good questions

7 Deepen understanding to go beyond memorizing facts and content

6 Make research meaningful & develop strong research skills

Google

Our program launched with a provocation in the form of a Zoom call with educator and author Trevor MacKenzie. He facilitated a session centered around a few of the characteristics of an inquiry classroom. Immediately after saying our virtual goodbyes, my colleague and I set a timer for three minutes and asked the group to individually respond to the following prompt: "What questions *do you* have about questions now?"

With the clock counting down, pens and pencils quickly wagged while small sticky notes stacked up beside each educator. As I glanced around the conference room table, I could see questions scribbled with language from the hour's worth of learning, with some brief pauses as teachers flipped through their notebooks, and I felt an energy buzzing with wonder. Walking over to the whiteboard on one end of the room, I drew the horizontal and vertical lines that would become the Question Quadrant we would be using for the remainder of the session together. No overthinking, revising, or editing allowed quite yet, it was now time to get playful with our questions!

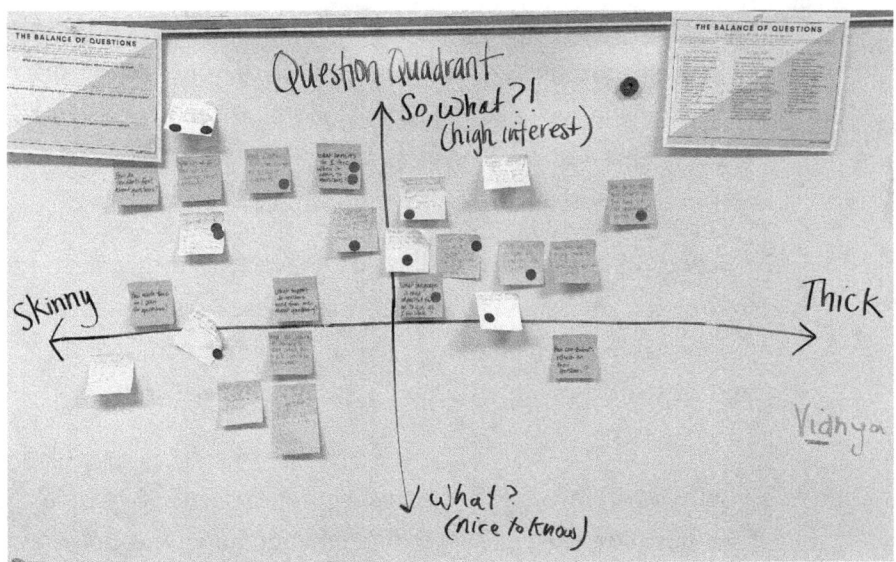

With the Balance of Questions resource in hand, I called the team of teachers to the whiteboard and gave them a brief introduction to the protocol. We spent time discussing indicators of each of the quadrants, outlining the roles that the types of questions (horizontal axis) and level of interest (vertical axis) had in classifying questions. With a basic understanding of the framework, the group started placing their questions on the quadrant while engaging in dialogue about location, similarities, differences, and even what new questions were emerging because of this playful exchange of ideas. As an observer, I carefully noted who confidently jumped into the task right away, listened for connections and current understanding about the role of questions in learning, and noticed a few trends that the Question Quadrant was able to capture that a traditional wonder wall could not.

Noticing #1: As questions filled the board, the teachers naturally engaged in reflective conversations about the questions that were already on the quadrant. An autonomous self-assessment unfolded right before my eyes as they discussed how the new questions measured up.

 Noticing #2: The structure allowed the teachers to get vertical—and let me step back and observe before asking targeted questions about their thinking. The collaborative nature of the protocol shaped my questioning, prompting deeper reflection and justification.

 Noticing #3: Questions that aligned with the left and lower side of the quadrant were placed with some hesitation and downward glances. Although the teachers were open to the experience and actively engaged, I could tell they were grappling with misconceptions around *good* questions.

Before stepping away from the learning wall, I asked them to share how the experience of working together and using the quadrant felt for them as learners. One teacher noticed that the framework became a vehicle for *even more* wonder, pointing out that they didn't stop generating questions simply because the timer had gone off. Another shared that because the task's primary focus was to play and sort questions rather than *be knowledgeable* or *be the expert*, she felt an increased comfort in the ambiguity of questions. Compared to the "parking lot" of questions they had tried previously in their classrooms, the structure allowed them to make more connections and gain a clearer picture as to what direction our learning about questions needed to take next. Although all of the reflections were glowingly positive, I didn't shy away from one obvious observation about the lower and left side of the quadrant.

The next step was to give the group another tool to help us unpack the common misconceptions about *good* questions. For that, I turned toward the "Power of the Post-it" or in this case, a similarly equitable stationary supply: a pack of circle stickers. The purpose of materials such as sticky notes and sticker dots is to provide instant, anonymous feedback. The activity allows us to nurture cycles of continuous feedback with a layer of safety that invites our learners to take risks and stand in the truth that we are all in this together.

Reminding the team that their voice would continue to impact what ongoing support and resources looked and sounded like, I gave each of the teachers two stickers and asked them to look at the landscape of questions before them, deciding which ones they thought would have the biggest impact on their practice and which they wanted to get started with right away.

The other facilitators and I stepped back to create some contemplative space. We watched to gauge the pulse of what was needed next for the team of teachers. Some of the questions they marked with stickers sparked immediate action in their classrooms the following morning, and other questions required more time to simmer and sort through with one another as a group of critical friends and thought partners.

What's worth noting here is that the learning didn't stop when the educators left the room that day—neither did the artifact we had created together. The group of sticky notes became the start of a wonder wall that our leadership team used to plan continued professional development across the campus. It became a resource to help us set intentions before heading out on learning walks or engaging in one-on-one coaching with teachers. Ultimately it became a driver for data collection we were doing to support district initiatives and campus-related goals. The longevity of the wonder wall spanned well beyond that half-day of learning, and its structure functioned as a space of wonder for us all.

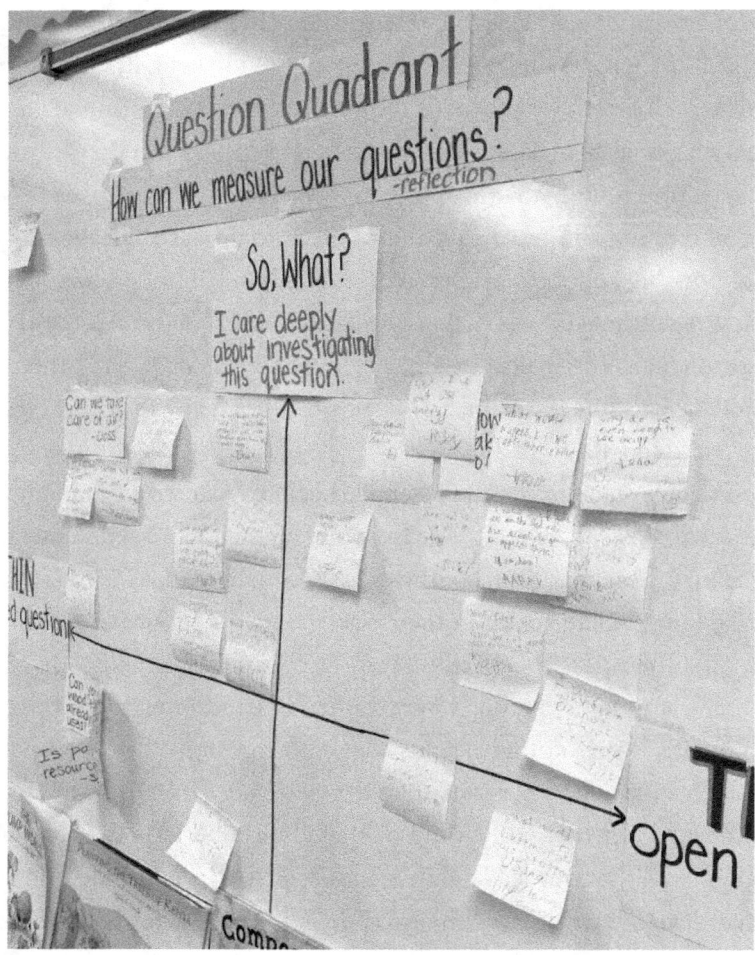

Source: Laurel Mountain Elementary, Austin, Texas

When learner questions arise, it can sometimes feel like too many cooks in the kitchen. I love the way a Question Quadrant helps us quickly sort, determine importance, and boldly, *yet easily*, move forward with learner questions in hand. The Question Quadrant here sits alongside one of the classroom learning walls and remains a staple in weekly classroom routines and lesson preparation. It is a practice that allows us to continue access to curiosity. In the many times that I have had the opportunity to walk into this learning space, I have seen the teacher use this quadrant, along with her wonder wall, in many flexible ways. The list below may be the reminder you need to reignite your practice, help you see an alternative perspective, or take the first step toward leaving more space for wonder.

Model the Model and Question the Quadrant

You're well into a whole-class discussion that's not *even close* to the topic you're *supposed* to be covering. And then there are the small groups of students who are all focused on different research topics. Oh, and next you know, you need to sit with a learner who is puzzled by a math word problem. We've all been there: juggling, multitasking, and bouncing between tasking and telling while facilitating and responding to learning. We balance our roles as classroom managers and inquiry leaders, leaning in, pulling back, and shifting the energy in the room with a powerful pause followed by just the right question. Modeling the model means we capture the curiosity in the room and demonstrate our thinking by adding the questions to the quadrant.

Take note of the large index cards on the quadrant above. These cards, kept in close proximity to the quadrant, house the questions that the teacher has lifted up from classroom conversations and while working individually with students. Model curiosity and reflection by pausing briefly, then reinforcing how to think about thinking through your language. Use phrases like, *It sounds like we're really interested in and wondering about . . .* or *What I'm hearing you ask is . . .* or even *Let's jot down that question and add it to our quadrant!*

The questions, in clear view, serve as a reference point for planning for the week as well as for reorienting in the moment. Students and teachers alike can reference the quadrant when the learning calls for it. The flexibility of the space means that as the questions are used, the index cards can be moved. Some will prove to be clearly connected to the learning, and others will lay stagnant and eventually be removed.

Welcome the Room

Inviting our learners into the learning is a mindful move that every inquiry educator makes. In the primary level, we create systems at the beginning of our days that help our learners know how to self-manage and organize themselves while considering other natural transition times in our schedules to prepare materials and organize activities that align with the energy levels of the day, while in the secondary level, we aim for transitions that are soft and ease learner mindsets into a different subject matter entirely.

Another way we use the Question Quadrant is by using a question (or a small collection of questions) as a provocation to welcome the thinking into the room. The list below offers a handful of ways to use questions from the quadrant to welcome the room.

- Grab a few sticky notes from the quadrant and put them on your front board. Ask students to find a thought partner and discuss the connections they see between the questions or jot down their thinking in their inquiry journals or notebooks.
- Have several closed questions that could use a bit of clarity or discussion? Try using the Tug-of-War thinking routine as your structure and have students determine where along the continuum they agree or disagree with the question. Encourage students to use evidence from the learning wall or other resources to defend and support their stance.
- If foundational knowledge has been established and you're looking to go further with connection making, try tasking students to ask the question you've pulled from the quadrant! This activity is great for stretching and flexing questioning skills and might also benefit from a list of question stems and collaborative time to work with a peer to generate a new wondering.
- Pull off a sticky note from the quadrant, then ask or write, *Yesterday, (name) was wondering . . . Stop and jot your thinking around this question. Be sure to include evidence to support your thinking!*

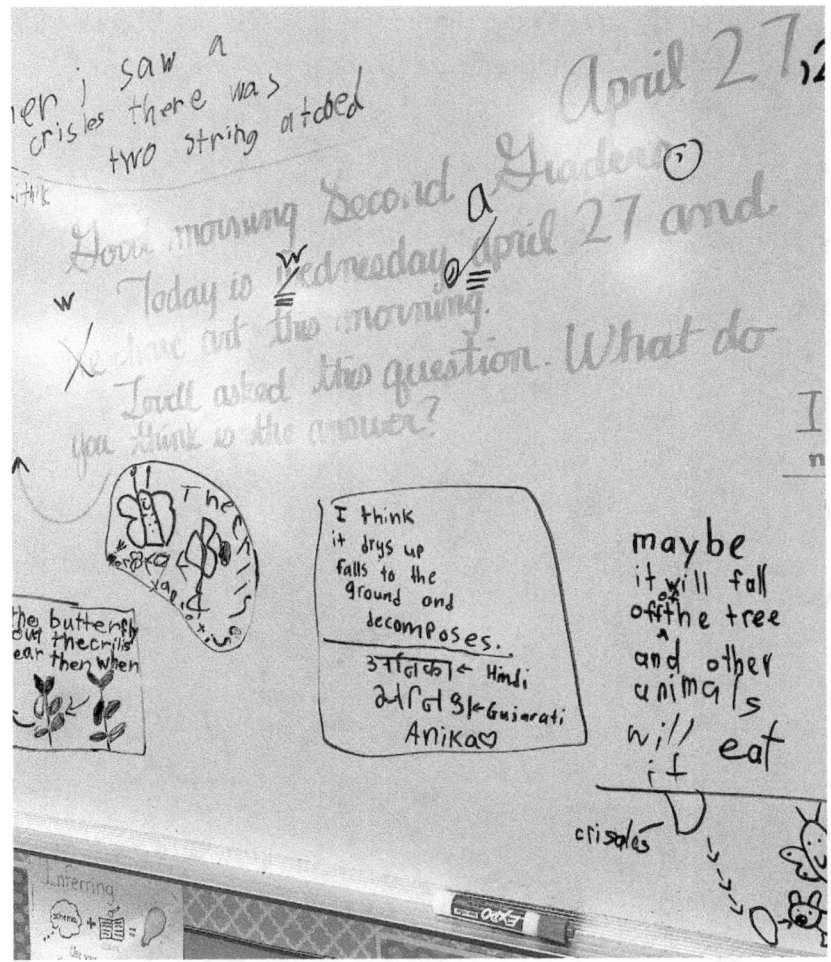

Source: Colleen Ruplinger, Second Grade Teacher, Laurel Mountain
Elementary, Austin, Texas

Clear for Clarity

If you've ever started or used a wonder wall in your classroom, you
know that after some time it can get quite saturated. It's easy to lack
time to refresh this space, or sometimes we simply have trouble letting
questions go in fear of undervaluing student curiosity, or we feel hesitation that taking down wonder eliminates the wonder in the room we
so mindfully try to nurture. I love this playful approach to thinking
about our thinking while getting students to do more of the heavy

lifting when it comes to determining what is still worth wondering about. I even find that this generates more questions in the room!

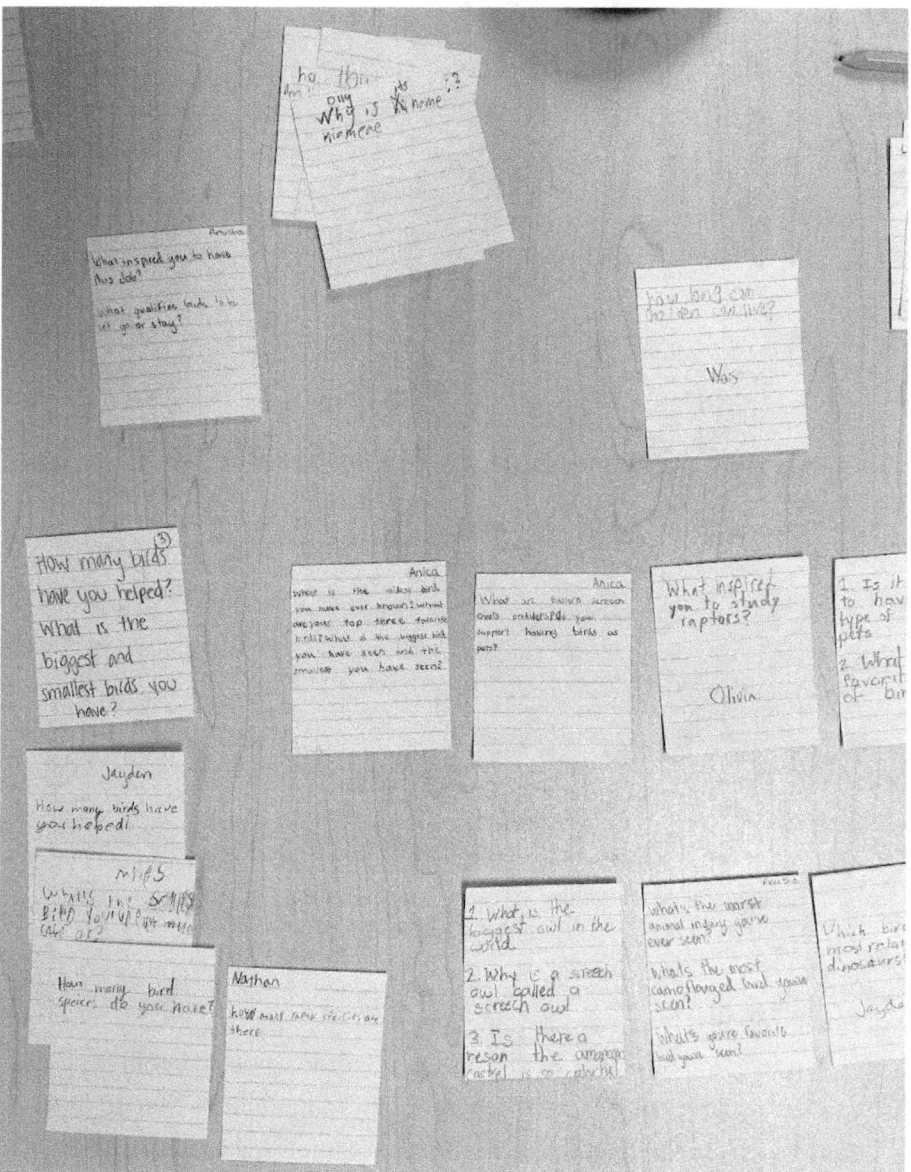

A helpful exercise to put into your lesson plans the next time you find your wonder wall looking a bit dense is to call up your learners to the wonder wall and have them take off the questions, sorting them into two groups, *keep* or *toss*. As students read each question aloud with their partner, tell them to consider whether this is still important to the learning. It might be helpful to work through a few of these together, modeling your thinking aloud with the group and inviting other voices to add to the collective reflection.

During the process of sorting, we let go of ideas, so be cautiously aware of the psychological safety in the room. Setting clear intentions, adding sentence frames to support student conversations, and creating essential agreements and assigning roles for students are critical steps in nurturing a community of connected learners. Once the stacks of sticky notes are in hand, introduce the quadrant to the students and have them begin to sort based on the indicators for each axis. While students are collaborating, listen for the types of questions they are drawn to, lift up ones that you know need a bit more attention, and use open-ended questions of your own to help nudge learner thinking along.

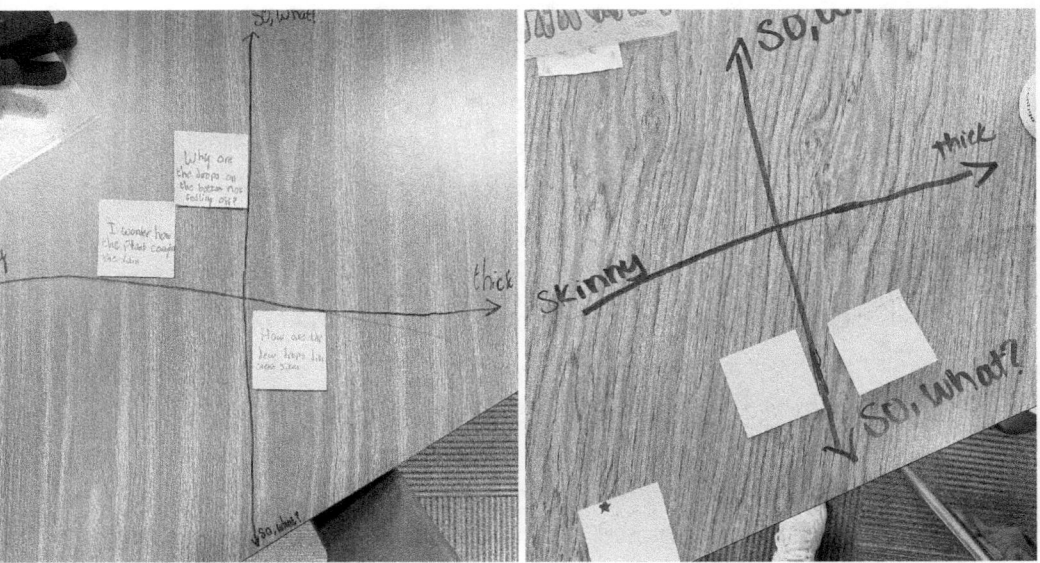

If multilayered sorting is not something your students are ready for quite yet or you don't have the time to allocate to this multistep approach, try clearing the wonder wall first. Pull out the questions related to the current unit of inquiry, concept, or other area of focus and give them to pairs or small groups of students to tinker with at their desks first. The two desks with quadrants drawn on them (on the previous page) belong to Grade 5 students who were sorting questions with their tablemates.

After this initial sort, the students were prompted to do a gallery walk around the room and then asked to bring their sticky notes up to the quadrant drawn on the whiteboard up front. More sorting, more conversations, more collaboration, and physical clearing of spaces made way for new questions, new thinking, and a renewed clarity in the direction of learning.

Return, Revisit, and Revise

Creating new habits for ourselves means retraining and rewriting our brains to think differently. In Adam Grant's book *Think Again: The Power of Knowing What You Don't Know*, he reminds us to find the joy in being wrong, teaches us how to detach from the final outcome, and inspires a flexibility in thinking only found when we define ourselves by our values rather than opinions.

These actions, mindsets, and awareness are "critical friends" of an inquiry teacher and leader, and structures such as the Question Quadrant allow us to befriend the lessons that come with *thinking again*. This last strategy is simple. Use the Question Quadrant to bring forth new routines to your practice. If you're a campus leader, consider constructing and keeping a quadrant on the back of your office door to house your learners' questions. Or create a quadrant in a virtual platform like Miro or Canva to help you look at and sort through feedback and reflections from your community or staff.

If you're a classroom teacher, I'd encourage you to take action in a similar way. Build a quadrant in a space that's within view of where you spend the most time in the room, or find somewhere that's easily accessible and reminds you to return to your students' questions, revising your lesson plans and staying open minded and curious about their curiosities. Set a reminder on your phone, a recurring calendar event at the tail end of your week, or call on a critical thought partner to keep you accountable to a way of rethinking thinking. The important thing here is interweaving a new pattern of action that roots us in wonder.

The Balance of Questions resource is one that Trevor MacKenzie and I created together to support the work we both do in schools and is one that I keep readily on hand. I am sure you will too. I encourage you to download this resource, use the reflective prompts, take note of the indicators that define open and closed questions, and try some of the teacher questions as you respond to your community of learners.

Question Matrix

Questions are a manifested action of curiosity. Select words help generate wonder and get us started on a new topic or area of interest. Playing with the order of language helps us in the sorting and making sense of what we want to know. There are layers of perspectives to explore as we continue to ask more questions about our questions. And just like any other skill that we develop, there needs to be some direct instruction, a scaffolding of support that gives us momentum forward, and feedback that helps us self-reflect and revise our actions accordingly. I love Chuck Wiederhold's Question Matrix for the way it balances these very things!

The Question Matrix shared in the photo from Amy Ing and Mark Minuk is used in tandem with the classroom's learning wall. The questions collected there after provocations nudge students to think about the topic in different ways. The intentionally large size of the matrix encourages a spacious and open-ended mindset while *physically* leaving room for wonder. As units unfold, different-colored sticky notes express layers of knowing, thinking, and wondering and bring to light the learners' strengths, stretches, and capacities.

Source: Amy Ing and Mark Minuk, East Three Elementary, Inuvik, NWT, Canada

I encourage you to refrain from the impulse to have students "fill and find" a question for each section of the matrix. Instead, set an intention for its use to be rooted in wonder. Data generated with question routines, like the Question Matrix, will show you how to move forward and *work with* your learners' curiosity. And although there are countless ways to reflect on and use the data collected in this matrix, I want to share a few suggested prompts that consistently move the learning forward. Employ the following questions as you consider the role questions play in your learning community. Or let them guide the reflection the next time you pull up a chair to the wall with a thought partner as you look at the data before you:

- Look at the landscape of questions. Are there areas in the matrix that are heavy handed? What provocation or skills might you need to plan for your learners to stretch this competency? How might you backwards plan and design for this across a span of time?
- Are you uncertain about the impact the matrix is having on the learning? Try asking your learners for feedback on this question protocol. What's been most meaningful or helpful for them? In which areas do they still feel stuck? What do they notice about the collections?
- Take a pulse of the room. What types of questions are your learners drawn toward? How might you plan questions that nudge and stretch them toward new dimensions of the matrix?
- It's time to sit alongside your learners! How have *you* added to this Question Matrix yourself? What do you notice happens to the questions in the room when you model your thinking and wonder? Are there open-ended questions you could plan to ask that ignite curiosity and push thinking a bit further?
- Take stock of how long questions have been "sitting" on the Question Matrix. Do your learners see these driving inquiry and the direction of the learning, or is the matrix lackluster and a pretty "wallpaper" for the room? How might you bring this framework back to life again?

You've seen several different iterations of wonder walls. Note the flexibility of the materials and systems used by each of these inquiry teachers and leaders. Wonder walls and question routines are not just something to check off a to-do list. In *Inquiry Mindset: Questions Edition*, Trevor MacKenzie dives deep into these question routines and several others that could support your efforts at leaving space for wonder. The teacher vignettes he includes highlight question routines that can be adapted to suit the context and readiness of learners. The great work of an inquiry leader is to get lost in the learning while maintaining a focus on the final destination. These routines can support you all along the way!

Spacious Learning

In Chapter Three, "Find a Blank Space," we explored the different questions to ask to determine where and what kind of structures to use for our learning walls. Whether we're looking for something physical or virtual, long lasting or short term, finding a blank space takes an expanded awareness and an intentionality around purpose, audience, and routine.

Leaving space for wonder means we are mindful of the physical layout and balance of empty space that our walls express. Walls filled with preprinted labels, posters, or students' final drafts of writing assignments from a past unit can quickly become visual clutter. A wonder wall bursting with questions and anchor charts can create noise that makes it hard for learners to determine what's most important or even worth learning.

And yet, I get it. The busyness of our days, the countless stops and starts that occur as we differentiate assignments or manage student behavior, the endless tasks we squeeze into the limited prep time we have in our schedules, and the boundaries we commit to creating for ourselves to honor the work–life balance of it all are factors that contribute to how we spend our time.

As inquiry educators, we know there is a beauty in the messiness of learning. The framework of the inquiry cycle helps to bring order. But even as we anticipate a messiness in the meaning-making, the stacks of sticky notes, large sheets of paper scribbled with students' notes, index cards with academic language and vocabulary, student questions, and other graphic organizers can all become a bit much. All too quickly, our learning wall's dense energy becomes a jarring space with no space to give our eyes (or brains) a rest.

I've had the pleasure of working with many schools and educators who are early on in their inquiry journeys. I love the opportunity in the never-ending questions, the surge of uneasiness that comes when learning something new, and the pull toward free inquiry. These learning communities are engaging in a sorting of their own, managing state or district expectations while reinventing what school could look like for their learners and choosing to do school differently.

Continental Colony Elementary, located in Atlanta, Georgia, is one of those schools. Their teachers and campus leaders plan with curiosity in mind. They regularly step back and take a critical look at their campus data, rethinking how they invite and co-construct understanding with their scholars. They use what they learn to revamp systems and structures to create ample space for teachers to reflect on their practice and use learning walls as a tool to support professional learning as well as the learning that happens with students.

While eagerly jumping into the challenge of documenting thinking and learning in an entirely new way, these walls quickly became overrun by anchor charts and student worksheets, were a jumbled collection of sticky notes and other artifacts, or sometimes were a complete afterthought lost to other dominating habits and patterns. We took a step back to brainstorm where these vertical spaces were stretching the teacher the most. Teachers vulnerably invited a group of their peers into their classroom spaces to have a closer look at what they had started. They sat around a conference table with their teams and shared honest reflections about what was making an impact on student learning and where they felt stuck. We took photos of learning walls, jotted down thinking, and collectively identified common challenges across the staff.

- **Challenge #1**: The *right* structure for a learning wall
- **Challenge #2**: Learning walls full of evidence with no clear purpose or room for more

These challenges became the provocation for revising their campus and classroom learning walls. I'm excited to share the steps that Continental Colony's staff put into practice. I hope their learning and honest reflections will inspire your journey too!

Challenge #1: The right structure for a learning wall

There is no *right* structure to use for a learning wall, but in my research and experience I have identified three frameworks that any learner can easily follow and find their way through:

- Timeline
- Spiral of Inquiry
- Spiderweb Map

As you read about these simple structures in the next few pages, think about the structure you are using and how it is working for you and your students. As you do, consider these questions for reflection:

- What would happen if you organized your collective thinking differently?
- How might an alternative structure invite more learners to this impactful resource?

Spacious Learning

Timeline

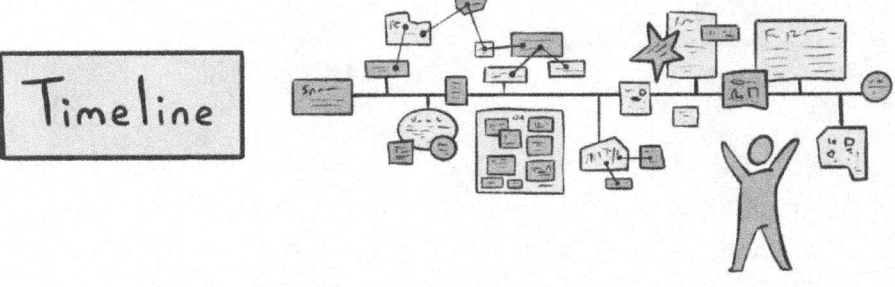

Spiral of Inquiry

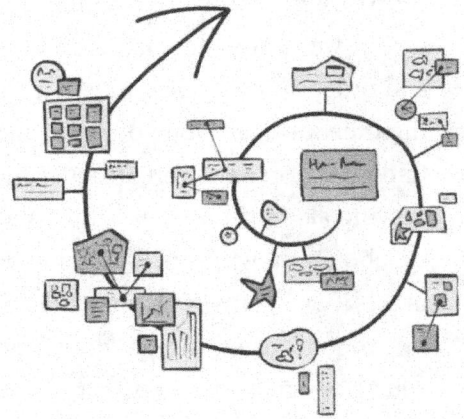

Spiderweb Map

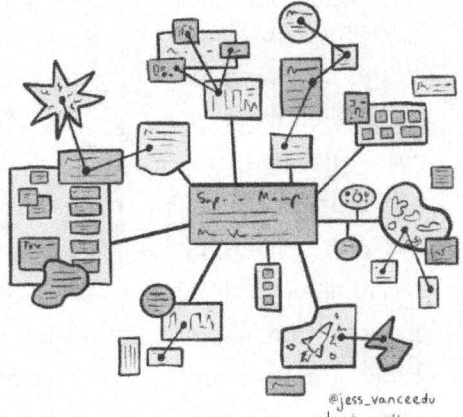

@jess_vanceedu
#leadingwithinquiry

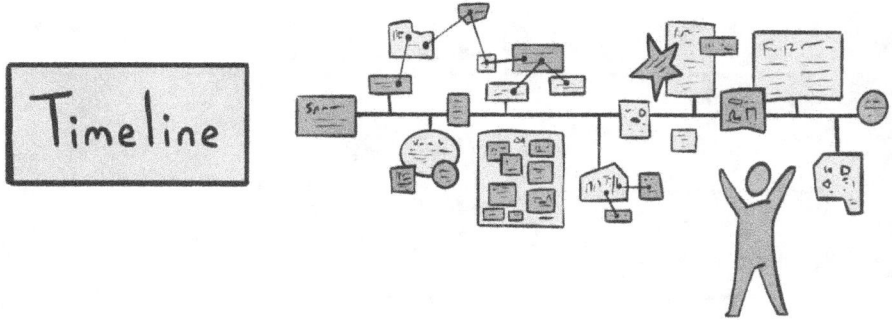

The timeline is a well-known structure that's used at museums or in other public displays of information, as well as in our textbooks. Timelines help students explore historical and social events and analyze story structure through plot diagrams. We can even find the structure at work in mathematics classrooms, where it is used to compare and order numbers on a line. The most spacious of all the structures, the timeline is also one of my favorites to offer to educators who are finding the organization of artifacts a challenge. The physical nature of moving along the wall as artifacts are added encourages motion and collaboration, which makes it a good choice for communal spaces. It makes it easy to invite anyone to engage with the vertical learning space.

To get started, simply draw or construct a line across the space you've designated as your learning wall. This line can be straight or a bit more playful and meander like a trail on a map; it's up to you. Leave open space on one end where you and your learners can add artifacts. Timestamps, dates, or other markers make great additions to this structure; for example, I've seen primary educators add numbers to reinforce counting skills. Transition words such as *first, next, then, after that,* and *last* support conceptual knowledge of sequence and order of events. If you are teaching a unit of inquiry centered on cycles or systems, building a collaborative learning wall to be used by teaching teams or different classes or groups of learners, or establishing a routine and organizational system for documenting learning, a timeline approach is a perfect choice for your learning wall!

I wonder what would happen if you chose one skill that was your focus for the work this year, supporting the development of a capable person?

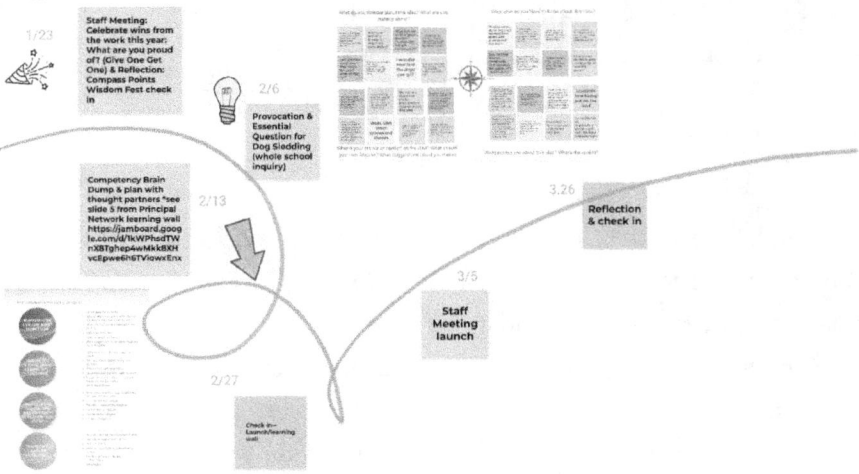

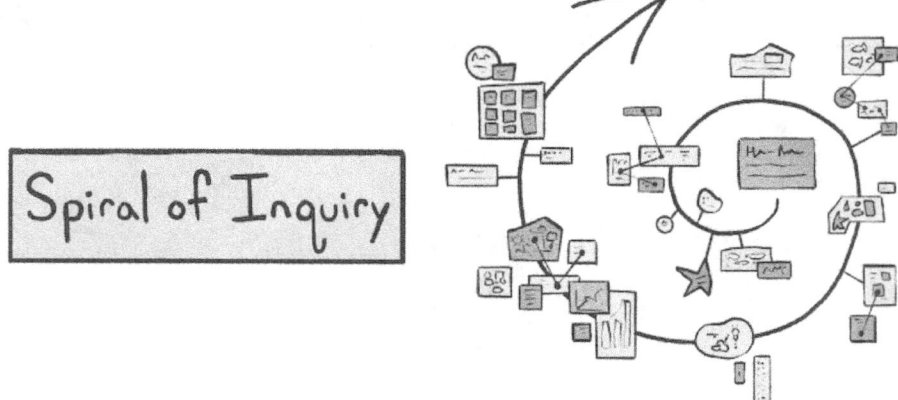

Spiral of Inquiry

Inspired by the work of Linda Kaser and Judy Halbert, authors of the book entitled *Leading Through Spirals of Inquiry*, a **spiral** is another great structure to use as a foundation for your learning wall. Rooted in Indigenous knowledge and traditional customs, the spiral symbolizes growth and the cyclical nature of time. Its outward expansion expresses a growth of knowledge, space for collaborative thinking, and as Halbert and Kaser outline in their publication, "requires a deep understanding of learning and appreciation for the experiences of learners."

A spiral framework gives you and your learners space to plot your learning journey together. You might attach string to the wall in this organic shape, draw a spiral on the paper or virtual platform, or hold this shape in your mind as you pin artifacts to your learning wall.

As with the timeline structure, leave empty space and consider markers and other labels to encourage mindful additions of evidence as the unit unfolds. If limited space is an issue, consider constructing mini spiral centered on related concepts, lines of inquiry or specific subjects, or topics in your curriculum. Don't get bogged down with perfection; instead, stay open to how this structure helps you redefine how you use your vertical spaces!

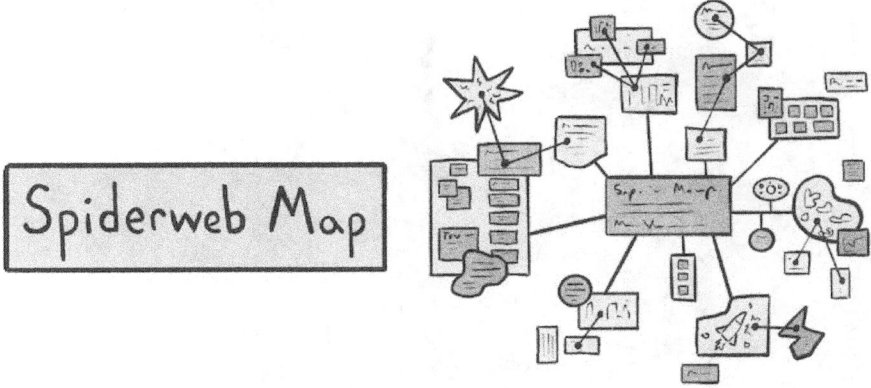

Spiderweb Map

Using structures that repeat themselves in other subject areas is an intentional way to support conceptual awareness and knowledge. A **spiderweb map** is a graphic organizer format. Students may have already used this kind of tool to record what they know about a topic, organize information, or brainstorm ideas. In Chapter Six, I shared an early years learning wall that used the spiderweb map as its beginning structure. Flip back and notice the simple, yet organized, start of that classroom's learning wall (page 58).

The spiderweb map starts with a central topic, concept, or small collection at the center. Artifacts are pinned to the learning wall, illustrating an unfolding of ideas. I frequently find that my most impactful learning walls start with this effortless structure.

> **Tip!** If you have trouble letting go of the learning and taking down these co-constructed artifacts, consider taking a photo of your spiderweb map learning wall. Keep this evidence close at hand for your learners (in a photo booklet, attached to the front board, stored in a digital folder, or added to a slide deck) so they can continue to find connections for even deeper learning.

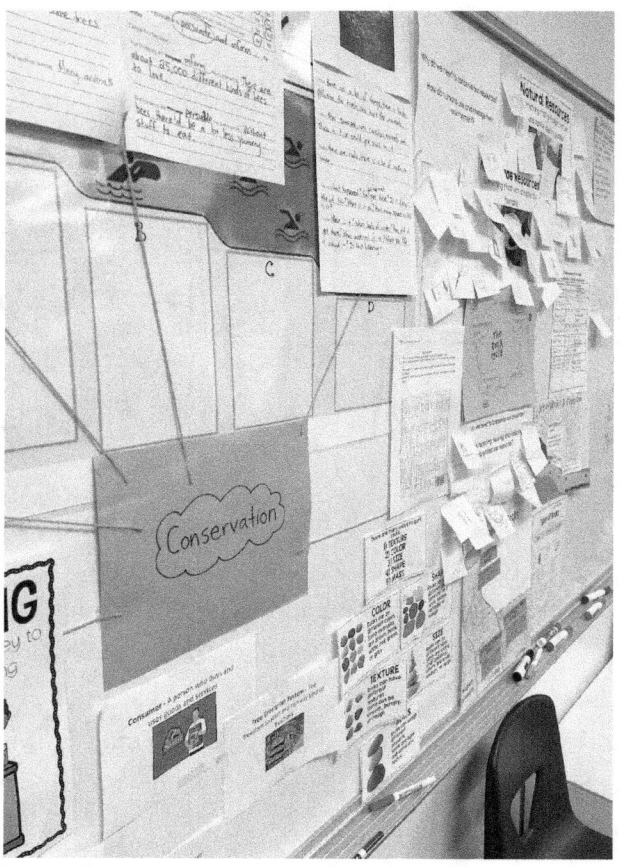

Source: Nicole Levitan, Laurel Mountain Elementary, Austin, Texas

*Source: Kristen Martin, Natomas Unified School District,
Sacramento, California*

Keep these three structures in mind as you build your next learn-ing wall or if you find that the structure you're using is not working and you need to reorganize. A disposition of an inquiry leader is being intentionally playful, which sometimes manifests in how we rethink and use our spaces. I've lost track of the number of times my initial vision for a learning wall didn't pan out or support the learning as intended. Once I adjusted the structure of the space, my learners and I both experienced an immediate impact and connection to the think-ing in a more cohesive way.

Challenge #2: Learning walls full of evidence with no clear purpose or room for more

"At what point are there too many artifacts?"

"Do you add everything or more of a representative sample of the learning?"

"How do you determine which evidence goes on the wall?"

"After each unit, how do you decide what artifacts to keep up and which to take down?"

Questions like these arise as we attempt to balance letting our scholars' interests lead the learning with our curriculum. After many years of building and rebuilding learning walls, I've asked myself those very questions. I've sat staring at bulletin boards, feeling a bit overwhelmed by the quantity of artifacts. There also have been plenty of times when I've been mentally exhausted after a day of teaching and lacked the capacity to untangle the messiness of learning exhibited on the learning wall. Inevitably, when we arrive at places such as these, it's an indication for us to pause, sift, and sort.

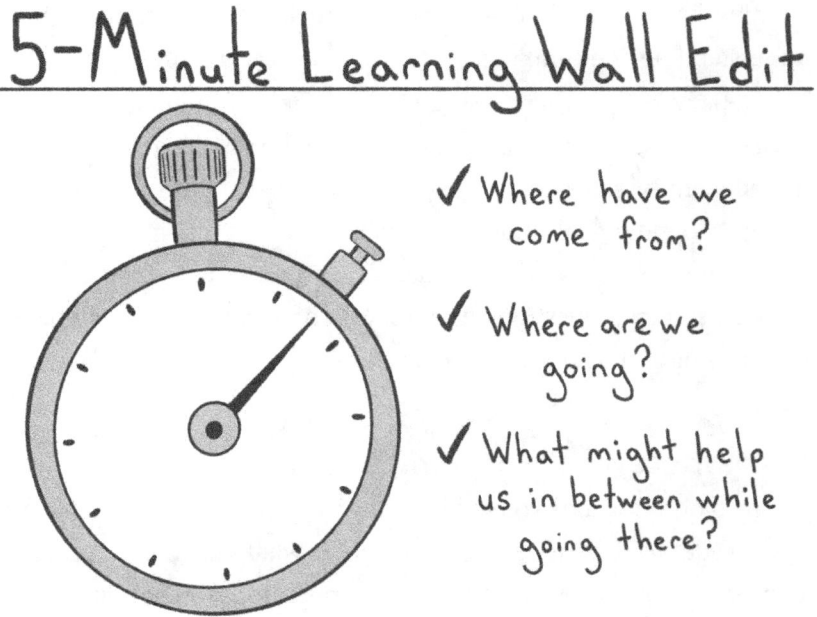

5-Minute Learning Wall Edit

✓ Where have we come from?

✓ Where are we going?

✓ What might help us in between while going there?

The *sift and sort* approach helps us quiet the noise so we can make sense of what the data are revealing. It is a purposeful way to create more space for wonder. Alone or with a thought partner, grab your inquiry notebook and pull up a chair to the learning wall. Give yourself five minutes to be curious. Asking just three questions rapidly transforms the space and evidence before you.

The three questions in this strategy are ones I routinely ask myself when I feel like I'm getting a bit lost in the messiness of learning or notice a stall in momentum forward. Use the sketchnote as a guide to putting the sift and sort strategy into practice.

Where have we come from?

This question invites you to slow down enough to reconnect with what you have explored with your community of learners. Let your eyes wander across artifacts and evidence. Reflect on what teaching and learning has occurred. Take stock of your learners' current stage of understanding and thinking.

Depending on where you are in your unit of inquiry, you might notice giant leaps in conceptual understanding. Alternatively, you might identify skills that need to be revisited, reinforced, or even retaught to individual students or groups.

I find it helpful to look at artifacts from provocations and to linger with the students' questions. These sparks of wonder are milestones in the learning and help me assess how far we've come.

Where are we going?

The next question asks you to look ahead. Open your laptop and check in with your lesson and unit plans. Confirm what's next in the progression of learning. Pause here with the same mindset that you employ during a formal, formative assessment. Consider what scaffolding is necessary to support and differentiate learning for your scholars. Make note of artifacts that might be useful for future direct instruction.

Make it a habit to skim and scan student questions to search for connections with your original plan. This alignment becomes part of the co-construction of learning. Add a reminder to lift up the connections for your learners, or simply start moving sticky notes and attaching them to new artifacts that have been added to your walls. Also notice what artifacts that, although they might have been purposeful in the moment, are no longer useful in propelling learning.

What might help us in between while going there?

This final question reminds you of the role of retrieval in learning—and what's important to keep for the long term. If you can't pinpoint a time that you'll teach from or with an artifact, let it go.

At this stage, you might post notecards to lift up essential questions, pertinent vocabulary, or sentence stems, or capture student noticings and wonderings that become a new focal point of the wall. If your aim is to help students visualize the connections between thinking and learning, you could reorganize artifacts and revisit them with your learners the following week.

Knowing what evidence to let go of (when) can be a challenge. One tip to help beat the sense of overwhelm is to think about how you can layer evidence to create more open space. Another tip is to remind yourself that you can *temporarily* remove an artifact and tuck it aside for the time being. The editing objective here is to be *swiftly reflective* and to detach from the notion that you have to keep it because you *might* need it.

Before
Source: Jocelyn Gore, Continental Colony Elementary, Atlanta, Georgia

I'm confident that you'll experience an immediate impact with these questions. The learning wall here belonging to a primary classroom teacher shows the outcome of this practice. Jocelyn Gore leveraged space as a third teacher. As we reflected together, she found ways to maximize the space by asking a few more questions:

- She planned to use the central idea structure for the six-week transdisciplinary unit but noticed that it bogged down her students' focus. She asked, *How might we capture this more simply?*
- Several examples of student-created timelines resided on the wall but weren't really applicable or meaningful to the learning anymore. She asked, *Could we file these away for the time being to create space for the next few weeks of learning?*
- The few math artifacts were not connected or essential to the overarching conceptual understanding. She asked, *How might we conceptually connect our math moving forward in the unit of inquiry?*
- The thinking routine See, Think, Wonder was full of rich evidence and needed a bit of a clearing out. She asked, *Where could we move and attach sticky notes to artifacts to celebrate and highlight the progress made in learning?*

Reflecting on the data made it easy to unpin, rearrange, and reorganize the artifacts on the wall. Working together, we grabbed string, created some new labels, moved graphic organizers, and pinned and stacked student artifacts. What remained was an expansive space ready for the learners to use. As you look at Jocelyn's learning wall "before" and "after" this revision, pay close attention to artifacts and track where they were moved, notice the overall feeling the learning journey evokes, and consider how this learning wall better meets the developmental needs of her young scholars.

Curious to see what revising a learning wall looks like in real time? Watch this time-lapse video of an educator editing her learning wall.

After

Source: Jocelyn Gore, Continental Colony Elementary, Atlanta, Georgia

There are countless ways to reflect on the artifacts you've collected along your learning journey. I've included a few common revisions that classroom teachers and campus leaders have made to their learning walls. Consider these as a launchpad for your reflective process as you engage in the sift-and-sort strategy!

Instead of . . .	What would happen if you . . .
Unpacking central idea or essential unit vocabulary at the start of a unit of inquiry	Simplified the unit and used only one or two essential questions or concepts or slowly revealed these as the unit of inquiry unfolded?
Adding all student examples	Clipped all of the pages together using a binder clip or chose a few select exemplars to add to the learning wall?
Keeping all student questions	Have students edit questions from your wonder wall with you? Can you group and sort questions in like categories and minimize space used?
Filling up all empty spaces with artifacts	Layered the learning, stacking similar anchor charts like a flipbook?
Keeping artifacts for the length of the inquiry	Took down artifacts that were not critical to the "long-term learning"?
Being the sole decision-maker of what stays and what goes	Asked students to share what artifacts they are most proud of, are a useful resource, or have been helpful in the learning?
Keeping artifacts in the same place	Moved artifacts around? How might that create the visual connections you are seeking?

Now that you have an idea of what's possible when you leave space for wonder, it's time to sift and sort your learning wall.

- How might this quick revision technique help your learners see themselves in the learning?
- What invitation does the physical space send to your community of learners?

- How does seeking more spacious learning help you live in a greater awareness of the culture of curious learning you are nurturing?

Leaving space for wonder is about more than collecting questions. It is a stance that allows us to hold on—but not too tightly. It means we unfold into new spaces yet manage to maintain a sound structure. It means we settle into the path and get more comfortable with the journey and the story being told right before our eyes.

We've unpacked almost all of the tenets of building a learning wall. I'm wondering how following this path has enabled you to lead and learn with a greater awareness of your learners' needs and interests. As you make your way to the last tenet of building a learning wall, how might you continue to leave space for wonder?

Pause and Reflect

* What do you notice about your mindset throughout this process? How does this tenet of building a learning wall enable you to lead and learn with a greater intentionality toward an inquiry mindset?

* Before you edit your learning wall, snap a photo as evidence for you to reflect on at a later date. What does this evidence reveal about your understanding, knowledge, and comfort level with building a learning wall?

* The sentence stem *I wonder what would happen if* . . . is a favorite of mine when I am feeling a tension or can't see beyond the barrier before me. The next time you are in a similar situation, use this playful sentence stem to help you generate ideas for how to collect artifacts and honor learners' wonderings.

Chapter 9

Co-Construct for
Personal Meaning

Constructivism is founded on partnerships and collaborative learning. It relies on an active approach to our pedagogy, or *how* we facilitate the learning. It requires our scholars to consume less in favor of *doing* more. Likewise, it demands trust between teacher and student that activates prior knowledge, incorporates new information and constructs, and builds new synapses of thinking through reflection.

The American writer and educator Margaret Wheatley reminds us of the power that lies within a community that works together around ideas that are uniquely important to the group with her words, "There is no power for change greater than a community discovering what it cares about."

We, of course, experience this when our interests are valued and drive our professional development. When administrators allocate time and resources that allow us to spend time away from our classrooms for professional development, we are able to get into learner mode. Spending time with our professional learning communities is a valuable, whether it is at a multi-day conference (of our choosing) or gathering for round-table discussions to let big ideas simmer. Other times, we might opt to tap into the power of group productivity to generate ideas and strategies, then follow up with immediate action that strengthens our practice. Meaningful growth occurs when we prioritize outcomes over outputs and fuse change through intentional action and curiosity.

Building a learning wall is a continuous act of co-construction. Throughout this publication, I've provided thinking routines, sentence stems, collaborative structures, questioning protocols, and strategies that allow you to immerse yourself in the process of learning *with your students*. As we unpack the last stage of building a learning wall, you'll recognize many of the strategies and approaches at work. This section, however, will challenge you to seek new perspectives and go deeper in your understanding around making and keeping learner thinking visible.

Prepare your mindset to approach the work of co-constructing with an intention that balances the ambiguity of inquiry with certainty. Let's first ground ourselves with the tools of co-construction, and for simplicity's sake, consider this your mental checklist as you reflect on how your learning wall functioned for you and your learners during the last unit of inquiry or determine what you *should do* with the most recent evidence collected from your learners.

Tools of Co-Construction

I. Know Your Curriculum

Getting to know your curriculum takes time. It's something that needs to be experienced firsthand through active planning, facilitation of learning experiences, exchanging ideas with other colleagues, and ongoing reflection about the layers of learning. When we know our curriculum, we can see beyond the five days that we have planned for, we are aware of prior knowledge needed to master certain skills, and we can easily adjust a lesson plan when our scholars are showing us they need to go deeper with a particular topic or concept. Being well versed in curriculum helps us better plan and select artifacts to pin to our learning walls, ensures that the documentation we choose represents the concepts we are building on, and reminds us how space "as the third teacher" is something we routinely rely on to help us facilitate learning in our classrooms.

If you have moved schools or changed grade levels, are currently experiencing curriculum changes, have newly adopted curriculum, or are just starting your professional teaching practice, the best way to get to know your curriculum is by embracing it with a mindset that you might not know how everything fits all at once. This stage of learning our curriculum can feel overwhelming, is often riddled with frustration and uneasiness, and leaves us only short steps ahead of our learners. While it's tempting to tell ourselves that we'll start "doing inquiry" or building a learning wall in the next academic year, we get to know our curriculum by playing with it right away! We experiment with new lessons, pull in critical thought partners to guide us through reflection and encourage a growth mindset, and remind ourselves that there is an unlearning and relearning that's required of us during this stage.

While writing this publication, in fact, I am challenged by several curriculum changes. There are disorienting feelings that internally bubble to the surface, countless questions from staff that are currently left unanswered, and future plans for campuswide learning that have been put on a brief pause until we are able to get a better sense of what's coming our way. As a school leader, I'd love to be able to field all of the questions with certainty, submit our professional learning plan to our area superintendent with a confident timeline, and have a deeper understanding of how all of the parts and pieces of the new curriculum align with the conceptual framework we've built as a school. These, however, are not truths that currently exist. We'll instead engage in an inquiry around the new curriculum we are receiving and ask ourselves a handful of questions as we collectively sort, find out more about the shifts in grade-level topics, and build a greater understanding around the "what" we are guided toward teaching. Guiding questions similar to the handful I've included below help orient us in what we know is needed by our learners, maintain a sense of curiosity, and integrate the well-versed inquiry moves we have ingrained in our practice.

As you read through these questions, ask yourself which of these you already use as reflective prompts and add additional ones to the list I've included for you. I encourage you to reference this list as you "pull up a chair" with your learners, bring them to your next team meeting, and keep them in a visible place as you plan for next steps in learning!

- How does this connect with what we already know?
- What are learner questions and evidence revealing over time?
- What are the skills and competencies that we can plan and align with the learning?
- What are the overarching concepts that might link learning and allow for deeper understanding?
- What are ways we can plan for collaboration and opportunities for co-designing learning?
- How might we evidence and document thinking along the learning journey?

2. Give Your Learners the Pen

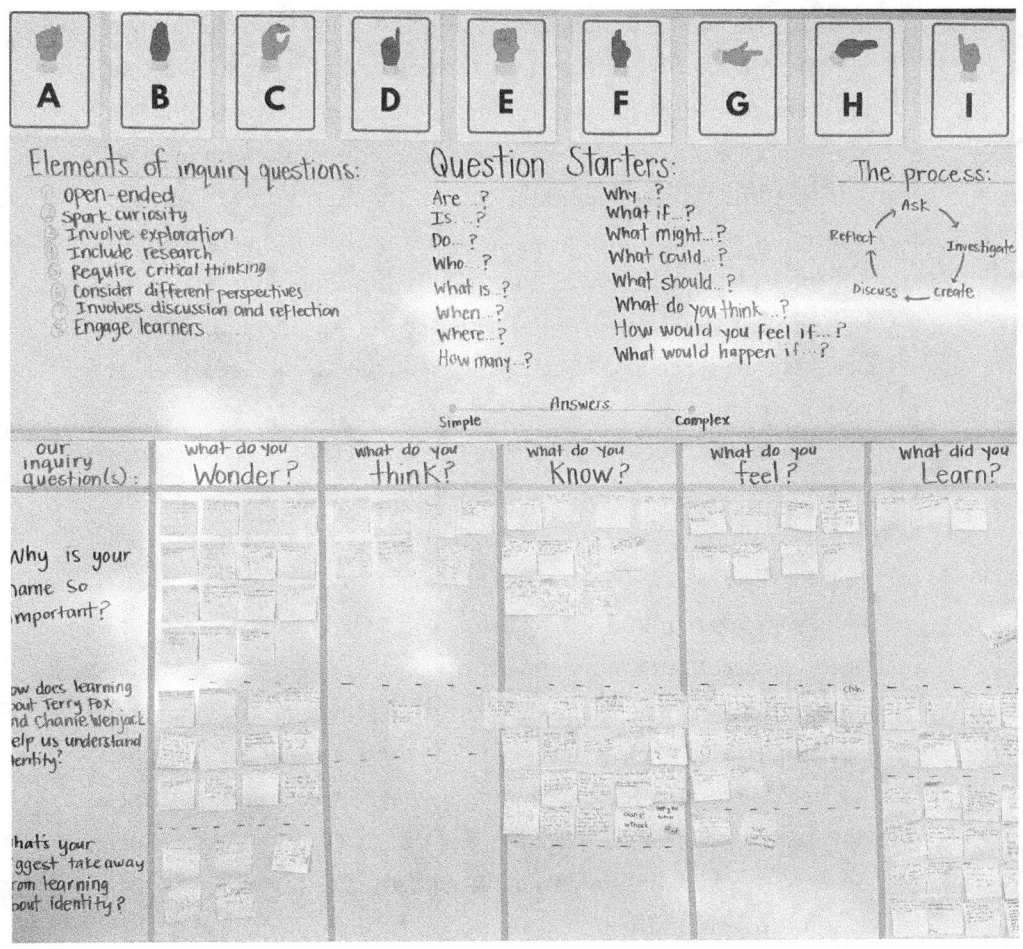

Source: Ashley Bodnar, Heritage Mountain Elementary, Vancouver, BC, Canada

With the best intentions, we occasionally fall into old habits of doing it ourselves, feel the pressure of time, and rush through the collaborative thinking to "get to the point" or underestimate the independence of our learners and do more of the heavy lifting than perhaps is necessary. Giving our learners "the pen," so to speak, comes in the collaborative structures we choose, the thinking frames and visible thinking protocols we plan for instead of the set of worksheets that come with our curriculum, and the systems and routines that reflect the value of agency and invite all voices to contribute to the learning.

We also *literally* give our learners the pen and other materials that enable them to use their voice. Supplies that include writing tools, sticky notes, or note cards have an open-endedness that encourages learners to authentically document current theories, give feedback to their peers, or pause and jot down wonderings based on the current state of the class's inquiry. Whether you are building a virtual learning wall or have one in your physical space, having the supplies and resources within reach and begging to be touched is an essential part of a co-constructive learning environment.

A tub of materials, or learning wall bin, is quick and easy to assemble and houses all of the tools you need to co-create learning walls in real time right alongside your learners. Simply get your tub started by taking a look at what materials you already have on your learning wall. With your initial list in hand, consider additional supplies that your learners could independently use, such as pushpins, binder clips, or clothes pins, and then begin corralling materials in a tub and small organizational bins, as necessary. The list below will help you get started, but I encourage you to also notice what materials your students gravitate toward, ask for their feedback about what might be missing, and observe the way that the availability of supplies invites more collaboration throughout the process of authentic documentation.

- Sentence strips
- Blank or lined index cards (I prefer blank for flexibility, but use what you have!)
- Markers
- Chisel tip or Sharpie Magnum (these markers are great for making bolded headings or vocabulary cards)
- Clothespins
- Yarn or string (I prefer bright-colored yarn for visual contrast)
- Pushpins

- Stapler and staples
- Circle sticker dots

Yeah, but how do I give my learners "the pen" when building a virtual learning wall? Just because you don't have a physical space as a learning wall doesn't mean you shouldn't consider what's in your learning wall tub too! Make sure your learners can easily access the space by scanning a unique QR code that directly takes them to the collection of learning, routinely drop the link into the chat of your virtual classroom, or have the digital tool linked on your classroom's website.

It's time to create your own learning wall "bin" too! Virtual whiteboards can sometimes feel overwhelming with the many bells and whistles, so be sure to keep things simple and easy. Consider and agree on some key tools that you'll use to add thinking and evidence, think about icons, and be sure to make use of the digital sticky note features too! Your learners should know how to use the digital sticky notes and be comfortable with adding emojis, icons, and arrows and lines to bring the learning to life in a whole new way. Don't be afraid to let your learners take the lead here, but be sure to pause and reflect to see how the tools are working (or not working) as a support for documentation.

 You don't have to have a physical space to build a learning wall with all of the same tools ready to go! Use this slide deck to co-construct and make meaning with the learning. Cut and paste the icons into virtual platforms, be playful with the structures, and give your learners access to the tools that make it easier for them to virtually document and evidence learning!

Questioning Skills

Asking questions that invite and inspire, welcome more than one voice, and extend ideas well beyond current thinking in the room are all intentions behind planning and leveraging phrases rooted in wonder. When we build learning walls, we plan for inspiring artifacts, pay close attention to what might be important to capture as authentic evidence, ask questions as a means to model curiosity, and most importantly, step aside so our learners can more actively step forward. When you continue to co-design your learning wall, you will notice the impact that asking questions will have on your learners and their agentic impulses to add thinking, make connections, and reflect on their learning.

Throughout this publication, I've included countless question stems and other prompts to help guide you and your learners through the process of building a learning wall. These questions include playful language and are open ended, are intentionally shared to help welcome different perspectives to add to the learning, and are hopefully questions you already have within your inquiry practice. I encourage you to revisit these questions now. Notice the gentle nudge they offer, how they stretch your thinking, and the easy way they integrate throughout the days with your learners. Use these questions frequently; play and rearrange different phrases and words and make them non-negotiable in your mindset and in your practice.

If you were to walk into my office space, you would find a sticky note with a couple of questions I'm currently using to help me grapple with my documentation practice. I encourage you to do the same! Grab a sticky note and jot down two to three questions that you want to keep top of mind, then put it in a place well within view!

3. Let the Misconceptions Lie

If you've sat beside me planning and reflecting on learning with your team, attended a workshop I've facilitated, or asked for guidance about what "happens next" after facilitating a provocation with your students, you have most likely heard me tell you, "Let the misconceptions lie." I couldn't tell you when exactly I became acquainted with this foundational prompt. I may have stumbled into this during my time as a PYP program coordinator struggling to support teams of teachers to push beyond the pressure of performance. Or perhaps it is a result of all the time I spent as a classroom teacher wrestling to balance authentic assessment with predetermined curriculum maps. Barriers and experiences such as these coupled with the influence of the research, writing, sharing, and expertise from a variety of educators, including Kath Murdoch (*The Power of Inquiry*), Edna Sackson (What Ed Said blog), Warren Berger (*A More Beautiful Question),* Margaret Wheatley (*Who Do We Choose to Be?),* and the late Ken Robinson (*Creative Schools)* were the root of this balancing phrase.

These four words are more than a direction, and they are more than a mindless routine or an actionable habit one checks off the list. These words underlie three critical values of co-design and co-constructing learning walls for personal meaning: *patience, vulnerability,* and *trust.* These values underpin the tone of the questions we ask, our mindset as we pull up a chair and sit alongside our learners, and myths we dispel about the space that direct instruction holds as we intentionally plan and leverage the four different types of inquiry in our practice.

Look closer at the values below and think about the ways these are similarly expressed in your practice and perhaps some you hadn't considered before. Some of these might be seeds you tend to through ongoing reflection and conversations with your colleagues or thought partners, and others may inspire new thinking that takes your practice to new layers of facilitating learning and a clearer understanding of how building a learning wall presents opportunities for integration and personal connection in learning. Let's dive into these three values now!

Patience

Patience presents itself when we carefully look at the questions our students ask and accept the negative space and the current representation of thinking as an opportunity for a clear direction for building on learning. We look for misconceptions in the collections of sticky notes and pause before jumping in to correct "mistakes" we hear our students share, favoring a slower approach and replacing the urge to overturn these "wrongs" into the "right" direction of learning.

We then backwards plan with these misconceptions and align the lessons and skills we already knew we needed to teach, reconsidering the misconceptions as part of the provocation for deeper learning. We add *all kinds of*, but not *all* of the evidence to our learning walls—the shallow questions that reflect a novice mindset or early stages of curious learning, early drafts of writing, and initial reflections of connection making as well as scholars' first attempts at defining academic vocabulary.

We remain patient with the process that unfolds and use all of this evidence as prime examples of integrating more student voice into the learning. We wait for collections of evidence to reveal direction and become curiously aware of what's being revealed by looking for patterns and inviting our learners in to help us identify connections we may have overlooked. I find critical friends and thought partners essential in remaining steadfast toward patience. Their alternative perspectives, nuanced wisdom, and distance away from the crux of the space of learning are an invigorating opportunity in patience one must consider inviting more than once in a while!

Take a look at the learning wall curated by an educator at the Sustainability Learning Centre in Tasmania as a space to make and keep her thinking about her practice. As a new teacher, she's using the vertical space to prompt reflection on her practice, document her lesson planning, and invite other educator voices into her planning and future programming. I've included a QR code that links to a post on social media that walks you through her learning wall and personal thinking.

Source: Louisa d'Arville, Sustainability Learning Centre, Tasmania, Australia

I encourage you now to take a look at the Instagram post that shares the breadth of Louisa's current reflections of learning and evidence. Notice how the thinking routine, What? So What? Now What?, she selected as the structure of her learning wall encourages patience and slowing down plans moving forward. I'm curious how structures you've chosen build the endurance necessary to build toward deeper learning and what Lousia's reflections and generous sharing inspire in your role and context!

Vulnerability

Letting the misconceptions lie requires a continuous willingness to let go and fall into the flow of learning. We might feel vulnerable when we see questions piling up that are unrelated to the topic at hand, feel a muddied mind as we take stock of our walls to determine what's needed next to push toward deeper thinking, or experience a pull to realign the timeline of learning with a scope and sequence that was not designed with our learners at the center.

We remain open and use a learning wall as a reliable tool that helps with sorting, connection making, and self-assessment. There is no waiting until we have all of the "right" artifacts, the perfect bulletin board prepared with our preferred color of butcher paper, large enough wall space, or even a full understanding of how we will use this resource to support and empower our learning community. Instead of stalling, we take action! The hands-on nature of this tool helps us continue to go further with knowledge and understanding and lean into the vulnerable space that requires a commitment to simply begin. Be vulnerable and dive right in—gather the evidence, pin, remove, or move artifacts, and step back to pause and curiously take note of what's emerging!

One way we gain the courage to embrace the discomfort is to create a ritual for ourselves. Rituals may include starting your day grounding yourself in the web of thinking and ideas displayed on your learning wall, ending the block of learning with a collaborative structure that gets your students talking and making sense of the concepts being explored, asking yourself a series of particular questions that ignite reflection and help you synthesize learning, or thumbing through the pile of artifacts you've collected throughout the week to assess the progress of knowledge and understanding. Rituals like these help us form new habits, let go of old patterns, and step into courageous new ways of thinking—welcoming misconceptions as part of the process of co-constructing personal meaning.

As you pause and reflect, consider what rituals or new habits might be helpful as you facilitate learning. Explore a short series of new habits and notice how they shape your mindset and way of being. Ask colleagues about their routines and take note of how these small actions collectively create greater clarity in purpose while helping to ease into unknown spaces. In time, you'll find a routine that suits and grounds you when the wave of ambiguity emerges in learning. Hold steady. Dig deeper. Remind yourself that vulnerability takes effort and requires a thoughtful prioritization for us to experience the joy, creativity, and authenticity that comes with curiosity-driven learning.

Trust

Sometimes the evidence we collect and artifacts we examine provide a clear direction that we confidently unpack with our students or community of learners. Other times the evidence before us remains a messy web that feels counterproductive, frustrating, and downright confusing. Inquiry educators know that both of these truths exist simultaneously, and instead of shutting down, we condition ourselves to trust the process and ask reflective questions such as, *What skills underpin what we are exploring here? What do I know about my learners that will show us the way forward?* Or *How can I plan for reflection and authentic spaces of feedback?* Questions like these help us gain confidence in the ambiguous mess before us, soften the cognitive resistance we're experiencing, and support us as we embrace trust to nurture spaces in which students feel a sense of agency and personal ownership over the learning.

Trust our expertise.

As we co-design next steps, reflect on evidence, and plan lessons for the weeks ahead, we trust the value in our experience, listen closely to our inner voice, and maintain a certainty that we will eventually get there. The countless hours we spend with our learners—engaging in collaboration, pulling small groups for targeted support, listening closely while students work in pairs, and our one-on-one conferences—shape our understanding in powerful ways. These daily practices add to the knowledge we gain from the professional books we read, the university classes we've taken, or the experts we hear on our favorite podcasts.

A critical friend and thought partner continues to tell me to this day, "Trust your expertise, Jess." This reminder is the generous pause I need to take stock of my experiences as an educator, recall previous feedback (both positive and areas of growth) that once shifted approaches to engagements with learners, and retrieve the strategies I know I have highlighted in some of my favorite publications. It is also the encouragement I need to stop second-guessing myself, let go of worries about not doing it the right way, and confidently choose my next steps.

We may use the scope and sequence as a guide to help us self-assess our progress and keep us on the path of learning, knowingly call in particular colleagues and critical friends to assure us that our thinking is aligned with pedagogical practices, or seek perspectives and knowledge outside of ourselves when we know we might need a bit more learning ourselves to approach the learning at hand. All of these strategies are ways we remind ourselves of the depth and complexity of our experiences and quiet the mind chatter that can all too often get louder than it needs to be.

Build a foundational knowledge in our curriculum and our learners.

As we begin our teaching careers, move to new educational systems, or make changes to our teaching positions or departments, we spend time studying our curriculum framework and standards. We might do this sitting with our colleagues unpacking new standards, attending professional development solely focused on particular skills or content, and referring to our guiding curriculum documents frequently to ensure that we are aligned with the expected outcomes of our province or state. Being well versed in our curriculum allows us to see its flexibility, identify the connections across subject areas, and maintain a cadence of learning that is uniquely attuned to the needs of our learners.

We build our foundational knowledge in time and *alongside* getting to know our learners. At its core, constructivism is a trusting of community that in turn means a trusting of our learners and starting with relationships first. Building relationships, however, doesn't stop after the first few weeks of an academic school year, the habitual "getting to know you" activities that fill time during our first interactions with our new learners, or the interest surveys we give as we settle into our new communities.

We get to know our learners by staying curious about who they are and what they uniquely bring to the classroom. This happens when we co-design essential agreements, invite them to share their passions through polls, and ask open-ended questions that uncover their past school experiences, strengths, and areas for growth. It also takes shape in the opportunities we create for students to turn and talk with one another. Structures like Four Corners or Fishbowl help scaffold collaboration, guiding students as they communicate and work toward shared goals. And sometimes, it's as simple and powerful as asking, "What are you curious about now?"

We build relationships through our instructional design and use that as a vehicle to observe peer-to-peer interactions as they use evidence from our learning walls to support the growth of their knowledge. We stand alongside our learners as they tackle a statistics word problem and glance toward the "Get Unstuck" wall we've been building across a term, as they choose a medium to showcase their understanding of habitats in their local community, or as they evaluate their feedback about a recent learning experience. The collection of the days across a semester, interactions, and one-on-one connections are the data we need to get to know our learners and find a trusted ease in partnership in learning. Take a look at four categories and ideas for action to get to know your learners. Consider these categories a framework to generate your own list of ideas as you continue to build a deeper understanding of your content and the learners you serve!

Notice
As your students engage with their peers during free play or recess, notice who they gravitate toward, and what games or loose parts tend to be a favorite. What stories of friendship or cooperation do they tell? How might the decision-making you see from the sidelines help give you a broader perspective of this student? What commonalities or differences do you notice? How might you leverage these relationships as you plan for collaboration and interaction with your learning wall?
Play
No matter the age, play comes to us all naturally. What are ways you can target more playful experiences? How might creating, making, or building bring your students together as a learning community? What skills or competencies might you see flexed through play?
Grab a bin full of LEGOs, provide a recipe to your students to cook or assemble some food, bring a game from home and teach it to a new friend, or get outside to take a walk on campus. Plant some flowers or herbs to freshen up an outdoor space. Consider how another service to the community might be a playful and meaningful way for your learners to connect with people beyond their grade level.
How might you choose to use your time blocks differently? What might happen if you asked your class to grab their belongings and head to an outdoor classroom space or other common area or excuse your class for a set amount of time to connect with an expert in the community?

Take the long way!

If you teach in the primary setting, consider taking a different route back to your classroom or to another area on campus than you usually do. Linger a bit longer, ask them what they notice, and give space for conversations to run freely. Does your context include building to support their learning during the "finding out" stage of their free inquiry project?

You might need to co-design expectations, but what an authentic opportunity for self-management and agency to be flexed! Notice what begins to unfold over a period of time; how does this impact what you know about your learners and their abilities to slow down and notice the world around them while establishing deeper connections with one another?

Greet

Soft starts are inviting, help us ease into the mindset that is ready for learning, and set the tone for what's about to begin. Close your laptop, hold off on sending the email, and put your phone to the side to start your day at the door. Greet parents, community members, and students with a warm smile and greeting. Be intentionally present for this short time in the day to establish connection and a focus for your day. I've seen school leaders greet families and students as they walk into the building, playing uplifting music to set a welcoming mood; early years teachers set up an invitation at their doors that gets parents and students engaging in conversation straight away; and support staff clock in for the day and find a hallway or other common space to say hello to teachers, connect with students, and settle into the joyful ways they want to spend their day.

Each of these creates opportunities in which students and staff meaningfully connect and learn more about one another's gifts and talents they bring to the world. We get to know our students and staff beyond their identification number or number on our rosters by asking questions as a means of connection and learning about one another. Think about ways you greet your learners. Are there times in the year these greetings wane for you? How might you recommit to your practice and your learners in a way that meets their needs while strengthening your relationship with one another?

Listen. Ask questions. Give it a chance.

We build the trust of our learners when they feel heard, know they can rely on us, and experience a sense of reciprocity. Think of a recent interaction you've had with your learners. Pause and take note of who was doing most of the talking. What do you know about them? Are they the loudest voice in the room? Does their sharing reflect other perspectives from the community of learners? What does the interaction tell you about the space and underpinning values of learning? Throughout the co-construction of a learning wall, we listen, ask questions, and optimistically give the learning a chance to slowly reveal itself. These three steps, *in their given order,* pave the way for a facilitation and plan for powerful learning.

Step One: Lean in and Listen

A classic Turn and Talk, carousel activity, or Give One, Get One has increased impact and leveraged traction when we lean in and listen to the conversations being exchanged by our community of learners. As we walk past pairs of students, we notice the academic vocabulary that students might be using in their discourse, carefully watch as small groups turn their heads to reference the sentence stems we've deliberately placed next to selected artifacts, take a knee to bring ourselves eye level with our youngest learners, or nod our heads and use other nonverbal cues to show we are attuned to the discussions at hand.

When we lean in and listen, we give ourselves space to get curious while quietly contemplating how to respond once we call the group's attention back toward us. I routinely use this strategy to create space for a bit more internal reflection, make more clarity for ways we might build on the knowledge we've already established, and include a pause to be guided by the artifacts that we've pinned on our learning wall after our initial provocation at the start of the week.

Within just a handful of minutes, I am able to listen to the land-scape of learning through observation and conversation and have just enough space for me to reflect, take action, and meet the needs of the learning.

Step Two: Whose story is not being told?

As you evaluate learner feedback in the form of wonderings, personal reflections, collaborative thinking routines, and question protocols, pause to ask yourself whether all perspectives are reflected in the evidence before you. Are there some students who may have over-powered conversations? Have you prompted students to share how they feel about the learning? Were there provocations or collaborative structures in your lesson design that nudged new perspectives and alternative ways of thinking?

When we plan for more learning and collection of artifacts, we also plan for listening and ensure we are prepared with question prompts that create a psychologically safe place for all voices to be heard. When you listen and believe in the capabilities of your learners, also ask, *Who or what might be missing from the learning? What additional ways could we explore and expand our thinking around this topic or concept?*

Step Three: Power of the Post-It

These three-by-three squares of paper have the power to create equita-ble space for all of our learners to share their thinking with us. They lift up voices that typically may not be heard, evidence thinking, and make the learning visible as it unfolds. Below is a resource that includes two ways I commonly use Post-it® notes when working with groups of teachers or students. How might these structures help you listen differently? What opportunities might present themselves when we lift up moments of equitable contribution?

 Grab a pack of sticky notes and choose a structure that helps you pause your natural inclination to lead with a heavy hand in a discussion. How does the power of the Post-It flatten the loudest voices while uplifting those of our learners who are less confident to jump in first.

I Do, We Do, You Do

If you are building a learning wall, you most likely have the following core beliefs about your teaching practice:

1. Students, no matter how little, are capable of great things.
2. How we learn has a greater impact on success than what we learn.
3. Constructivism and co-design are powerful vehicles that develop these skills.

How we think about *and use* the four walls of our spaces are the pivotal moves that bring these beliefs to life and transform the way we continually move away from a checklist-based approach to documentation. We resist the compulsion of tasking and telling as our primary mode of instruction and assessment of learning in the classroom. We move into a space that allows us to revisit and experience the core beliefs listed above with more frequency in our practice.

We build learning walls to integrate meaningful exchanges between our scholars that reinforce the value of community and the benefits of "two-way teaching and learning" while simultaneously creating rich opportunities for a greater understanding of self. Within these frames, we find ourselves "doing less" while gaining "more" as a result of a gradual release of responsibility. We take inspiration from a familiar structure most of us learned in our university courses and student teaching experiences—I do, we do, you do—as our guide for the "last step" of building a learning wall.

As you read about the three possible approaches to building a learning wall below, keep in mind the intention you have for building your wall. Depending on the needs of the cohort of learners, time constraints, and number of students the learning wall will serve, you might find yourself needing to flex in between a few of these states. All of these have their own benefits that are unique to the learning community in which they are built, so stay open-minded and flexible here!

I Do

Modeling how to solve a math problem, reading a passage aloud while orally annotating key vocabulary words, editing a writing exemplar, or demonstrating the first steps toward research and experimentation in the science lab are all conscious decisions we make in the planning and facilitation of learning. Modeling, or direct instruction, provides the initial and equitable scaffolding needed toward a gradual release of responsibility and is one we also consider as we plan with learning walls in mind. It is a natural first step when orienting learners.

We begin building learning walls by modeling how to add artifacts—purposefully pointing to pieces of evidence that show connections in learning or shifts in thinking over time. As chart paper is layered, moved, or taken down, these small actions show learners how the wall can support their growth. This intentional modeling becomes the mental model they return to as we gradually release responsibility and invite them to take more ownership of the learning wall. We wax and wane from explicitly calling out these moves with language such as *I noticed that the strategies we've listed here might be important; Let's revisit some of our questions we had last week before we begin our day!;*

This is reminding me of something we added to our learning wall yesterday—let's go take a peek together! or even *I might need some inspiration before I start writing; where might be a good place to look on our wall?* while also ensuring that we habitually plan and teach with evidence displayed on our walls.

It's time now to take a look at a few learning walls to see how the I Do strategy might be supportive for your own context and community of learners. As you look closely at these walls, it's important to remember that as we co-construct for personal meaning we think about where we are in an academic year, the early moves necessary to support the skills we are nurturing, and we can't forget to take a pause to consider our own mindset around what we think our scholars are capable of. All of these are assets we employ in our planning process and use as points of reflection. Look for each of these as you read about the learning walls below and make note of the connections you see in your practice. Circle elements that pique your interest and jot down questions that you can return to as you continue to refine and revise how you evidence and actively document learning. I'll outline the unique (and sometimes surprising!) benefits of each of these learning walls and suggest you also use these as a provocation for reflection and application in your practice. Let's tune in to the first learning wall now!

The start of this small learning wall began when I was presented with the opportunity to support the learning of our paraprofessionals. While looking ahead at the academic calendar, I quickly realized that the infrequent cadence of our allocated time might prove to be a barrier to what I had hoped we would accomplish. Fully aware that administration had clearly defined goals, I knew that because of our limitation with time there were two critical factors that heavily influenced how this learning wall would need to be built.

1. Pinning artifacts, determining important evidence, and making decisions about this vertical tool would be a "me job." I would need to be doing more of the heavy lifting when it came to actively documenting and building our learning wall.

2. Spacing, visibility, and routines around learning were unlike a "traditional" learning space. Planning for the process of retrieval would be particularly important for this group of learners.

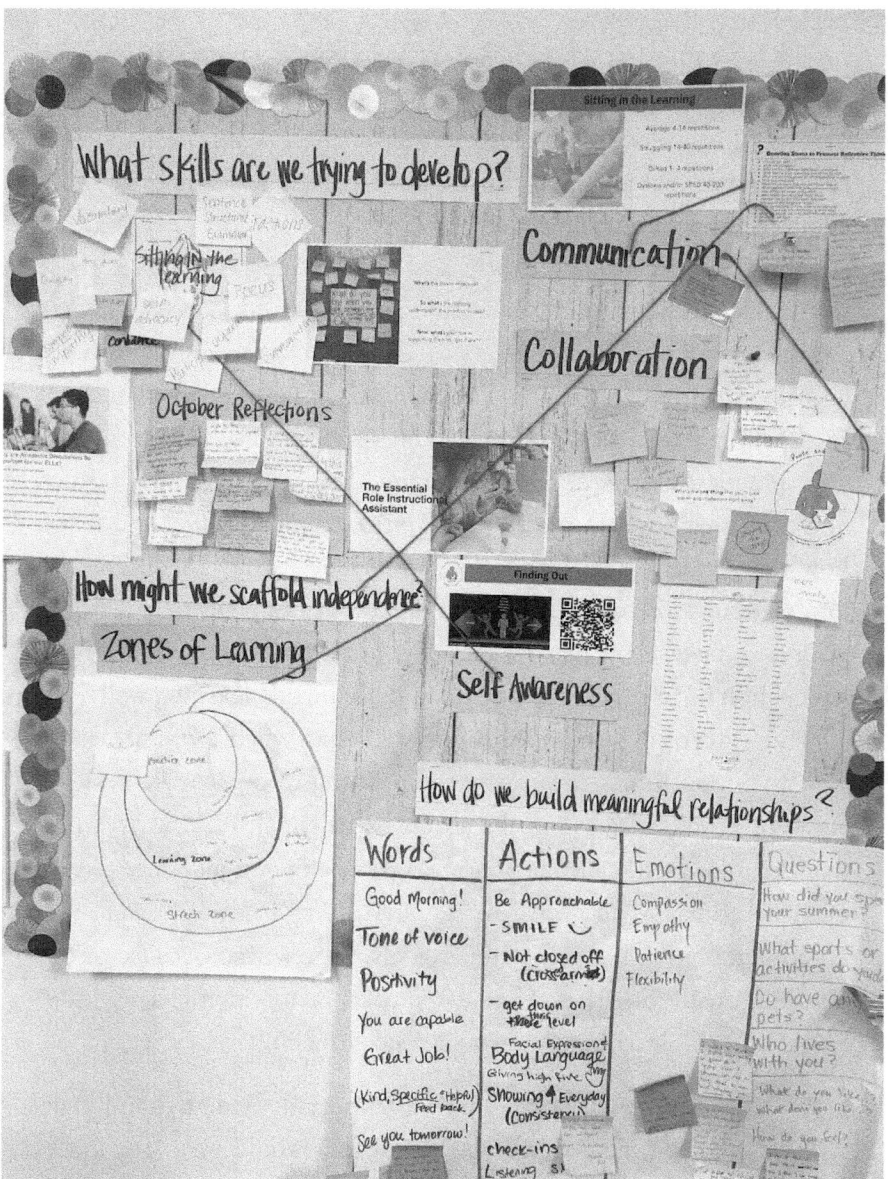

With an intention to keep the narrative of this learning wall simple and easily accessible, I've anchored this vertical space with three essential questions that emerged from an early provocation as themes of interest and areas required for the growth and development of the group. Scribbled on sentence strips and pinned to the bulletin board, these questions became the pillars for planning. They were used to help us summarize and synthesize learning and to assess connections, and they eased us all into an organic cycle of reflection.

If your circumstances necessitate that you build your learning wall without your learners' active contribution, as mine did, use the planning structure Plan, Retrieve, Reflect to ensure that your display of learning reflects the rich tenets and values that these teaching tools provide.

Plan

Pulling up a chair to the evidence is always a step I encourage educators to engage in during their planning and reflection routines. With sometimes several months in between our sessions and paraprofessionals unable to take stock of the learning wall in between our times together, this ritual of recalling became a critical part of my process for designing next steps in the learning. Looking at the evidence I had pinned to the wall, thumbing through the small stack of anchor charts and sticky notes that I kept tucked aside, and scrolling through my slide deck was the familiar routine I returned to each time I sat down to organize my thinking for what was ahead.

I compared the evidence and reflections of learning with the overarching objectives I had for the cohort of learners and used the three essential questions as my compass toward planning. If one goal was to identify the skills for independent students in the classroom, what were the skills *the educators* needed to flex during our sessions together? If another goal was to identify strategies for strong relationships with students, what experience did they already bring from their time in the classroom, and what opportunities might their collective wisdom provide for the landscape of learning? With these reflective planning questions in mind, the group was asked to go on learning walks throughout the building to identify different ways space might be a third teacher as they supported students, tinker with loose parts to experience the benefits of play, and flex and refine their approach to using questions as a medium to support more independent learners. They dug into research and explored new learning around best practices for our emergent bilingual population, and they were asked to collaboratively reflect using structures I knew were familiar to the classrooms they supported, such as a Turn and Talk, Give One, Get One, or Texas Two Step.

Retrieve

Choosing artifacts with the constraints of space became my biggest teacher for this vertical teaching tool and challenged me to really become clear on what was most important to lift up in the learning. I used color and sentence strips to anchor the big ideas and concepts I wanted learners to remain focused on. I chose artifacts that reflected what I hoped would remain "sticky" in their classroom practice. Simple invitations as the cohort entered the space for a morning learning, such as, *Orient yourself with our learning wall and recall the small goal you set for yourself last time.* and *Which of our essential questions are you most curious to revisit and unpack more today?* supported retrieval. Nudges toward active reflection with the encouragement to *Find some evidence that connects with a story of learning you can share about your week*, fostered co-construction of thinking across time and created wells of deeper understanding and personal meaning-making that might have been overlooked had I not been clear with the skills and concepts I wanted learners to walk away with.

If you are building a learning wall without your learners in the room, be sure to revisit the structures and strategies presented across Chapter Five. Use the reflective prompts, question starters, and other examples of learning walls within that chapter as a guide when considering what actions are necessary with the evidence before you.

Reflect

I have a rule for myself when it comes to reflecting on learning . . . *give it space.* Although my enthusiastic and curious self has the urge to immediately begin unpacking, making connections, and synthesizing what's next, I find that taking a step back and returning to reflecting on the evidence the following day helps me see opportunities with much more clarity and a refreshed perspective. Give yourself permission to pause too! Stack the evidence, mindfully step away from the learning space, and save the process of adding, editing, and moving artifacts to another day. Once you are ready to return to the evidence, consider the following list as possibilities for reflection. Although not exhaustive, this list includes common practices I see experienced inquiry teachers engage in and are ideas I encourage you to take on and include in your practice too!

Move or take down evidence. Whether because of old habits of creating traditional displays of learning or hesitation about making mistakes, I find most educators miss this opportunity for reflection!

The physical act of shifting, moving, and removing artifacts brings a refreshed mindset and pushes us toward a playfully reflective practice. If you are building a learning wall in the physical space, don't be afraid to unstaple anchor charts, unpin other evidence, or change up the structure of how things were initially displayed!

Bring in an outside perspective. Try inviting someone outside of your typical learning circle to the evidence before you and ask them to help you reflect and brainstorm possible connections. While building this learning wall, I was fortunate to collaborate with an instructional coach who supported our campus one day a week. As she asked me questions about artifacts and offered her expertise toward the landscape of learning, I gained a better understanding of the value of some of the evidence I was displaying and was more easily able to edit and revise the vertical learning space.

What does this make you wonder now? This simple prompt is a favorite of mine, and I find myself frequently asking program coordinators, school administrators, and classroom teachers this simple and open-ended question when they invite me into their space and settle into planning next steps for learning. Before you jump into planning, pull out your scope and sequence to compare timelines, or align assessment dates, briefly pause to look at the evidence and ask, *What does this make me wonder now?*

Let your eyes wander, and the questions spill, leaning into a playfully curious mindset as you dance across what's before you. I'm sure that in less than five minutes you'll uncover connections that provide a clear direction for next steps in planning and easily identify opportunities to lift up and model your own wonderings when your learners walk back into the room. This exercise is also a fantastic one I favor as a start to team planning meetings. I love how it recenters the student as we plan for learning while asking us to put our habits aside and tap into our own curiosities too!

Celebrate and Share: I'm a big fan of using social media platforms like Instagram and LinkedIn as a way to grow our professional learning networks while celebrating our students and their growth. I've seen honest reflections of where the learning "went wrong" and new paths were taken, felt the joy in the carousel of photos that reveal big aha moments in understanding, and discovered displays of intentionally planned provocations. Inspired, I bookmark these ideas to refer to later. In fact, many of the educators presented to you here in this book are from virtual sharing and celebrations!

Even if you are not on these platforms or don't choose to share your practice in this public way, as you examine the collection before you, celebrate and share what you see! Take the time to slow down and notice, start off your next department-level planning meetings by celebrating one another and the growth of your scholars, and settle into the ways that your intentionality is making a big difference in the development of the whole child. The pressures of compliance, timelines, and the traditional school system itself doesn't often leave a lot of space for the acknowledgment of the growth forward, the small wins along the way, and the general sharing of how we are nurturing the minds and hearts of our students. In an effort to nudge you not to overlook this important part of learning and meaning-making, I've listed a few prompts to help you celebrate and share the bits of your practice and share what the evidence before you is making you think more deeply about!

- What's something that surprised you this week?
- How have you seen learners stretched?
- What growth have you experienced? What makes you say that?
- What artifact are you most proud of?
- What are you excited to unpack next in the learning?

Benefits of I Do

- Helps with understanding the inner workings of how to build a learning wall without the pressure of performance in front of a group
- Acts as a planning and teaching tool that encourages an unrushed process of reflection
- Improves collaboration between additional collaborative support systems provided to the learning community
- Explicitly models to learners how learning walls can be used to support learning

We Do

Most of the walls I help educators plan for, implement, or reflect on fall into this category of co-design and co-construction; however, I recognize that context, culture, and individual or school values impact how these walls are collaboratively built. You've already seen collections of vertical spaces that have been built with this joint effort yet range in how they have been contributed to, and while nothing can quite take the place of seeing these learning walls being assembled "in action," the following list provides several different systems one can consider when planning for and teaming up with your scholars to build a learning wall.

Context

Whole-class additions: Whole-class additions to learning walls is a great place to start when adding evidence and documentation of learning. Once you get going with your documentation, however, I encourage you to get playful with this approach too! Consider co-constructing an anchor chart but give your learners the pen while you do it, using a spider web diagram to document the ebb and flow of a whole-class discussion, transcribing wonders that have piqued your younger learners' interest as a means of reflection or a form of assessment, or tasking your scholars with an exit ticket that uses powerful sentence stems such as *I used to think . . . now I know . . .* or *One thing that's important to remember tomorrow . . .* to effectively use time and ensure that all students have a space to enter into the learning.

Be playful with the medium in which you gather this evidence too! How might a Padlet digitally capture end-of-day reflections or photos of students working? Give your students stickers or circle labels to "vote" or highlight important thinking. *Whole-class contributions* simply means we consider ways we invite our class to engage and interact with the collection of evidence before them. Habits such as these are what learners will take with them as they continue to make meaning of these organic spaces!

Selections from group work: An inquiry-based approach to teaching and learning means that our students often have their desks and chairs turned toward one another to synthesize meaning around the latest text we've presented them, are collaboratively solving a complex word problem on vertical surfaces we've placed around our classrooms, or have pencils in hand, generating ideas and thinking with one another on the large sheet of paper we have provided. We observe our students working with one another, lean in to listen to exchanges in conversations, or collect small stacks of chart paper at the end of a learning block and determine what's important to lift up in the learning and to add to our vertical spaces.

In Chapter Six on retrieval, I shared one of my favorite strategies for gathering selections from group work: *layering the learning*. Sometimes, it's not necessary to collect *all evidence* along the way. Whether I am trying to conserve space on my wall or the evidence that's been generated isn't hitting the learning target I had in mind, I'll oftentimes just grab one piece of evidence from a group that most clearly aligns with the direction that's needed while asking myself a familiar question I introduced to you earlier in this publication—*What's most important to lift up in the learning now?*—which helps me quickly decide what to keep and what's okay to let go of and recycle. It's important to note that the selection process described above is not done in the presence of learners. This reflective sorting is reserved for planning periods or after school as I plan and assess for next steps in learning.

Individual student contributions: Do your students share learning-inspired action taken after stepping away from the four walls of your classrooms? Do you have reluctant learners who could benefit from some celebration amongst their peers? Is there something you heard during your one-on-one conference with a student you know the rest of your class could benefit from? All of these are fantastic opportunities for you to extend a personal invitation for learners to add to your co-constructed space. Knowing your learners' preferences and needs, being mindful of language you use, and ensuring there's a balance in the types of artifacts we choose to display are all factors we keep in mind as we ask for individual student contributions. I love the way that keeping these artifacts in mind helps build a community of learners while honoring individual needs and growth opportunities!

Archive for skills: If you teach several different sections within a subject area or are an educator within the arts, you know that it's impossible to collect every sticky note, student wondering, or group assignment along the way. The sheer volume of paper and time to manage materials while teaching within your short block of time immediately eliminates the benefits of building a learning wall! Instead of thinking about documentation for content in the traditional sense, look at your curriculum and identify the skills that are essential and enhance the content that you teach.

How might a learning wall archiving skills support multiple levels of learners? I've observed science teachers build skill-focused learning walls that support students as they engage in laboratory research or other hands-on experimentation, physical education teachers leverage rapid co-construct lists for self-assessment and reflection before sending students off for independent practice during group rotations, and art teachers enhance peer-to-peer feedback with collaboratively generated success criteria, helpful sentence stems, and word banks filled with academic language that support studio thinking and process art from the start! These learning walls are interwoven into classroom systems, often have a longer lifespan that extends across terms and semesters of learning, and remind us of possibilities for deeper learning when we plan with skills in mind.

Culture

With a commitment to foster a love of learning, it is our responsibility to recognize, welcome, and honor the unique school cultures in which we serve and design learning experiences wherein everyone can find an entry point, creating a place of understanding that extends well beyond institutional requirements and boundaries. Well-designed and well-planned learning walls ensure equitable participation of our scholars and can become the vehicle for culturally responsive discussions. The work and expertise of educator and author of the publication *Culturally Responsive Teaching and the Brain,* Zaretta Hammond, reminds us of the power that these protocols have in the classroom to nurture more equitable classrooms and learning communities. Asking yourself questions similar to the ones listed below helps you further move toward building the capacities of individual students. As you learn more about the cultural learning styles of your scholars, I'm confident that you'll return to this list to help you deepen your knowledge and understanding of culture and these visible displays of learning.

Source: East Three High School, Inuvik, NWT, Canada

- How do you know what feels relevant and impactful to your scholars?
- What is the current culture of thinking in your classroom?

- How are students' cultures or the community's culture reflected in your learning wall and the artifacts on display?
- In what ways do you intentionally invite multiple perspectives that honor unique gifts, talents, prior experiences, and knowledge?
- Are there cultural calendars of elders in your community from whom you can seek advice and perspective?
- How might you consider storytelling, games, collaboration, or social interaction to nudge your learners to engage with the learning wall with more ownership?

Values

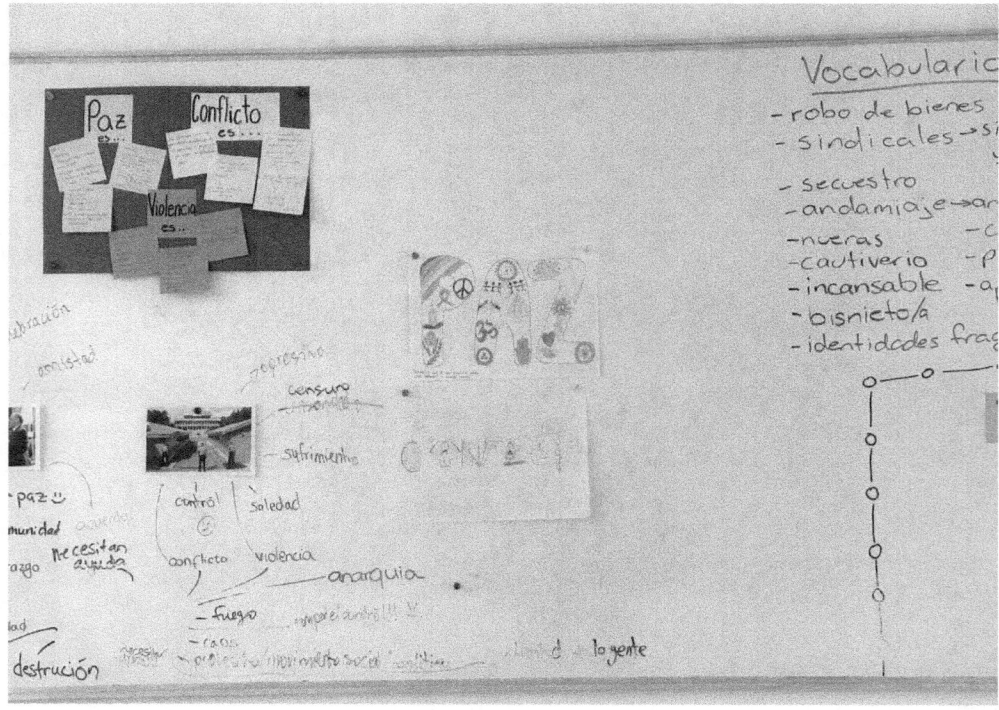

I have a handful of questions that I routinely return to each time I begin new partnerships with schools, classroom teachers, or program coordinators. I find that this curated list of questions is an authentic way to get to know one another, and it allows us to enter into spaces that honor unique expertise and experience. The questions are open-ended enough to invite, engage, and activate conversations that lift up an essential focus for our work with one another and bring forth the vision of the partnership and values of the educator or organization. Knowing our values is foundational to the work we do to ensure that we don't get caught up in the limitation of the systems out of our control. It allows us to co-construct learning experiences, make decisions that are in alignment with the vision and values of the organizations we are a part of, and bring an awareness of self that nurtures the core of who we are as educators.

As you continue to evaluate how you leverage "space as the third teacher," determine how to best organize your learning space, and build learning walls that are meaningful for all of your scholars, it's important to be clear on your values too. Use the values inventory resource included below to help you reflect on your core values, then return to your learning wall and assess how they are reflected in your space. With a curious eye, consider the following list of reflective questions to help you continue to evaluate how values permeate your practice and influence your mindset as you strengthen new documentation habits.

- Where is there alignment in your documentation practice with your values?
- Do you notice any unintentional misalignment?
- What would your students or community say you value based on the physical displays of learning? What makes you say that?
- How are your school values reflected in your space?
- What's one thing you want to shift in your practice or change completely based on this reflection?

How do you ensure that your actions and values are aligned? Use this resource to quickly inventory and assess alignment, misalignment, and possible opportunities moving forward!

The systems described in this section are flexed in greater detail in Part Three of this book as over a dozen educators share their personal journeys of building a learning wall. Their stories range from evidence that reflects the interests of our youngest learners to artifacts that demonstrate the power of a whole-school inquiry. As you look at their learning walls, pay close attention to how their distinctive contexts, cultures, and values are revealed in their spaces, and use their experiences as inspiration for how you will continue to co-design your learning walls too.

Benefits of We Do

- Shows learners how to use the evidence we collect as an essential tool to support independent learning through shared roles and ownership of action
- Fosters deeper understanding toward an agentic learning environment
- Reinforces psychological safety, risk-taking, and a community of learners

You Do

You Do doesn't mean *you do it all alone*. The intentional creation, active modeling, showing interest, and aligning actions with internal motivations such as curiosity are all intentional actions we plan for early on to ensure that our scholars experience the value a learning wall brings to the landscape of learning. When our students are given the tools they need, we see their agentic nature soar! Let's take a look at three possible pathways for this gradual release of responsibility now without losing the quality reflection, meaning-making, and skill development.

As you look at the learning wall examples below, pay close attention to the initial moves and scaffolds put in place for all students to achieve (and feel) success. I'm curious where you see your own practice and students within these examples and what new ideas and possibilities they spark for you!

Setting Goals

In the last decade, social and emotional awareness, strategies for self-management, and internal reflection have thankfully become more mainstream within our schools. Students are asked to collect artifacts of learning and slowly construct process folios instead of collections that comprise only final products or achievements. Schools are rethinking their traditional approach to conferences and a more student-centered approach with student-led conference structures and morning meetings or other "slow starts" are more commonplace than they have ever been in modern education. I love seeing these small yet powerful shifts in the way we are approaching the collaborative nature of learning, and I see seismic shifts in schools' agentic culture when they begin to restructure old and outdated systems to better align with what's best for all learners. Asking students to set goals aligns with this more student-friendly approach and is a fantastic way to have our students practice more of the heavy lifting when it comes to co-construction of our vertical spaces.

Using language from the learner profile we have adopted as a school, Grade 2 students were called on to determine indicators and other descriptive language to define these traits. As part of the community-building process at the start of a new academic year, students collaborated to illustrate icons and images, sorted and organized photos, and brainstormed collections of ideas and other colorful language that best describe each of these attributes.

These student-designed posters were then attached to a bulletin board and took on new life for personal meaning-making! Each week

as students entered the space, they were invited to reconnect with this wall and one another to determine a goal for the week. Students moved individual clothespins to different areas on the wall and set a focus for themselves.

Scaffolds to support decision-making and nudges toward thinking about their thinking in new ways expressed themselves during mid-week check-ins during morning meetings, end-of-day peer-to-peer reflections, and brief student-to-teacher one-on-one check-ins.

We design opportunities like this goal-setting learning wall as a means to establish the habits and ways of thinking about ourselves as learners. Scholars tune in to take notice of how they are feeling about themselves and the day ahead and learn the patterning of setting goals that include evaluating the evidence, communicating growth, reflecting on experiences, and becoming more aware of the ebb and flow when it comes to personal development. Practices such as these infuse a greater readiness toward spaces where a culture of inquiry can thrive!

If you teach within a context in which your learners are a bit older, I highly suggest that you pick up a copy of Trevor MacKenzie's *Inquiry Mindset: Assessment Edition*. Within this publication, he shares several ways that he uses similar frameworks to help his students set goals. From using a desk calendar to collectively set "target windows" or deadline goals for upcoming projects and assignments to a learning display of competencies as critical evidence toward the reflective process that ensues when collaboratively writing report card comments with his students, you'll find several strategies that pave the way for learners who are able to self-manage and more confidently self-assess their strengths and stretches as a learner. No matter how you adapt the ideas described here in this section or where you start with goal setting as a means of building the reflective muscles of your students, know that these agentic actions nurture opportunities and mindsets that are necessary for the process of co-construction.

Group Displays of Learning

Learning walls are meant to serve the unique culture, context, and group of learners in which they serve. We define a need, target a selection of skills, and reflect and revise as we go. Unlike with a traditional

Sarah Scott, Primary Teacher, Scone Grammar School, Scone, NSW, Australia

presentation that is assigned at the culmination of a unit to summarize learning, in this Year 5 classroom, Sarah Scott chooses to take a different route with her eleven-year-olds to support co-construction and personal meaning-making.

Using an essential question as the starting prompt, she tasked students with gathering evidence from their notebooks. They collected and organized sticky notes from several "pause moments" that she had nudged them toward at different points in the unit. They were encouraged to use thinking routines to show the unpacking of big concepts, photos of models from an earlier Makerspace design challenge, key vocabulary highlighting different artifacts, and wwws that linked to videos students made that explain broader systems from their research. These walls are bustling with an agentic energy that's hard to miss!

Look more closely at the learning walls above and you'll notice student-created labels using language from the inquiry cycle (tuning in, finding out, etc.) whose purpose is to categorize the different stages of learning, pushpins that encourage a flexibility with the placement of documentation, and stretched ribbon carefully attached to selected artifacts to demonstrate the new connections being made based off of conversations with their peers, whole-class reflections, and feedback from Sarah herself.

We of course don't jump into the deep end of this sort of documentation without backwards planning toward this type of deeper learning. Working closely with Sarah over the past few years and having been to her classroom connecting more personally with her students, I know that building and modeling how to use learning walls was not a step she waited for until this unit of learning unfolded; rather it's an integrated daily practice and routine that she and her students are very familiar with.

Early in the year, Sarah models how to use a learning wall each time she adds some evidence of thinking and learning, she plans her lessons in a way that ensures that she's calling on students to use the evidence to support and defend their thinking, she organically points to the learning wall during direct instruction moments of teaching to reference key vocabulary as a means to refine understanding, and she synthesizes her own learning by taking stock of the evidence on her camera roll she's collected throughout the week. Over time, these routines are the scaffolding that supports students to confidently construct these group displays of the process of learning.

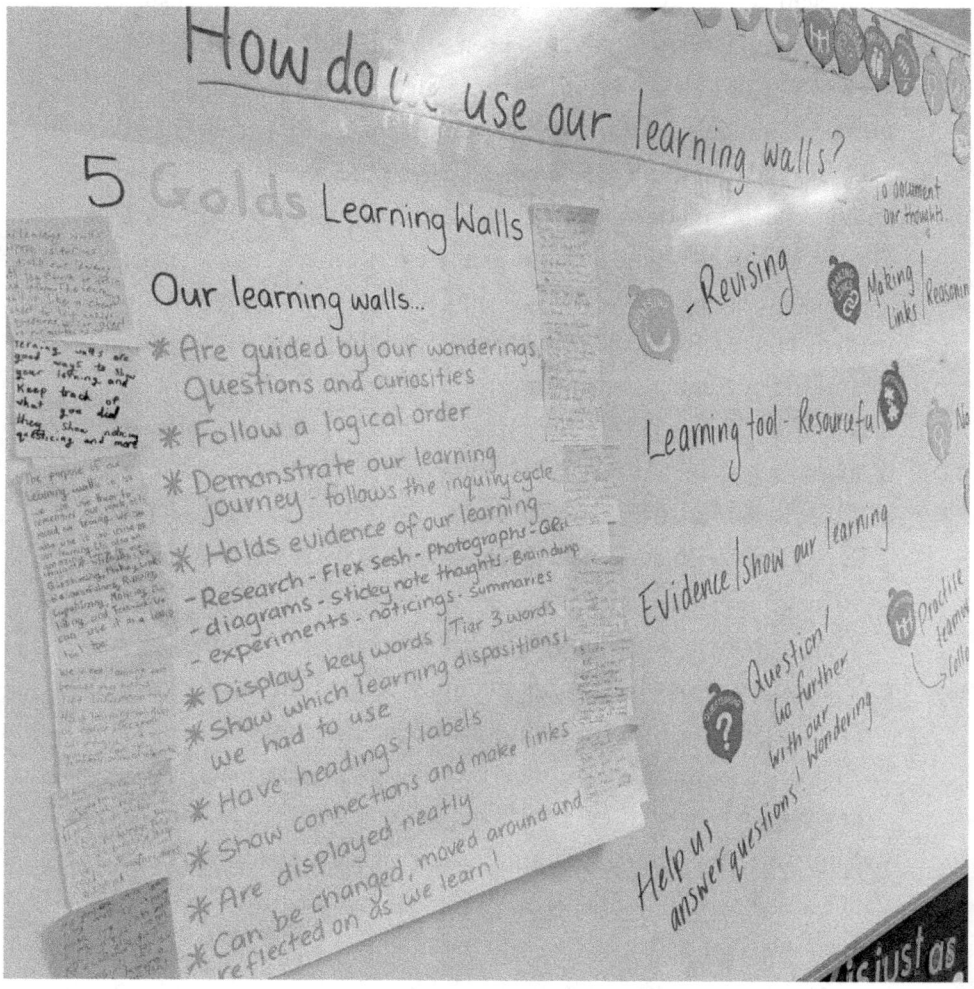

Source: Sarah Scott, Year 5 Teacher, Scone Grammar School, Scone, NSW, Australia

In Part Three of this book, you'll have the opportunity to take another look at Sarah's classroom and a learning wall she built early in the academic year. As you read about the learning wall from Sarah herself, take note of her process and early moves she shares with you. Look for her personal reflections as she plans for materials and considers agency as part of her plan. Notice how she seamlessly integrates curriculum and student curiosity. These actions all contribute to the independent actions you see evidenced in these learning wall examples.

Collective Reflection

Those who facilitate adult learning in schools know that planning and creating meaningful opportunities for synthesizing and reflecting on big ideas, new strategies, and application in the classroom is an essential part of the design for learning. Unfortunately, midweek or end-of-day staff meetings, time pressures to check things off our lists, and the assumption that a two-hour training means we've mastered a strategy can all contribute to rushed or shallow reflection. As a result, we often omit the critical step of co-constructing for personal meaning and miss valuable opportunities to do what's best for all learners.

We nurture work cultures that honor the value of adults as learners and model the process of building onto knowledge through actions of collective reflection, hanging onto the evidence with a stronger permanence and routinely asking ourselves, *what might we **keep learning** about their learning*? These artifacts of reflection are the starts of learning walls to add to throughout the academic year. They remain in communal spaces to nudge us toward thinking about our thinking. We bring them to the table as reminders when we plan opportunities for continued learning, identify needs for one-on-one coaching support, and formatively assess progress toward larger district or campus goals.

Thinking routines are fantastic options to consider as a start toward collective reflection. Once they are introduced, they become self-guiding, honor the slower pace that's needed for deeper connections and application of big ideas, and are easily replicated in classroom spaces with students. The Compass Points thinking routine is a favorite of mine, and making use of an outdated bulletin board in our mailroom became the perfect location for us to house this reflective space.

Its proximity to our administrators' offices and central location in the building made it easy for staff to add reflections after campus-related learning opportunities. It became a reliable tool for goal setting and ongoing support of learning because it reminded us, as leaders, to continue to ask for feedback and tune in to the needs of our staff.

In the example below, you'll see a wall at several different stages across a school year. With prompts at the end of a full day of professional learning, calls toward reflective action to summarize thinking from PLC sessions, or nudges after grade-level teams engaged in learning walks during their allocated planning time, this wall ebbed and flowed with evidence and a natural ease toward reflection.

As leaders of learning, we prioritized time to take a closer look at the thinking that was being displayed and demonstrated interest in the collections of reflections with mindful actions that included the removal of sticky notes to add to our greater campus learning wall, identifying common themes in feedback, organizing sticky notes accordingly, and pulling up a chair to the thinking as we were analyzing campus data and completing district reporting systems. Having a framework so visible and easily accessible made it easier to lean toward reflection and honor the wisdom that was being displayed before us.

Compass Points is not the only frame we can use to invite collective reflection. Several other thinking routines and other scaffolded structures provide similar benefits. I've used many of the organizational tools below and encourage you to playfully try one of them in your practice. You're sure to find their open-endedness and reliable structure easily adaptable for any group of learners or context. I'll let the walls "do the talking" and take it from here!

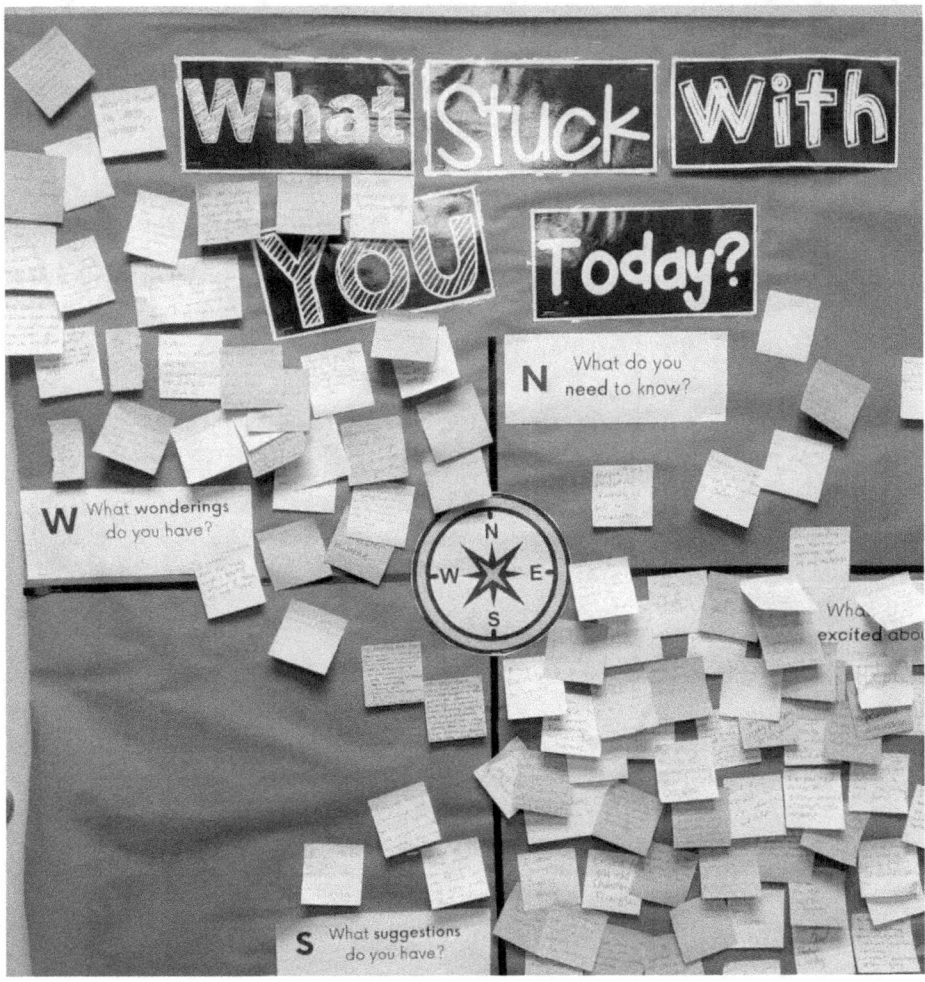

Plus/Delta/Wonder

I love the way a Plus/Delta/Wonder encourages continuous improvement and nudges us toward forward thinking. Take a look at how this Grade 3 teacher used this structure to ground her learners in reflective action toward challenges they were currently facing as a community of learners. Notice how she anchors the structure in student feedback that encourages a growth mindset and ownership over learning moving forward!

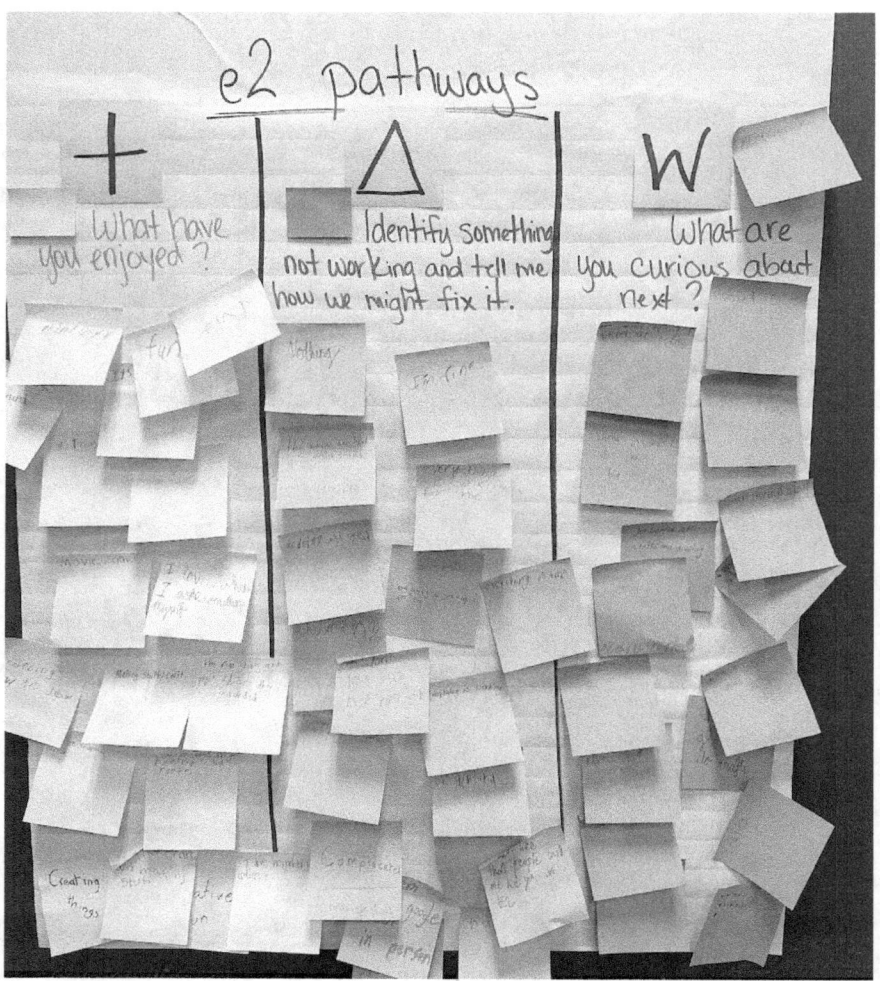

Know-Value-Wonder-Need

Seeing leaders model the model and use their empty spaces to document the adult learning in the building is always inspiring. I love how the leaders at Tarvin Elementary use their PLC room to unpack big ideas and take stock of action steps needed moving forward. Using a quadrant and the prompts you see here, reflections rooted in values and vision easily emerged and created powerful opportunities in learning moving forward.

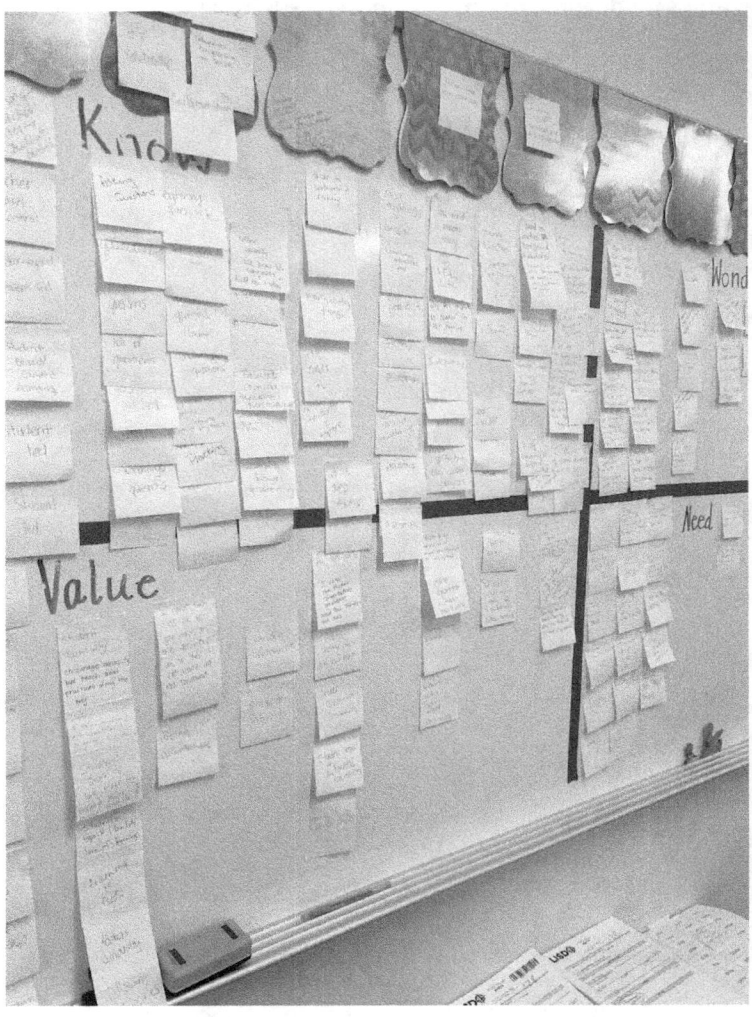

Tarvin Elementary, Leander, Texas

Stop-Start-Continue

While building the language and defining indicators for the profile of a
learner, the reflective frame Stop-Start-Continue was a helpful routine
to help this group of educators determine common practices that supported the development of desired competencies of a learner, other
practices that were deemed no longer necessary, and new perspectives
and ways of teaching toward these attributes. You can see how sticky
notes have been moved from the original reflective structure to a larger
learning wall devoted to unpacking these essential skills.

Regardless of whether you facilitate learning for groups of adult learners or if your practice is more scholarly focused, I highly recommend you construct your own version of a reflective frame to establish the value of this skill and work toward independent reflection and action. As with all thinking routines, differentiate how you introduce these structures, give thought to supportive language or sentence stems, carry some of the cognitive load for your learners, and be playful in ways that you approach and invite engagement.

Thinking routines are phenomenal tools that invite engagement and ask us to think about the thinking we desire to unpack, but sometimes we need a different kind of mental model to spark reflection and to reinforce overarching concepts. I am also a big fan of sketchnotes for that very reason, and I find that this visual resource is another foundational tool to strengthen collective reflection while synthesizing and supporting meaning-making.

The Types of Student Inquiry sketchnote from the work of Trevor MacKenzie and Rebecca Bushby anchors this staff reflection as school leaders take inventory of several campus-wide goals. The symbolism of the pool, the invitations toward further growth with language such as "stretch," and the specificity of feedback all lend themselves toward co-designing next steps in learning. What are the sketchnotes that anchor your practice? How might a visual display help support a more robust reflection and provide equitable access for all learners?

 If you need a bit of visual inspiration to start or add to your next learning wall, this robust collection of sketchnotes is an asset to surely spark wonder and new thinking among your context and group of learners. Simply download the sketchnotes and choose one to anchor your reflective process.

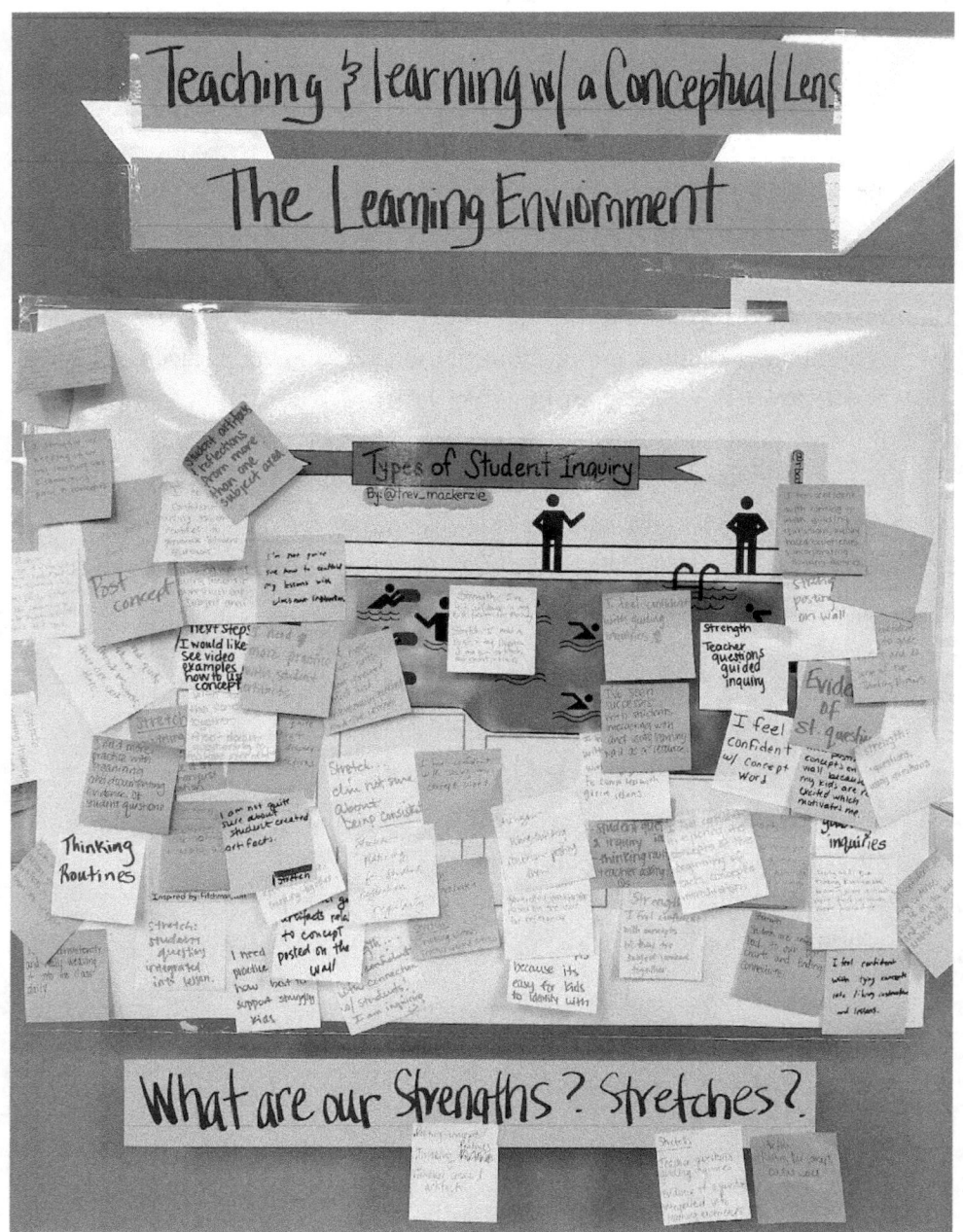

Benefits of You Do

- Multiple opportunities for learners to self-assess and live in the "deep end" of the Inquiry Pool
- Vertical spaces built by learners for a richer formative assessment practice
- More frequent opportunities for feedback and flexing the skills of reflection throughout the cycle of learning
- Competent and confident learners who are more conscious of *how* they learn

In time, as the tangled bed of idea of ideas gets sorted along with the layers of sticky notes we methodically attach to our vertical spaces, the tension we feel as we navigate the varied needs and readiness of our learners become clear. We feel more certain about how the puzzle pieces will fit together. We gain confidence in knowing by calling in expertise outside of ourselves and welcoming the voice of our learners while thanking them for their perspectives and the unique experiences they bring to our landscape of learning.

By using the provided protocols, reframing your approach to gradual release of control, and trusting your expertise, you will become more confident in stepping back from the messiness. With practice, you'll notice that the cognitive resistance untangles organically. As you play and make meaning of the visible learning before you, share your reflections with thought partners and friends. Contribute to the global conversation using #learningwalls to experience the freedom and impact that authentic documentation brings to the culture of learning!

Pause and Reflect

* By now you're ready to move further away from a learning wall that's Pinterest-worthy and instead favor a vertical space that "piques your learners' interest." What's one thing you're ready to let go of to make more space for co-design?

* What do you need to scaffold the process of co-construction (I Do, We Do, You Do)? What skills would you backwards plan for what this looks like across a term? A semester? An academic year?

* It's time to take notice the next time you are with your group of learners and look at ways the intentional creation of a learning wall supports scholar thinking, understanding, and communication throughout learning. How might you get feedback from the learners themselves to help illustrate this benefit in a timely manner?

* Sometimes we all need a spark of inspiration, so head over to social media and scroll some inspiring learning walls using #learningwall. I'm curious what strikes you and how our PLN supports you and what you need!

Part 3

Stories of Learning Journeys

Inquiry is a collaborative practice, both with our students and with our peers. We respond to the sharing of ideas, notice and name critical elements in the learning, and anchor environments in curiosity. This book is designed to add to your collaborative experience with stories of learning journeys from educators who teach in schools around the world. Several have been woven into the first two sections of this book as we've explored what learning walls are and how to build and use them effectively. I'm sure many of you have dog-eared a few pages and made notes to remind you to revisit ideas and share them with your colleagues. My very sincere hope is that you have been (and will continue to be) inspired to adapt the ideas and strategies you read about here to fit your unique context and role.

This final section is packed with stories of learning journeys to give you additional insight into how authentic documentation can look, sound, and feel in a variety of contexts and roles in both traditional and nontraditional education settings and almost two dozen schools around the globe. I've chosen the thinking routine What? So

What? Now What? as the framework for their reflections, and I'm confident that their vulnerable sharing, aha moments, and commitment to action will embolden and inspire you to move forward with your evidencing practice.

The contributions are grouped into categories and lift up foundational themes of inquiry. The stories highlight multiple entry points, so no matter your context, experience, or comfort level when it comes to inquiry, you'll see how simple it can be to integrate this transformative documentation practice. Here's what's ahead:

- Stories of Co-Construction
- Stories of Skill, Competency, and Approaches to Learning (ATLs) Development
- Stories of Teacher Agency
- Stories of Virtual and Digital Learning Walls
- Stories of Conceptual Understanding
- Stories of Assessment

After reading each of these vignettes, you'll have the opportunity to engage in your own reflective practice, using the same prompts that brought you these learning journeys. By the end of this section, you'll have a deeper understanding about where you are in your practice in documentation. I'm sure too that you will feel more confident in planning your next steps with your learners and will be delighted by your perspective.

The educators represented in this section are exploring new parts of their practice. They, too, are on a learning journey, and the examples they share represent where they are in the various stages of the cycle of inquiry. Their vulnerability in sharing the new strategies they're exploring—and making sense of—in their own spaces is powerful. So is the growing understanding they're developing about the impact of inquiry on their approach, mindset, and learners. All of it is part of their ongoing reflection and learning.

Let's take a look!

Stories of Co-Construction

Erin Boughner

Junior Kindergarten / Kindergarten Teacher
East Three Elementary School | Inuvik, NWT, Canada

Learning wall intention: This learning wall demonstrates what we know about birds, our questions about them, and the learning we explore/gain during the unit. We were conducting a whole-school inquiry into birds and what they mean to us as a community, but this learning wall was specifically for my JK/K class to demonstrate their learning. This unit lasted the month of May. We did have some special activities, and guests came in the first week of June, but most of our unit was done throughout May.

What? We begin each inquiry unit with a provocation table, which encourages students to think about what they know about birds and what they want to know. The table includes books, pictures, and hands-on manipulatives.

We then explored what we already knew about birds, and my students drew a picture or wrote a word to describe what they already knew. As we were learning about birds, I organized our learning into a tree, where we put what we already knew around the roots to help begin and guide our learning journey.

From here, we explored what we wanted to know about birds, formed them into questions, and organized them into topics or themes, with each theme becoming a branch on our learning tree: nests, the life cycle of a bird, flying, ptarmigans camouflaging, parts of a bird, and what birds eat.

Now that we had explored what we already knew about birds and what we wanted to know, we used blue sticky notes to draw photos or words of resources we could use to help us answer our questions. Resources identified included our parents, books, tablets, elders, hunters, going into the forest to look at birds, and more. We added these to the trunk because they would be the core of our learning.

Now that our classes had identified the themes/topics they were interested in, I started with the biggest topic, introducing them to birds, and then let them decide what we focused on next. For us, we focused on different features of birds first, which led us into their wings/flying and why ptarmigans camouflage. This led us to birds flying to their nests and why birds build them. We then explored birds laying eggs in nests and what birds fed their babies.

So what? One of my biggest goals for this unit was to ensure that my students were very involved in building the wall and adding to it as learning happened (so that it was *our* learning wall, not just my display of their learning). The way I did this was by taking as many pictures as I could of the learning we did that day, and printing off ideal examples. The following morning, I would lay out the images I had taken on the carpet and ask my students to tell me what was happening in the photos in their own words. This let me determine what photos they gravitated toward and what learning they remembered.

I would then take the photos they chose and add their learning in captions underneath. I also added any of my learning that I noticed, such as conversations they had or observations they made. Students could also write words/labels for any of the pictures they wanted.

In the afternoon, we would take the photos (with the captions) and add them to the learning wall. My students helped me decide where the pictures would go for each of the topics. We would then look at our learning and recap what we had learned so far and our favorite moments, allowing us to include anything else they remembered or wanted to add.

As I was writing this reflection, I had the idea of getting the students to do their final reflections using the learning wall. I had students take an orange sticky note and post it to their favorite memory of the entire unit. I loved watching them point at pictures while recalling what happened that day and sharing moments I didn't see or hear. This was also a final check for me to explore what they took away from the unit.

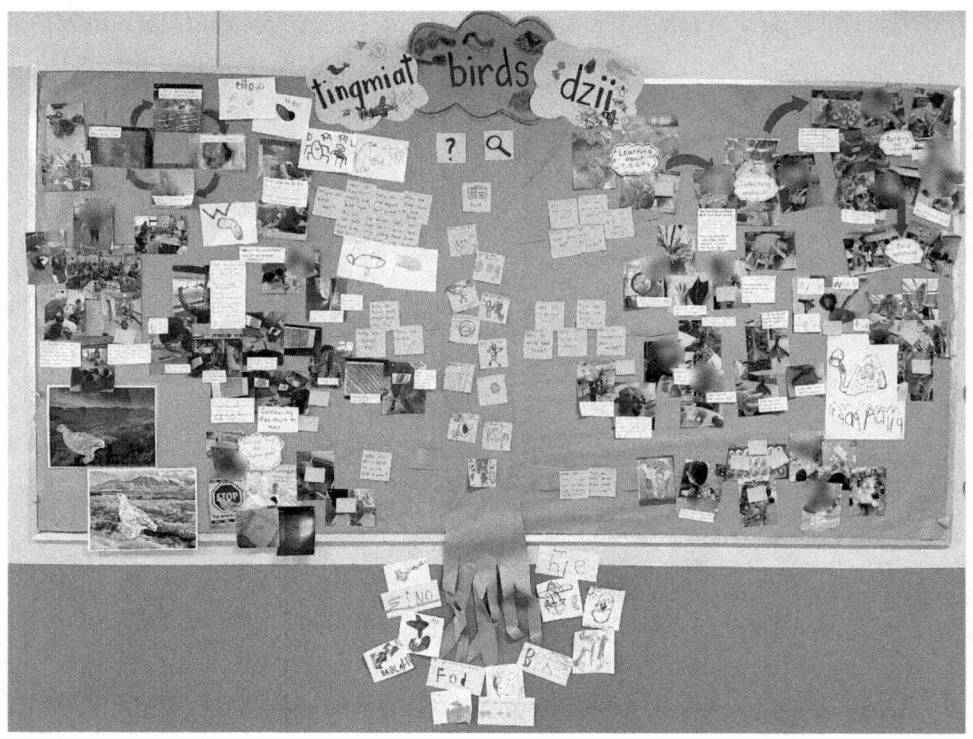

Final Learning Wall

Now what? My major takeaway from building this learning wall is to include students as much as possible, regardless of age and abilities. I think we (myself included) underestimate what students are capable of and the connections their brains are able to make, especially in kindergarten. I loved visiting the learning wall every day (or every couple of days) to recap what we had learned so far and add new information. This made the wall become something that we built together and not just something I did.

The one thing I struggled with was the fact that our learning wall was outside of our classroom (where the bulletin board/most space was). I would like to bring it into the classroom so students can interact with it during play/snack time in the classroom. I am not sure that they will because not every student is engaged with the learning wall to begin with, but I would like it to be an option.

I also wonder whether a learning wall has to be a wall at all and how this might look in kindergarten because we might not have as many "products" that demonstrate our learning. Maybe each question theme could be put on a cardboard box, and we use the boxes to build during play. Our bird unit, for example, had six main themes and a couple of mini lessons, so students would have six-plus boxes with their photos, words, and learning taped to them that they could then use to build during play.

The goal would be that they would be reviewing the learning while in play. This is one of the ways I have considered bringing learning walls into the classroom. I look forward to trying a few ideas next year!

Sarah Scott
Primary Teacher (Years 1 through 6)
Scone Grammar School | Scone, NSW, Australia

Learning wall intention: The intention of our learning walls is to create a "third teacher" in the classroom. Our walls create a visual, and sometimes sensory, representation of our learning journey. They help students make links throughout their investigations and spark emotive connections to experiences that support memory retrieval, helping to eliminate the "doorway effect." Our walls are used to create and display anchor charts with working examples that can be accessed, referred to, and transferred across different lines of inquiry or curriculum areas, providing a resource that promotes independence and agency within the classroom. Our walls symbolize our view of learning as a journey, our collaborative classroom culture, and the reflection that learning is not something we have to do alone. Students co-construct purposeful learning that is displayed with the intention for it to be shared, accessed, and used by everyone. Our walls guide our curriculum, provide insights into students' wonderings, interests, and understandings, and allow me as the teacher to plan for learning experiences that break down misconceptions and build up foundations of knowledge. Our walls give my students a voice, allowing their questions and curiosities to guide the learning process, and provide an outlet for them to celebrate, share, and contribute their discoveries.

As a primary teacher, I work with students ages five to twelve years, teaching across all curriculum areas, with class sizes ranging from twenty-four to twenty-eight students. Recently, Year 5 embarked on a fascinating science inquiry into space, aimed at answering the question *What's beyond planet Earth?* This learning wall serves as a visual representation of our exploration journey. This was the first time these students had been exposed to inquiry-based learning, so our learning wall played a pivotal role in supporting their understanding of the inquiry process, including routines, structures, dispositions, and skills they can refer back to, build on, and practice throughout the year. Additionally, it helped students grasp the purpose of a learning wall and fostered a culture of collaborative learning within the classroom. This wall also celebrates our term's focus skills of "research" and "summarizing," providing an outlet for students to practice their skills, share their findings, inspire, and learn from others. The lengths of our units are dependent on student interest; however, this particular inquiry line went on for eleven weeks.

What? These learning wall photos showcase the introduction to our science inquiry journey, investigating *What's beyond planet Earth?* The intentions behind our first couple of lessons were to spark curiosity and wonder in the students, establish their prior knowledge and existing theories, use their curiosity to develop rich questions, and provide a foundational background knowledge and context for students to build on as they progress through their inquiry journey. Additionally, this learning wall features co-constructed anchor charts and photographs with working examples of inquiry-based routines and protocols introduced for the students to refer to and retrieve from throughout the year.

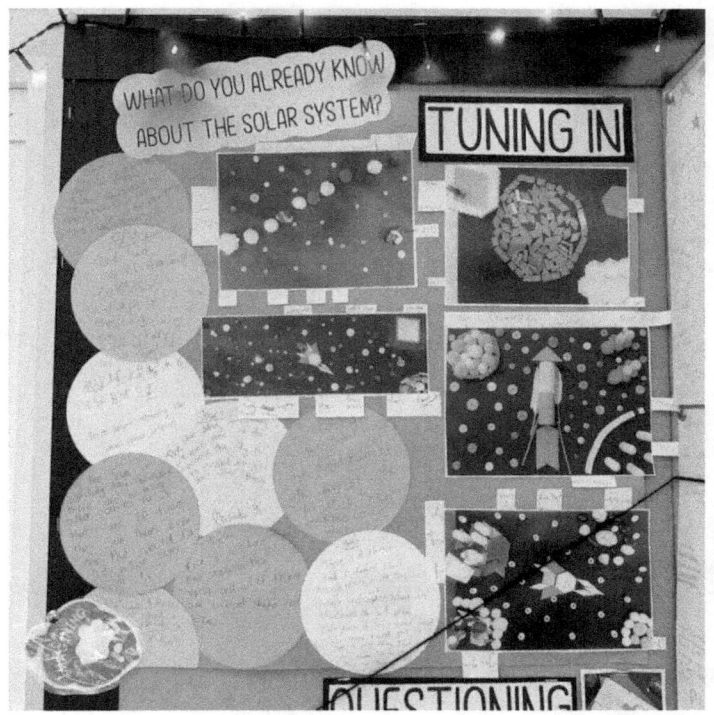

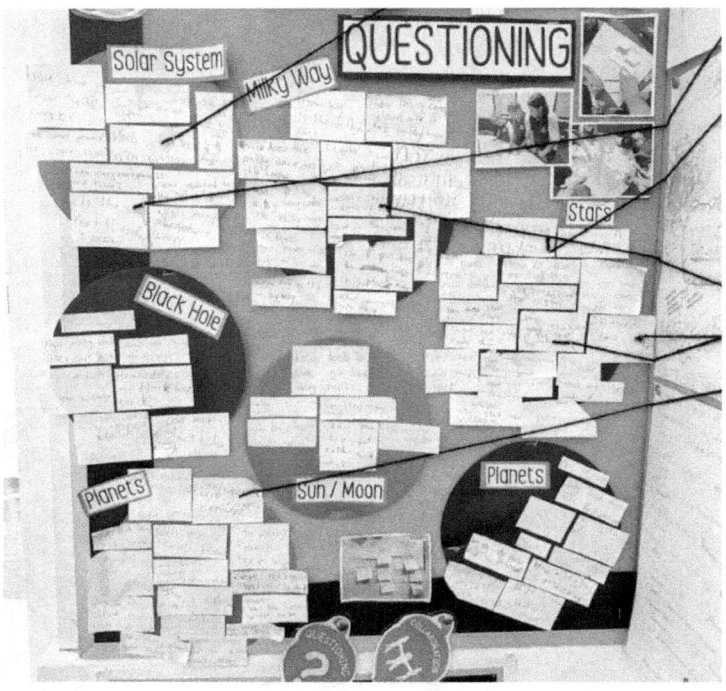

I facilitated activities to enhance students' knowledge and theories about space and encouraged them to connect with prior learning and life experiences. This process helped me identify any misconceptions and establish foundational understandings we needed to build on before diving into further investigations. To practice communication and collaboration skills, students worked in groups of three, using loose parts to answer the question *What do you already know about the solar system?* Students photographed and labeled their creations, then wrote accompanying theories to present to the class.

Our next step was to spark curiosity and wonder through a captivating provocation aimed at stimulating the development of rich questions to guide our inquiry journey. While watching a "Wonders of Space" mini clip, students were prompted to tune in to their curiosities and write any questions that arose. They referred to our previously co-constructed "Questioning Wall," where they were encouraged to ask both open and closed questions. After this, I introduced a new questioning routine called the Question Formulation Technique, where students learned how to sort their questions according to depth and interest. In small groups, students sorted their questions into quadrants and contributed the questions of highest interest to our class collection.

Photos from this routine were placed on the learning wall to serve as emotive memory triggers, facilitating recall of the experience when revisited. As a class, we sorted the questions of highest interest into topic categories, and these formed the basis of our inquiry direction and exploration.

So what? The tuning in pre-assessment revealed that my students had superficial understandings of the solar system, possessing limited knowledge beyond their own planet, with only one group creating a representation of the solar system. With this insight, I planned several

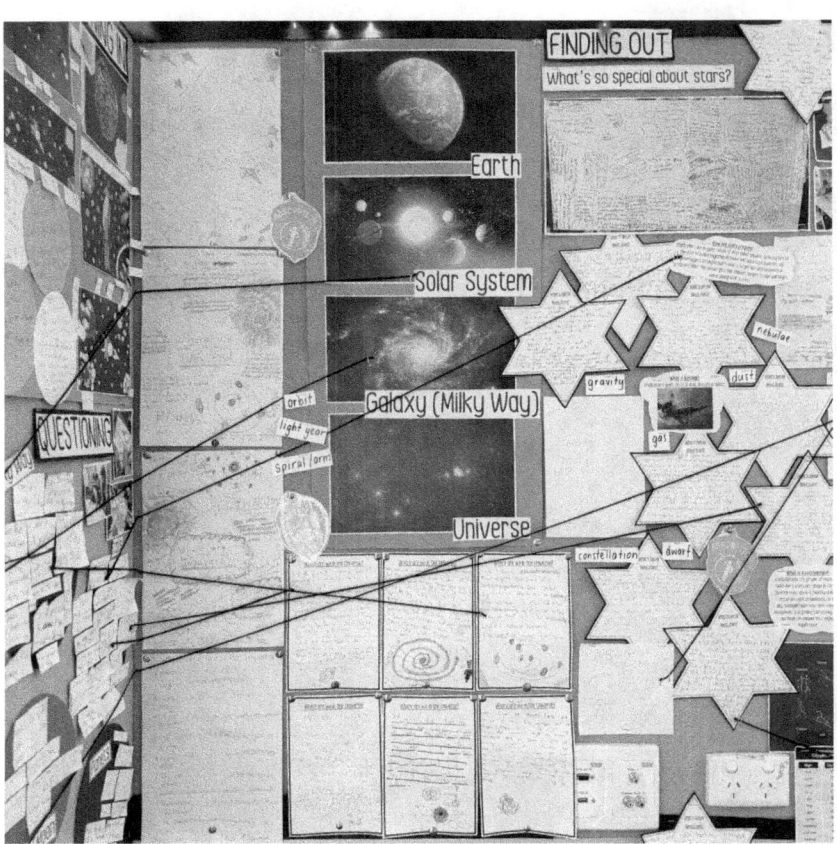

whole-class investigative lessons and research activities to help students develop foundational understandings of our place in the universe that could be built on throughout inquiry investigations. Evidenced on the learning wall are pictures from video clips we watched, tier-three language we defined, and student notes taken during their research, accompanied by a "show me what you know now" flex session summarizing their new understandings of space. It was fantastic to see students already drawing connections between their original questions and their new learning, evidenced by black string connecting their questions to the newly found answers.

My next steps involved using student questions and my syllabus to plan potential learning experiences that would enable my students to investigate their inquiries. This included borrowing a variety of books from the school library, sourcing and uploading appropriate

website links to our class page, consulting with our school science teacher, identifying potential excursions, and gathering hands-on resources or experiments for students to play with and further develop their understanding.

Our "questions of highest interest" data showed that my students were particularly curious about stars and wanted to begin our investigations there. With the goal of honing their research skills, the students collectively decided that the wall would serve as a collaborative information hub. During each lesson, students dedicated time to researching a specific topic, then used their summarizing skills to create a "flex sesh" to be displayed on the wall for sharing and use by their peers. This approach allowed students to exchange research findings, highlight inspiring discoveries, draw connections between their findings, and generate new questions. Consequently, our investigation expanded from stars to encompass topics such as zodiac signs, constellations, and Aboriginal astronomy, all driven by student-led exploration.

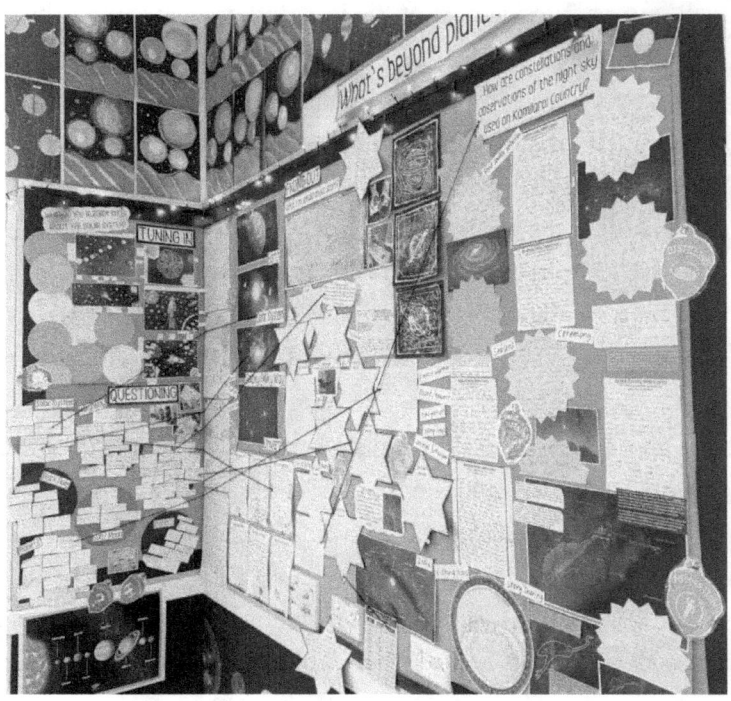

Now what? The next step was to refer to the interest data and select another topic that would cohesively link into our investigations, accommodate syllabus outcome requirements, and allow my students to continue practicing their research skills. Evidence made it clear that students held misconceptions about the planets in our solar system and how they rotate around the sun. To ignite curiosity, I needed to find a provocation that not only highlighted the differences between all the planets but also provided context using factual comparisons with things on Earth. We discovered a sensational book called *Big Questions about the Universe* by Alex Frith and Alice James, which sparked student curiosity and encouraged them to want to learn more.

Now that my students are starting to grasp the purpose of the learning walls, I'm eager to give them more control over the space, layout, and design of our next learning wall. I envision a more interactive space where students can actively engage with the wall as a physical resource. They should have the freedom to add, remove, change, edit, and use the evidence displayed on the wall. My goal is to transform the wall into an integral part of the learning process, rather than just a representation of the learning achieved. This shift will empower students to take ownership of their learning journey and foster deeper engagement with the material.

I am left wondering about the best ways to display our walls and am curious about the most effective methods for evidencing our learning on those walls to encourage more active interaction. I'm considering providing a trolley of loose materials such as Blu-Tack, Velcro dots, sticky notes, colored card, QR code creators, evidence folders, surfaces for interactive brainstorms, magnets, pegs, and string. My hope is that this approach will allow for more student connection and agency, fostering increased interaction while still ensuring that we authentically document the learning process in a cohesive manner. I wonder whether this will promote deeper understanding and connection to the learning. I look forward to experimenting with my students and finding out what works best for them.

William Polan

Fifth Grade PYP Teacher, Math Curriculum Learning Leader
International School of Ulaanbaatar | Ulaanbaatar, Mongolia

Learning wall intention: The aim was to document, support, and guide our inquiry of shapes, angles, and area. In addition to documenting and guiding learning, the wall also aimed to establish and bring meaning to the conceptual drivers of the unit, supporting the application of understanding through the documentation of learning and skills. The unit lasted approximately four weeks, with students inquiring into properties of shapes, area and perimeter, and angles.

What? The learning wall was a collection of provocations, thinking routines, and student work. When beginning our inquiry into shapes, we unpacked our standards and used some AI-generated images as provocations to tune in and create unique lines of inquiry as a class (pictured below).

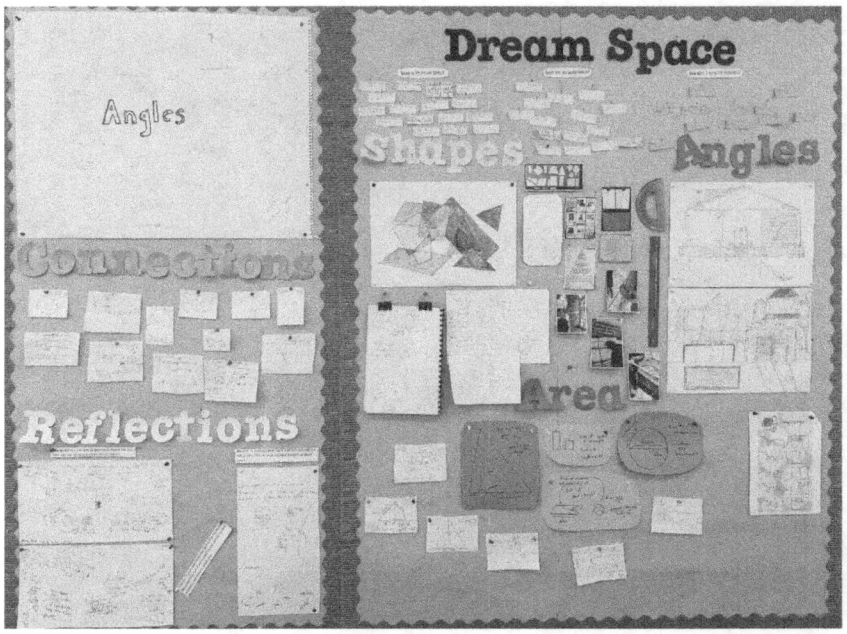

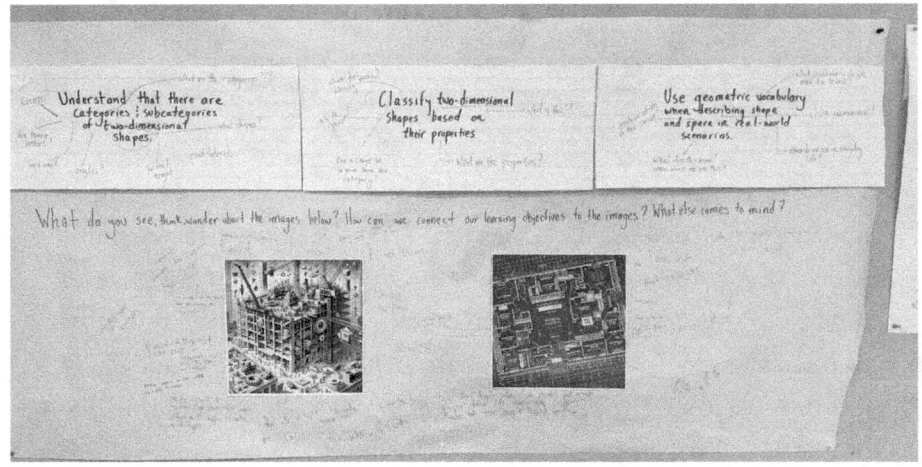

The collaborative products from students were then put on our learning wall. Short reflections underneath helped students reconnect with previously learned skills and knowledge. A note: Many of the products of student inquiries were far too large to fit on the board. Ultimately, I ended up taking photos of them and printing them out in a shrunken version.

As the unit progressed, we used a Chalk Talk routine to better make conceptual connections to angles. This Chalk Talk was put on the main learning wall. Importantly, it allowed the class to see and understand that as learners, they each have unique connections and perspectives when it comes to math learning. This, along with all of the different learning products of the unit, was a celebration of the diverse learning styles of the class.

The "connections" section of the learning wall was an important one. It began blank, and as students would make realizations in their inquiries, I would ask them to pin them up on the learning wall. These connections were related to any time a student made a discovery in which angles, properties of shape, and area were interconnected. This documentation and sharing played an important role in the progression of our unit.

Finally, I wanted to further guide my students into a culminating, inquiry-driven project that would ask them to apply their understanding of shapes, angles, and area. The class arrived at the idea of designing their own dream space. In small groups, they answered some reflective questions that would support them in their "dream space" creation.

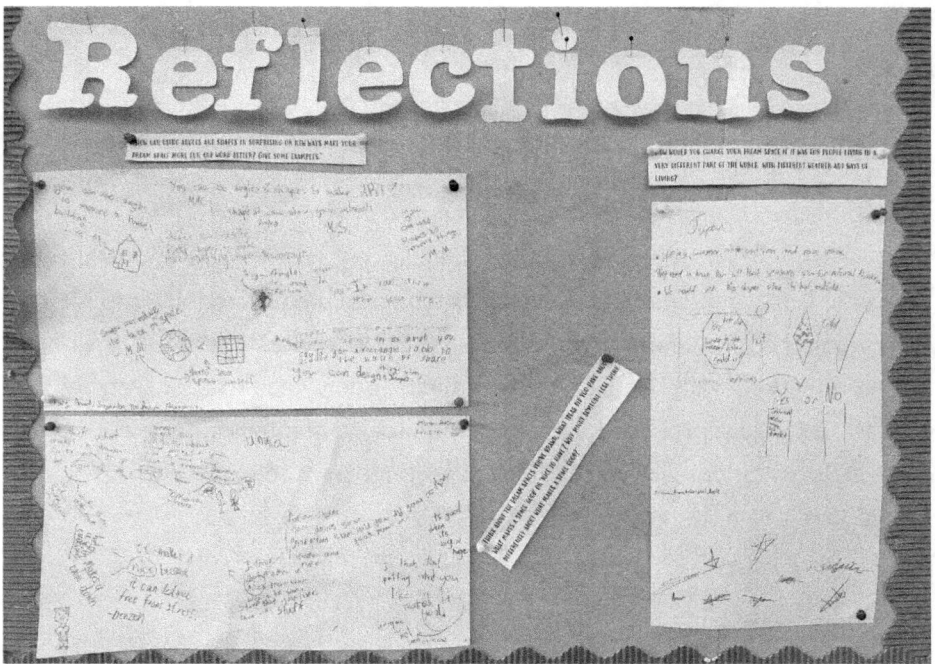

So what? My students responded to the learning wall in several ways that greatly benefitted the collective learning of the entire class. First, it documented and empowered student voice, interest, and learning, bringing a sense of ownership and agency to the unit's learning. Secondly, it ultimately guided and supported the class into a culminating inquiry that asked them to apply all the skills and understandings that had been documented on the learning wall.

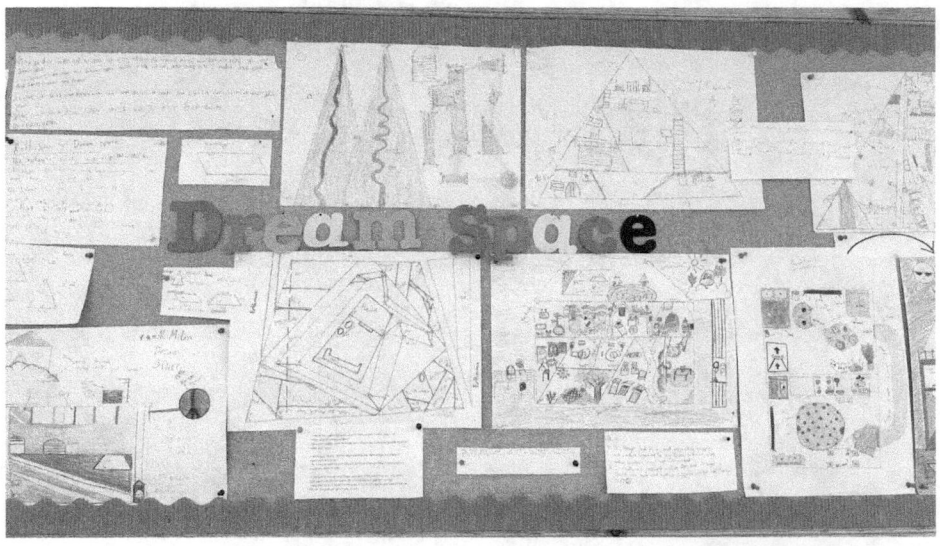

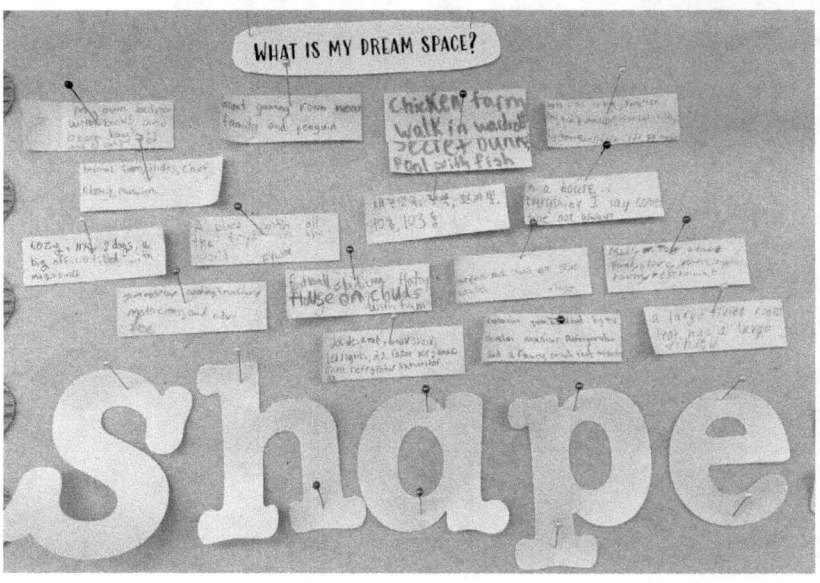

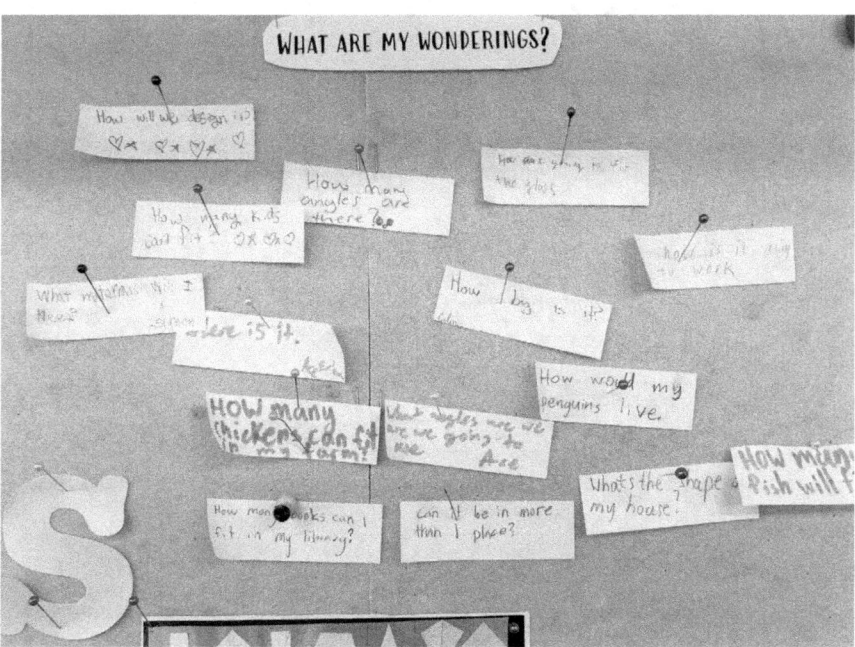

The benefits of the learning wall were tremendous for both myself as a teacher and my class as learners.

I was able to effectively understand the needs, perspectives, and interests of my students, supporting my students through questioning and provocations that met their needs and wants. Through the various thinking routines on the board, I was also able to harness the collective creativity of the class as well as their unique connections to guide and support as needed.

The students greatly enjoyed the "living nature" of the board, and their sense of pride when filling the board was evident. "Mr. Polan, can I put this up in the connections section?" And "Can you take a picture of my inquiry into shapes and art to put on the board?" Perhaps the biggest benefit, particularly in a math context, is that it allows students to see the different perspectives and thinking of their peers. Mathematical thinking, not mathematics, was on display throughout the unit; this is important to students in their understanding of mathematics as a creative, thinking-driven endeavor. As a teacher, I was filled with a sense of pride in observing the class's collective pursuit of understanding, their documentation of learning, and ultimately, what led to further inquiry and applying their learning from the wall to a culminating "dream space."

Now what? Moving forward, I certainly plan on using learning walls for future math units. The benefits were clear: empowered student voice, interest, and thinking. The benefits of documenting and revisiting learning were also very beneficial to both the class and myself. Allowing students to record and share their connections and perspectives allowed us to harness the cognitive diversity of our classroom.

I wonder what would the learning wall look like if I only used it for provocations and thinking routines, putting less emphasis on capturing different learning products? What would the learning wall look like if it were viewed more as a "thinking wall"?

Matt Fletcher
English Teacher/ CAS and MYP Projects Coordinator
Léman International School | Chengdu, China

Learning wall intention: The area for display in my classroom is one long glass wall that runs across the back of the classroom. My learning wall was set up for two classes: a Grades 7 and 8 English language and literature class and a Grades 9 and 10 English language acquisition class. The main concept of the learning wall was for students to see how the key concepts connect with their inquiry journey (even within subjects). I am an English teacher in both the International Baccalaureate middle years and diploma programs. Additionally, I am responsible for the core course of CAS and the MYP projects in Year 3 and Year 5 of that program. This unit of inquiry is running for eight weeks.

What? At this juncture in our unit of inquiry, we find ourselves amidst the second week of exploration. The learning wall stands as a testament to our journey thus far, adorned with a mosaic of questions, artifacts, and student reflections.

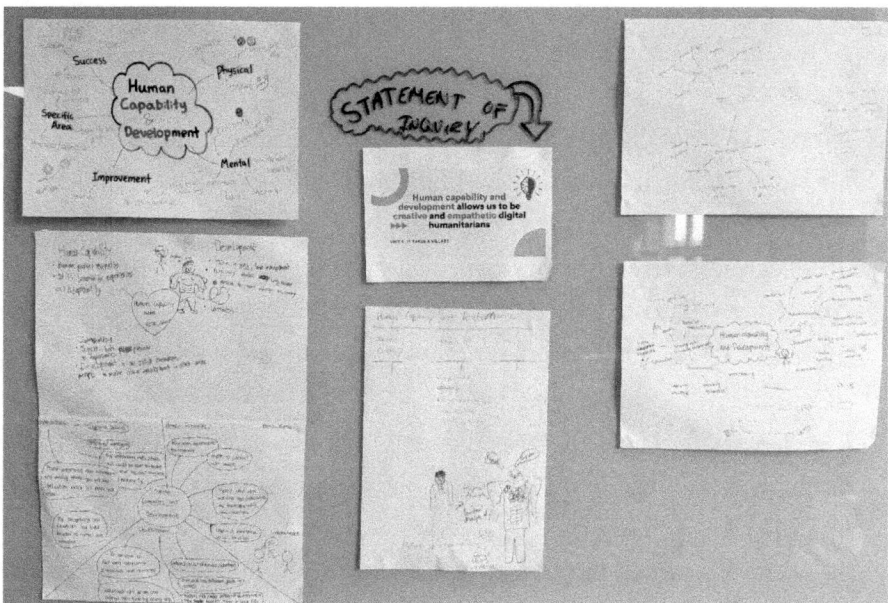

At the outset, the wall was adorned with printed questions, serving as a springboard for inquiry. As students delved deeper into the unit, they began to curate their own questions and select artifacts that resonated with them. From poignant song lyrics to evocative poems, from insightful fact files to thought-provoking questions, the learning wall became a canvas for their collective exploration.

Each artifact on the wall represents a thread in the tapestry of our learning journey, weaving together diverse perspectives and insights. Students' work adorns the wall, showcasing their responses to questions and their connections to the unit's statement of inquiry.

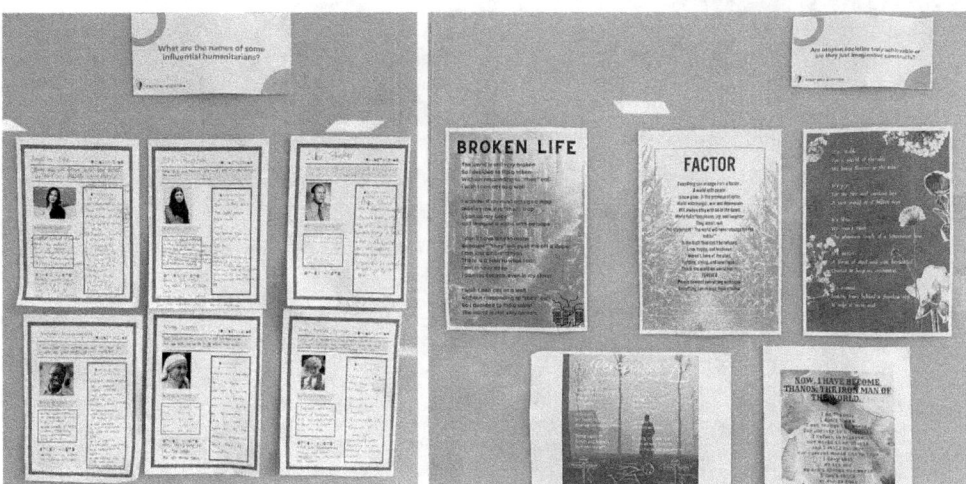

The initial provocation for our English language and literature class was the iconic song "Imagine" by John Lennon, igniting discussions on themes of imagination, creativity, and the power of language. In the language acquisition class, we embarked on our journey with *The Boy Who Harnessed the Wind*, delving into themes of resilience, innovation, and the power of storytelling.

Throughout our exploration, thinking routines and provocations have been integral to our learning process. From employing the See, Think, Wonder routine to provoke curiosity to using the I Notice, I Wonder routine to deepen understanding, these tools have enriched our inquiry and fostered critical thinking skills.

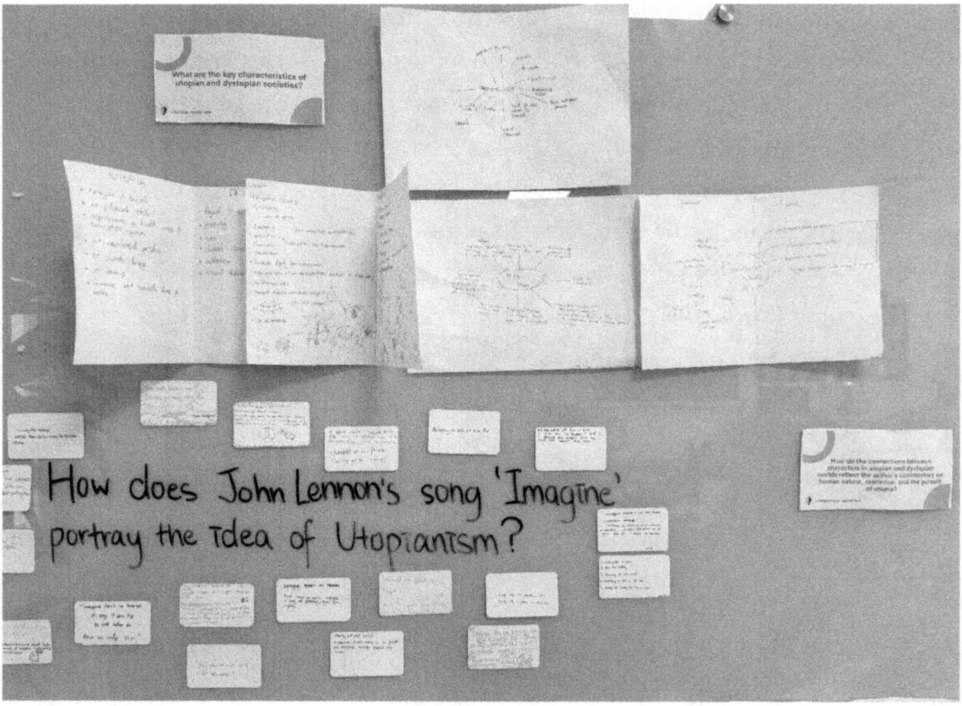
What are the key characteristics of utopian and dystopian societies?
How does John Lennon's song 'Imagine' portray the Idea of Utopianism?
How do the connections between characters in utopian and dystopian worlds reflect the author's commentary on human nature, resilience, and the pursuit of utopia?

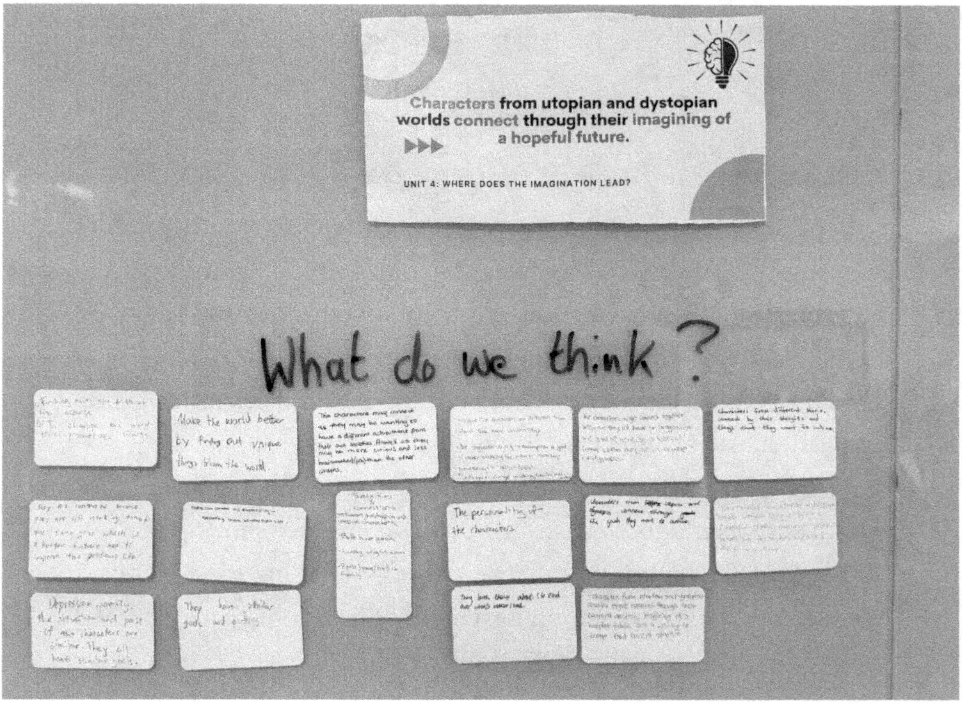
Characters from utopian and dystopian worlds connect through their imagining of a hopeful future.
UNIT 4: WHERE DOES THE IMAGINATION LEAD?
What do we think?
Make the world better by finding out unique things from the world.
The personality of the characters

So what? The evidence gleaned from the learning wall has been invaluable in guiding my planning and shaping the trajectory of our unit. Specific artifacts, such as the song lyrics, poems, and fact files, have provided rich insights into students' understanding and engagement with the material. As questions are answered and connections emerge, it becomes evident how students are grappling with the key concepts and their relationship to the statement of inquiry. Surprisingly, some artifacts sparked unexpected connections and discussions, enriching our exploration of the unit's themes.

Learners have responded enthusiastically to the learning wall, eagerly engaging with the curated artifacts and using them as catalysts for discussion and reflection. The wall has become a dynamic space where ideas are shared, perspectives are exchanged, and deeper understanding is cultivated. Witnessing students' curiosity and active participation in the learning process has been immensely rewarding. Their thoughtful contributions to the learning wall not only showcase their individual growth but also foster a sense of collective ownership over our inquiry journey.

Through this process, I've learned to appreciate the power of visible learning environments in fostering meaningful engagement and reflection. The learning wall has served as a mirror, allowing me to step back and gain valuable insights into students' needs and understandings. It has informed my instructional decisions, guiding me in tailoring future lessons to better meet the diverse learning needs of my students.

Overall, the evidence from the learning wall has reinforced the importance of creating interactive and student-centered learning spaces where inquiry thrives, connections are forged, and learning becomes a collaborative endeavor.

Now what? In planning our next steps, I'll focus on how the evidence from the learning wall can inform our exploration of deeper questions and misconceptions. By employing techniques such as the Question

Formulation Technique, I can encourage students to delve into more profound inquiries, challenging their understanding and uncovering any misconceptions they may hold. The spiderweb discussion, using the evidence on the learning wall as a central point of reference, will facilitate collaborative exploration and critical thinking.

The impact of this process on my planning has been profound! It has provided clarity and direction, ensuring that our discussions and activities remain aligned with the overarching goals of the unit. Additionally, it has helped me identify areas where students may need additional support or clarification, allowing me to tailor my approach accordingly.

Looking ahead to the next unit, I'm intrigued by the idea of using more visual provocations to stimulate discussion and engagement. By incorporating images, quotes, and other resources, I can encourage students to make connections with the key and related concepts in a more tangible way. This approach not only appeals to different learning styles but also deepens students' understanding through visual representation.

As I reflect on this process, I'm struck by the potential of the learning wall as a dynamic tool for inquiry and exploration. Its ability to capture the essence of our learning journey and serve as a catalyst for deeper thinking is truly remarkable. Moving forward, I'm eager to continue leveraging its power to enrich our learning experiences and foster a culture of curiosity and collaboration in the classroom.

Stories of Skill, Competency, and
Approaches to Learning (ATLs)

Fiona Hudson

Visual Arts and LOTE (Languages Other Than English) Teacher

Henderson College | Irymple, Victoria, Australia

Learning wall intention: In the art room, the intention of the learning wall is to bring student thoughts and products together. I teach students from ages five to twelve, so there is a wide range of abilities and prior knowledge across the realm of students. In Australia, our school year is divided into four terms, approximately ten weeks each. Each term, I introduce a new topic that is the inspiration for all of the artwork covered over the ten weeks, rather than the art medium or style to focus on.

What? These photos were taken about three-quarters of the way through our Australiana unit, looking at all concepts related to Australia. This included Australian artists, artwork based on Australian animals or landmarks, native flora and fauna, and tapping into the Indigenous culture through their seasons wheel. Many of the different age groups participated in the thinking routine of See, Think, Wonder or Ask This Picture a Question to help guide their thoughts and spark their prior knowledge. Through the actual artwork process, the students were less guided by set materials and were encouraged instead to produce their artwork using mediums of their choice. I would often put out five or six choices for them to use to add color to their piece, and they would choose the material that they felt suited their artwork best. It opened up conversations about what materials students were already confident using and which materials they were hesitant to use or reluctant to build their skills with.

The Kind, Specific, and Helpful display has been left up from our last unit in the previous term, as we have been focusing heavily on giving each other feedback. It serves as a visual prompt for me as a teacher but also gives students some prompts to help guide their feedback when sharing with a partner. The speech bubbles were pieces of

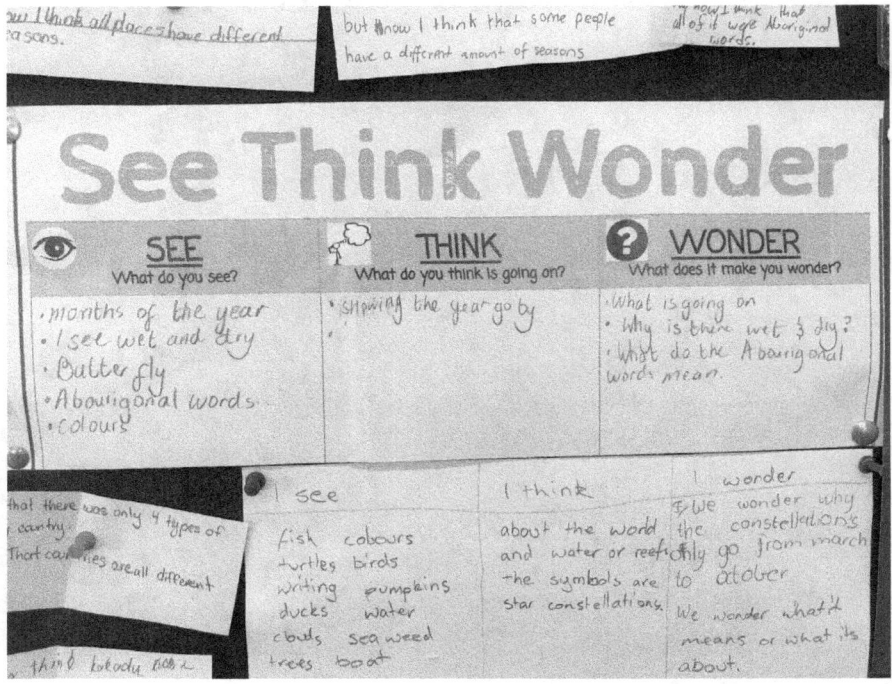

feedback that were brainstormed over a variety of year levels, and I have just created the learning wall around them to demonstrate the importance of this positive language in the Art Room.

So what? Students loved referring to the learning wall, but with limited time each week, I had to ensure that we were still allowing enough time for the actual art-making process and not just spending the entire lesson talking and thinking (despite the power in that!). The information that stemmed from the thinking routines has guided me to include short videos in my lessons to help explore some of the wonderings. I've also used the poster section in our library to share information with students, which I've been able to add to our learning wall—even though it hasn't been co-constructed with the students. By using it in the explicit teaching part of the lesson, students are able to form connections and build understanding.

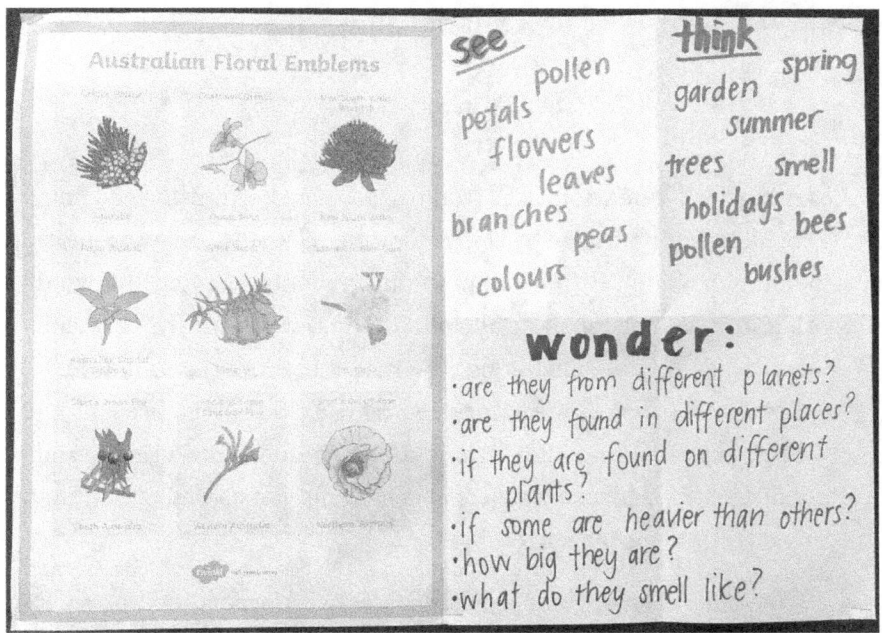

It's been amazing to see students from different year levels come in each week and want to look at the wall to explore what all the other classes have added to it. Because they all share the same topic, they love to see the connections between their artwork and the artwork from other classes. It was difficult to accept that my walls wouldn't be covered in just "finished products" anymore! A small sacrifice, but the wall now reflects student understanding and the process behind the final piece. It's certainly a case of "process over product."

Now what? My goal is to revisit my eight different units/topics, which I rotate over two school years, and ensure that I am allowing enough connections and choice for each topic. I'm excited to introduce one or two more thinking routines to my students' repertoire of thinking and build on their skills. In my next units, I want to include more photos of student work and more visual timelines of how the art pieces are formed. It will mean photocopying my students' work each week along the way, but I feel it will add more visible learning opportunities.

Graham Laing
Grade 5 Teacher
ISG Jubail | Al Jubail, Saudia Arabia

Learning wall intention: Classroom walls can be transformed into powerful learning tools by incorporating elements that promote active inquiry and self-reflection among students. (I avoid the word work as it is so general and unhelpful. Rather, we think critically and analyze what we are actually doing—reading, writing, communicating, creating, assessing, reflecting, feeding back, deciding, discussing.) By strategically adding language, vocabulary, questions, visuals, and student-created artifacts, teachers and students can co-create a stimulating environment that encourages students to

- **remember** key concepts and ideas through visual cues and reminders
- **reflect** on their learning journey by revisiting past thinking, observations, and assumptions to seek deeper understanding through open-ended prompts
- **notice** patterns, connections, and relationships within the learning materials
- **make decisions** about their learning paths and strategies
- **understand** their own learning process through metacognitive reflection

This learning wall was specifically created to encourage students to remember, reflect, notice, make decisions, and understand the learning that they are experiencing. The intention is that the children will be aware of the different elements of the learning that they are involved in. They will be aware of what, how, and why they are learning. A part of the intention was also to help students see the connections between different elements of their learning.

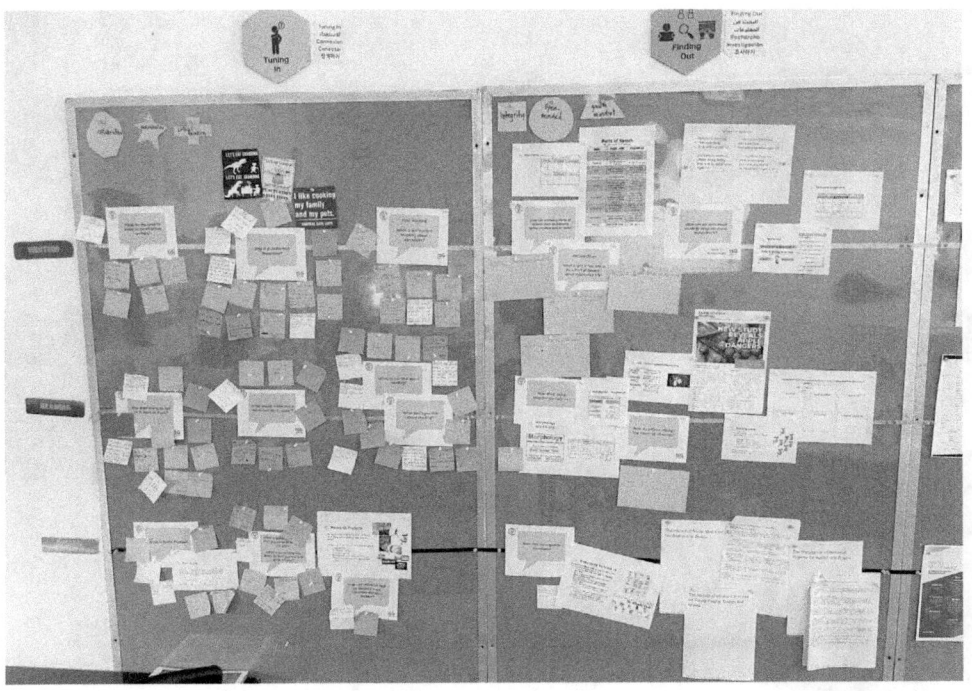

What? This unit was a beginning-of-year unit based on students becoming more aware of themselves as individuals and as individuals who are part of a community (Malaguzzi-Gandini and Edwards, 2011). A class discussion resulted in the questions *What are things that we could do that are helpful for us, yet we don't do them?"* and *What are some things that we know are not helpful for us, yet we do them anyway?* And the overall question: *How do the decisions we make impact our bodies and brains?*

The children then researched their responses, which included screen time, video games, reading, exercise, sleeping, eating fast food, and drinking soda. The learning wall helped us track our journey, with a specific focus on the elements above (remember, reflect, notice, make decisions, and understand). This unit was four weeks long.

The image above was taken at the end of the unit of inquiry. It shows the following elements:

- **Timeline**—It shows the connections between the different elements of our learning—reading, writing, and social studies.
- **Split screen**—This helped us see the what, how, and why of the learning. This transparency led us to greater understanding, engagement, and better questions about the learning process.
- **Reflection**—The children reflected continually throughout the unit on the learning skills, strategies, and dispositions that helped them at particular times of the unit. These were highlighted in color-coded sticky notes on the learning wall.
- **Questions**—The learning wall helped us inquire into and generate questions that led to specific use of learning from reading, writing, and social studies standards as well as specific content related to life skills, learning skills, and knowledge about bodies and brains.

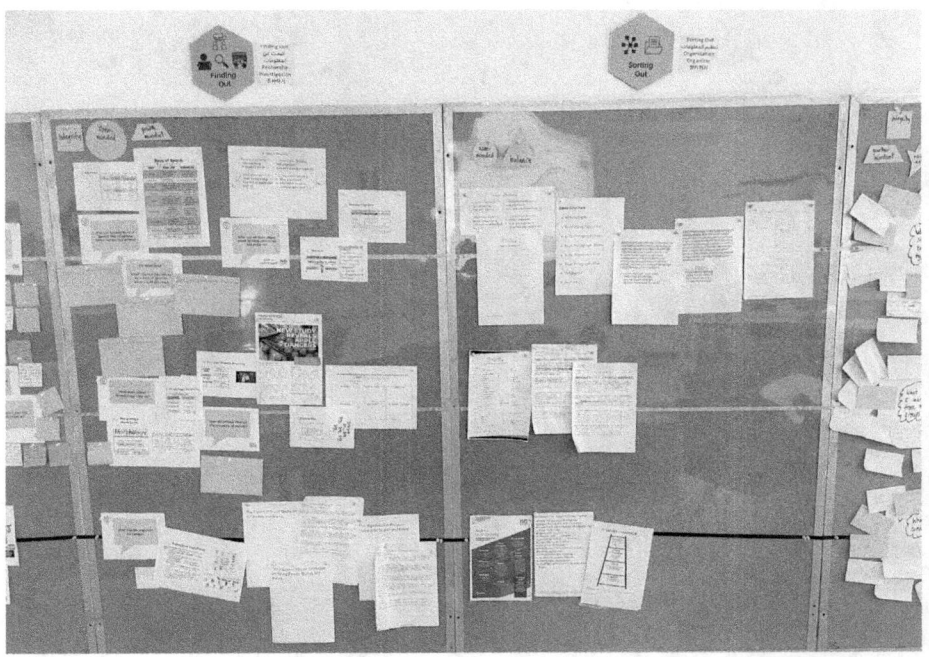

Inquiry Cycle

1. **Tuning In**—Initiate the inquiry process by capturing students' prior knowledge, initial thoughts, questions, and curiosities. This is typically done by the use of a provocation. The provocation in this case was a discussion and collection of pictures about identity.

2. **Finding Out/Investigating**—Engage students in active exploration of the concepts, gathering evidence, and making observations. The children researched what they were interested in.

3. **Sorting Out/Analyzing**—Guide students in analyzing the collected evidence, identifying patterns, and making connections.

4. **Making Conclusions/Reflecting**—Encourage students to reflect on their learning journey, considering their findings, questions, and evolving understanding.

5. **Taking Action**—Empower students to apply their newfound knowledge and understanding to real-world situations or further inquiry.

So what? This learning wall allowed us to raise awareness of our learning in real time.

Now what? Now that the unit is over, the students will all use this completed wall as a prompt to reflect and for retrieval practice in terms of all the learning that happened in the unit.

The learning also helped me, as a teacher, reflect on the unit and the specifics of learning skills and standards within subject-specific areas of our curriculum. After reflections and assessments based on what is on the wall, I am now better placed to create specific learning plans for our literacy and social studies learning. Learning walls can effectively minimize assumptions made by both students and teachers.

Challenging Student Assumptions

- **Visible Questions**—Prominently display open-ended questions that encourage students to question their initial assumptions or first thinking and explore alternative perspectives.
- **Divergent Thinking**—Incorporate visuals and examples that represent diverse viewpoints, challenging students to consider multiple possibilities rather than making quick assumptions.
- **Evidence-Based Thinking**—Encourage students to gather and analyze evidence to support their claims, discouraging reliance on unsubstantiated assumptions.

Reducing Teacher Assumptions

- **Student-Led Inquiry**—Allow students to drive the inquiry process, fostering a culture of student ownership and reducing teacher-centered assumptions.
- **Multiple Perspectives**—Encourage students to share their unique perspectives and experiences, providing teachers with a broader understanding of individual learning styles and backgrounds.
- **Reflective Practice**—Encourage teachers to reflect on their own assumptions and biases, promoting a more inclusive and equitable learning environment.

When evidence of learning is visible and prominent in a learning space, it gives everyone daily opportunities to notice and react to what is happening in the classroom in real time. Teachers and students do not need to assume, guess, or struggle to remember what, why, and how they learn and think. Student and teacher decision-making is more informed and relevant.

Trevor MacKenzie

High School English Teacher

Oak Bay High School | Victoria, BC, Canada

Learning wall intention: These learning walls were created with high school students in a Grade 12 English course. My intention was to have a visible and collaboratively created space in the classroom where students could share their ideas and thoughts throughout our unit of inquiry. I wanted students to learn from one another, to see evidence of learning that could impact their own ideas, to invite them to make connections with their peers in safe and equitable ways, and to give them time to reflect and engage in deep thinking. This unit of inquiry was eight weeks in duration. Students examined the concept of identity through the lens of resilience, conflict, and story as we read the novel *Three Day Road* by Joseph Boyden. Students were tasked with writing a literary analysis essay, a common assessment agreed on by our faculty for this course.

What? These photos were taken throughout our unit. Students had identified three main characters that would be the focus of our examination of the questions *How might conflict, loss, and trauma shape one's identity? How could someone's response to these challenges reveal their identity?* We made three learning walls in our space, one for each character. I asked for volunteers to create artistic representations of the characters Niska, Elijah, and Xavier.

For each learning wall, we used painter's tape to create sections around the character sketch that allowed us to sort our ideas into categories. This design proved to be incredibly helpful when it came to students organizing their ideas into the structure of their essays. In planning for what evidence to lift up and add to our learning walls, I considered what areas of their summative task, the essay, might be best supported by visibly sharing evidence of their learning. I felt that evidencing their thesis statements, strong quotes from their reading to support the essential questions, and powerful language, word choice, and vocabulary would likely be most helpful for learners. I wanted whatever we added to the learning walls to reflect evidence that could go directly into their essays.

So what? The evidence on our learning walls provided many opportunities for us to reflect, revise, and grow throughout the unit. Seeing

one another's thesis statements, for example, gave some of my more reluctant writers a chance to see a whole range of examples, all from their peers, that they could use to provide context and understanding. Several times during this particular lesson, I stood at the learning wall and asked students questions about what they were noticing, what they were considering doing with their own thesis statements, and what specific things they could take away from the evidence on the learning wall. We were using the evidence on the learning walls as formative assessment to drive next steps.

When it comes to our summative task, one specific challenge senior-level writers encounter is determining the strongest evidence to include in their literary analysis essays. Students do not have trouble finding quotes and paraphrasing details from their reading, but they are challenged in finding more powerful pieces to circle their ideas, evidence from the novel that allows for a more sophisticated interpretation of the text. To help in this area, I called on students to share their strongest evidence to the learning wall through a Give One, Get One thinking routine. This resulted in thirty to forty powerful quotes that students could dissect, discuss, and consider using in their own essays. By making the evidence visible and engaging in a Give One, Get One, students had a myriad of great examples before them. In having conversations with students at the learning wall, I noticed that even my stronger writers benefited from the activity. I heard students share reflections about refining their ideas, revising their choices, and making connections with their peers' quotes. This was exciting!

Now what? At the end of the unit, I called on students to add some reflections on the process of writing their essays. This reflection was done as a final page of their summative task. One prompt I provided them was to reflect on whether and how their essays were impacted by our learning walls. Students shared that the learning walls gave them ideas they had overlooked or didn't think of on their own. They were able to make connections and have conversations that we don't usually have in class. They shared that the process of using the learning walls was engaging, helpful, and fun.

From my perspective, all students benefited from the structure. My reluctant writers gained ideas and made connections that they may not have arrived to on their own. My strongest writers were stretched in their thinking and revised their writing as they went. It was as though the waterline of writing was slowly rising as we continued to make our learning visible to our learning walls.

Alona Yildirim

Early Years Teacher (four- and five-year-olds)
Bilkent Laboratory and International School | Ankara, Turkey

Learning wall intention: Document the experiences of young learners, making it simple and clear to support young learners' ability to "read" the documentation, creating a learning space to ignite curiosity and promote inquiry, encouraging communication, creating a reflective practice in the community, celebrating young learners' perspectives, encouraging documentation as a process, facilitating parents' involvement, supporting self-directed learning, connecting to a larger community, and making the thinking and learning of young citizens visible. The unit of inquiry under the transdisciplinary theme "How The World Works" (IB PYP) with a focus on nature is a year-long exploration.

My role: As a documenter, facilitator, and learner, my role is to capture and celebrate the expressions of curiosity and learning among young learners.

What? Our learning wall diverges from the traditional single-wall display, with documentation elements placed on surfaces throughout the learning environment—halls, classrooms, windows, and doors. Despite the familiar challenge of limited space for showcasing learning, I choose to view it as an advantage, intentionally leveraging the available space. In this context, multiple sections of the learning wall significantly enhance the visibility of the "Discovering Beauty" inquiry project within the community. The documented actions and collaborative efforts of families and children exploring "Discovering Beauty" beyond the school are showcased in the school hall, providing an accessible platform for school members to engage with these narratives. Additionally, these narratives find expression on windows, inviting passersby (other members of the school community) to take

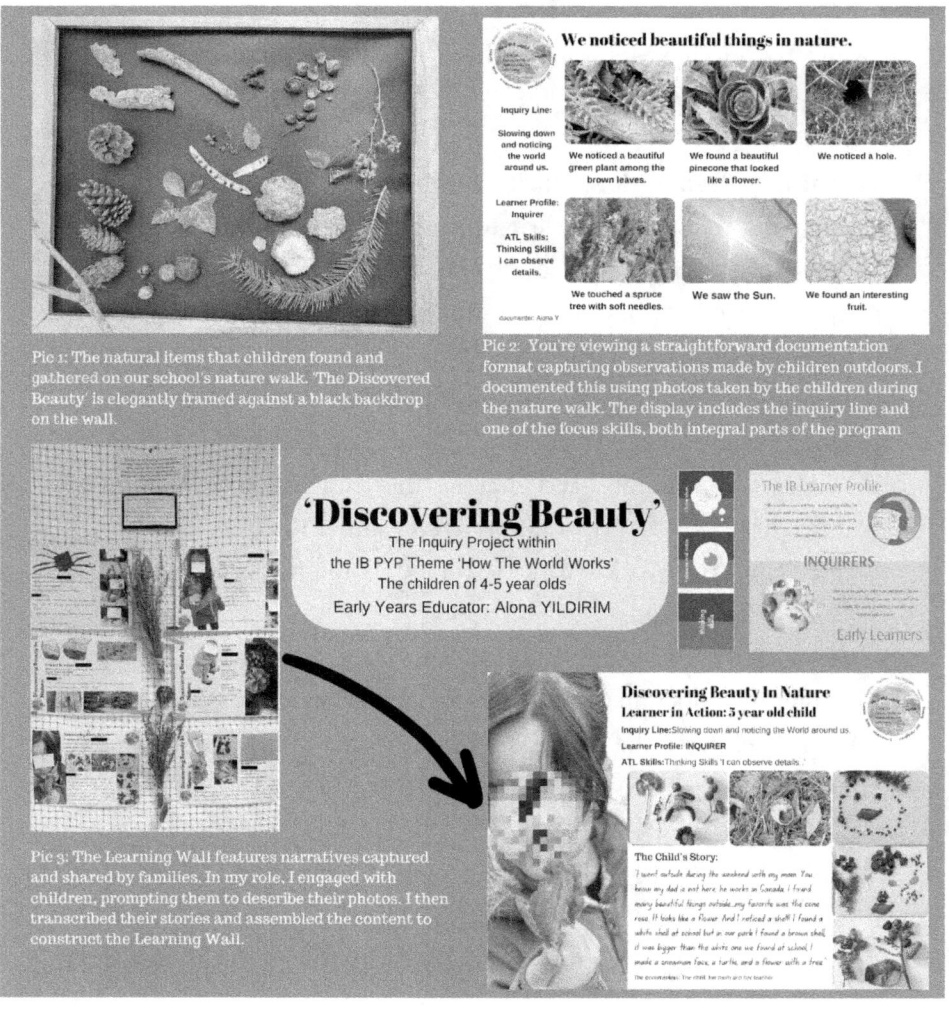

Pic 1: The natural items that children found and gathered on our school's nature walk. 'The Discovered Beauty' is elegantly framed against a black backdrop on the wall.

Pic 2: You're viewing a straightforward documentation format capturing observations made by children outdoors. I documented this using photos taken by the children during the nature walk. The display includes the inquiry line and one of the focus skills, both integral parts of the program

Pic 3: The Learning Wall features narratives captured and shared by families. In my role, I engaged with children, prompting them to describe their photos. I then transcribed their stories and assembled the content to construct the Learning Wall.

notice and potentially delve into the children's stories. The shared documentation phase corresponds to the tuning in and finding out stages of the "Discovering Beauty" inquiry project, fostering increased engagement from learners eager to share their discoveries.

In a deliberate departure from the initial decision to collect and present artifacts, I embraced a dynamic approach at the inquiry's inception. I invited young learners to partake in a nature walk around the school—a deliberate provocation aimed at tuning in to the inquiry. This experiential journey not only sparked curiosity but also fostered a deeper connection with nature, concurrently strengthening observational skills. Before the walk, I prompted the children to brainstorm ideas about what they might observe in nature, recognizing some misconceptions in their responses. I anticipated that the collective nature walk would serve as a clarifying exploration of these theories. Throughout the walk, guiding questions were employed to highlight vocabulary, such as *I am curious about . . .* , *I notice . . .* , and *I wonder. . .* , enriching the learning experience with thoughtful observations and reflections.

So what? The evidence collected from our learning initiatives highlighted the inherent fascination young children possess for nature and the discoveries we made together. Beyond the act of collecting natural items, the children actively engaged in posing inquiries about their findings. Notably, the discovery of a hole in the ground prompted a series of questions and imaginative musings about its origins and potential inhabitants. The natural progression of the children's questions and discoveries seamlessly guided our next steps in the inquiry process.

Our exploration shifted toward delving into the realm of living creatures dwelling underground as a direct response to the children's curiosity. A concurrent observation during our nature walk added another layer of depth—the resilience of certain plants remaining green in winter, in stark contrast to deciduous trees shedding their leaves. This particular observation became a catalyst for diverse learning engagements, encompassing topics such as evergreen plants, the intricacies of the color green and its shades, seasonal changes, and various other explorations.

Continuing the documentation process, I consistently added the children's evolving insights to both the physical learning wall and the school's online platform. In a collaborative spirit, learners were extended an optional invitation to continue their exploration beyond the classroom, involving their families in the process. The response was indeed contagious; most families actively shared photos capturing their children's discoveries, labeled as "beautiful things," and some children went the extra mile, persistently collecting and presenting these findings to share with their peers at school.

This evidence not only emphasized the engagement of children with nature but also revealed the relationship between the learning wall and the active involvement of learners and their families. The surprising depth of their responses and the interconnectedness of various aspects in their explorations affirmed the efficacy of this inquiry-based approach in fostering a comprehensive and collaborative learning environment.

Now what? The identification of a misconception among some children regarding "things that belong to nature" has notably influenced the trajectory of our inquiry planning. This revelation has been instrumental in unveiling significant concepts related to distinguishing between living and nonliving entities. In the upcoming nature walk, my intention is to guide children toward a more immersive experience by engaging their other senses—specifically, hearing, smell, taste, and touch. I anticipate that this approach will facilitate the exploration of different textures and scents, enabling us to delve deeper into the sensory aspects of our surroundings. *What do you hear when you close your eyes and just listen? Are there any edible plants or fruits you can try? Can you find something that smells sweet, and something that smells strong? Can you find something smooth, rough, soft, or prickly? What do* *you think the clouds look like today? Can you see any signs of animals or insects in their natural habitat?* are the guiding questions I think of.

Our nature walks have unveiled another layer of awareness, particularly concerning items discarded by people, often deemed as "ugly things" by the young learners. This discovery has propelled our discussions and learning toward broader global issues and environmental awareness. Presently, we have introduced the concept of "beautiful and ugly things," providing children with a framework for effective categorization. The ongoing inquiry project has garnered a satisfying level of engagement from the children, prompting contemplation on what nature might surprise us with next.

Reflecting on the current state of our inquiry, I am content with the children's enthusiasm and curiosity, prompting me to ponder the natural evolution of our exploration. As a recent development, the discovery of the first crocus flowers outside, notably early for the season, has added a delightful element to our ongoing nature observations. Moving forward, the challenge lies in harnessing this momentum to craft future provocations that not only address current misconceptions but also spark fresh wonder and curiosity among the young learners.

Stories of
Teacher Agency

Becky Carlzon

Community Designer

Learning Pioneers | Bristol, England, UK

Learning wall intention: Learning Pioneers is an international learning community committed to being the positive change in education. Practitioners from across the world connect in our community to discuss what matters in education and embed intentional pedagogy into our schools and classrooms. We highly value diversity of thought, context, and perspective. My role is to connect ideas and people across Learning Pioneers and to spark, facilitate, and highlight provocations, connections, and conversations.

We learn from a diverse range of leading educational thinkers, focusing on what matters in education, including quality inquiry-led practice, learning-to-learn, and prioritizing relationships. Having learnt from Jessica Vance and Anne van Dam on ways to make teacher learning visible through documentation, an obvious next step for our community was to visibly document our learning journeys with lead thinkers.

Our next line of inquiry, after our learning with Jessica and Anne, was *What might education look like in 2030, and how can we make steps toward that?* with Yong Zhao and Valerie Hannon. We chose this as our first inquiry to document learning across our community. From book studies to masterminds to Campfires to community discussions to provocations, we wanted to find a way to gather key thinking and ideas all in one space.

Our intention for our digital learning wall was to connect ideas and learning together across the Learning Pioneers community in one clear, easy-to-access space. We have so many incredible discussions and ideas developed across the Learning Pioneers community. The key ideas to carry forward and embed into our settings can get lost in threads. Having a learning wall means that we can gather these key ideas in one shared space and therefore be able to refer back to them over time. As we build up these learning walls for each inquiry, we will be able to make links between them and deepen and connect our thinking even further.

A key value of Learning Pioneers is that we are co-creative. We hoped being intentional with our learning wall would spark opportunities to create new ideas and thinking in current and future inquiries. The duration of this learning journey was twelve weeks.

What? We wanted to value conversations from all areas of our learning community and bring those together in one space.

One aspect of our community is regular "Campfire" meetups. To plan the focus of our Campfires, we invite members to share key grapples to practically embed ideas shared by our lead thinkers. From this feedback, we plan Campfire discussions on Zoom, where practitioners can connect with members across the world to unpack moving from inspiring ideas into action. The conversations are always really rich and build a bank of collective expertise and practice to solve our biggest problems in our roles. Our community members had highlighted that time was a potential block to making space for the kinds of learning they wanted to develop. We wondered *How can we create more time and see time as an abundance model rather than a deficit model?* Using a short video provocation from a previous "live" with Trevor MacKenzie, we opened up a discussion as to how we could rethink time in our busy school days. Using the thinking routine Give One, Get One, we each shared a top strategy and also took one away from our colleagues. After a rich discussion sharing strategies to create more time in our lives and the school day, each member reflected on and shared their favorite strategy (their "Get One") on our learning wall.

We also linked in student voice from interviews with students about how we could improve education, which included slowing down.

Combining thinking from our lead thinkers (in this case, Trevor MacKenzie) with student voice and our own range of experience, we became "unstuck" and were able to find new strategies to approach time in the school day. By documenting this on our learning wall, those who couldn't make the Campfire could still draw on the strategies we shared.

Both video provocations from Trevor and the students and the ideas shared in the Campfire were documented on our thinking wall page on "slowing down."

This is a visual of the documentation from Becky's Campfire. You can see her full digital documentation process by scanning the QR code.

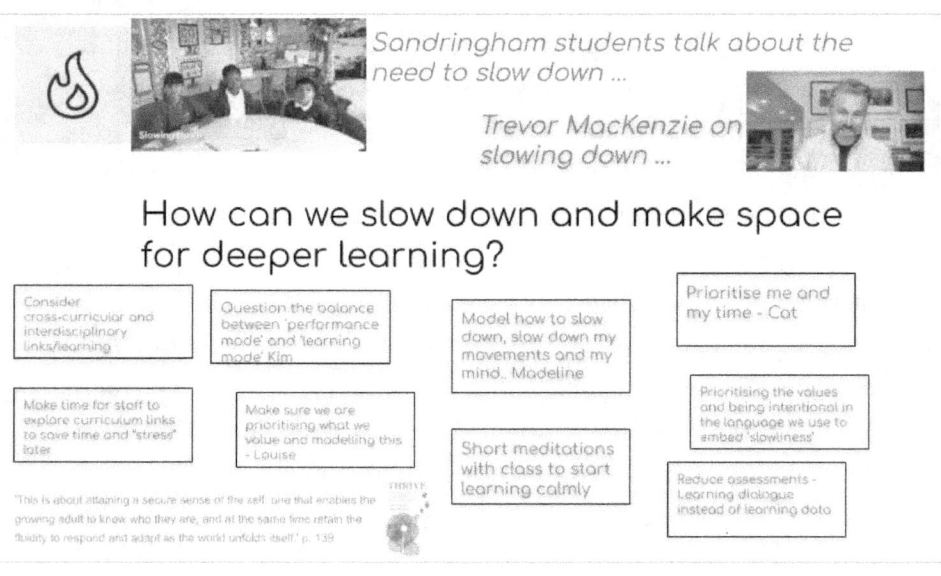

Sandringham students talk about the need to slow down ...

Trevor MacKenzie on slowing down ...

How can we slow down and make space for deeper learning?

Consider cross-curricular and interdisciplinary links/learning

Question the balance between 'performance mode' and 'learning mode' Kim

Model how to slow down, slow down my movements and my mind.. Madeline

Prioritise me and my time - Cat

Make time for staff to explore curriculum links to save time and 'stress' later

Make sure we are prioritising what we value and modelling this - Louise

Prioritising the values and being intentional in the language we use to embed 'slowliness'

Short meditations with class to start learning calmly

Reduce assessments - Learning dialogue instead of learning data

'This is about attaining a secure sense of the self: one that enables the growing adult to know who they are; and at the same time retain the fluidity to respond and adapt as the world unfolds itself.' p. 139

So what? Using a thinking wall grounded ideas and placed emphasis on the "Get One" part of the thinking routine, so the focus became, *What are you going to take away and put into practice?* This made the Campfire not only energizing through the sharing of rich ideas but also impactful for each individual. We made time in the Campfire to document that learning meant everyone's voice was heard and included and that members had a role in building up a bigger picture of our learning.

One of our key values in Learning Pioneers is "intentionality." Using a digital learning wall in this way has enabled us to be more explicit with our intentionality in Learning Pioneers and evidence learning and key takeaways in one document.

Now what? This was our first attempt at visibly documenting learning. It has been a useful way to bring thinking together into one space and to give a quick and easy overview of some community discussions and thinking. We are able to refer to prior key points and make links between them. There are a few challenges we are grappling with and will fine-tune as we go:

1. Co-creation and collaborative involvement—This is a huge challenge as we have a lot of learning opportunities and rich discussions in Learning Pioneers! We want learning walls to be intentional and meaningful and to clarify and add to the value we already have in our community—for learning walls to be integrated into learning and not an "add-on." We will continue to work on how to make this a collaborative process with our community members.

2. Discernment—One of the biggest challenges was deciding what should go onto the learning wall and what to leave out. The richest discussions in Learning Pioneers often pop up spontaneously in threads. It's impossible to include all of this on a learning wall! It would be great to hyperlink in these discussions so people could go from the learning wall to those deeper, richer, more detailed conversations to gain even more inspiration and reference back to the source of the discussions.

3. Making use of the learning wall throughout the inquiry—Our learning wall grew organically, based on key ideas and discussions that bubbled up throughout our inquiry. With the focus on connection, discussion, and the generation of new ideas, it was a challenge to refer back to and use the learning wall. One key way we reflected the learning back was at the end of the inquiry, using the thinking routine *I used to think . . . now I think . . .* and inviting our community members to refer to the learning wall as inspiration. Here is one of the reflections we gathered:

> I used to think that all was lost and that the change needed in education is too overwhelming and unsurmountable.
>
> Now I think that by opening these conversations and circling round to ideas in the book *Thrive* and from the "live" with Yong and Valerie, there are opportunities for us, our children, our school communities, and our national education systems to adapt and respond intentionally to an ever-changing world. I have found asking "why?" and coming back to my/ our values helped guide my thought process as we have gone deeper into this inquiry.

Moving forward, I would like to find more ways to refer back to the learning wall in mastermind and Campfire discussions so we can use and build on the ideas we have gathered.

4. Examples of practice—We share examples of impact in an area of our community called "Pioneers in Practice." Now I'm wondering how we can document and thread in the practice we've created as a result of the learning in our inquiry.

Catherine Place

Head Teacher
Jubilee Park Primary School | Newport, South Wales, UK

Learning wall intention: As leaders, we are driven by a strong moral purpose and are developing an ecosystem that values the development of individuals, our community, and the wider society. Since we opened the school in September 2017, we have been focused on our purpose, which is articulated through three vision principles. Our vision principles are the foundation for our strategic purpose and our aspirations for the future. We are committed to

- igniting a passion for learning
- creating the conditions to thrive
- growing together with the community

We are a learning organization and value an inquiry approach to learning and teaching. The practice of documenting learning through a learning journey is well established within our classrooms. Through reflection, we decided we wanted a space to document the learning of the adults within our school. We place great emphasis on professional learning and development, and our intention was to create a learning wall dedicated to sharing our self-reflections and the impact on our pedagogical decisions. The learning wall documents learning from across the school year; it is regularly updated and flexible to respond to the needs of staff and their professional learning and development.

What? The learning wall shares the types of professional learning and development on offer for our staff, for example, leadership days and CAIP (Collaborative Approach to Improving Practice, Reading, and Research). It also displays prompts and reflective questions from *A Guide to Documenting Learning* by Silvia Rosenthal Tolisano and Janet A. Hale. This book has challenged our thinking regarding adult learning and how we can map meaning, understanding, and reflection to share with our school community.

We value a *slowliness* approach to learning for our children and are trying to advocate the same philosophy for our staff. As leaders we recognize that we need to ensure our rhetoric is matched by action (*Leading with a Lens of Inquiry*, Jessica Vance, 2022). This firstly requires trusting relationships and a culture of inquiry across the school. Our learning wall documents our intentionality for adult learning and development based on the foundation of trusting relationships.

We recognize that inquiry learning is messy! As such, we wanted our learning wall to reflect our processes of learning and provide a space for immediate feedback and provide points for consideration.

"The overarching purpose for documenting learning is to allow learners to fully participate in their own learning processes."
Play Inquiry
C.A.I.P
Documenting OF Learning

days
What is worthy of being looked for and captured during this learning opportunity?
What media platforms and tools will provide the maximum effect for capturing, reflecting on, curating, sharing and amplifying my personal learning or the evidence of others?
Practitioner's are learners too

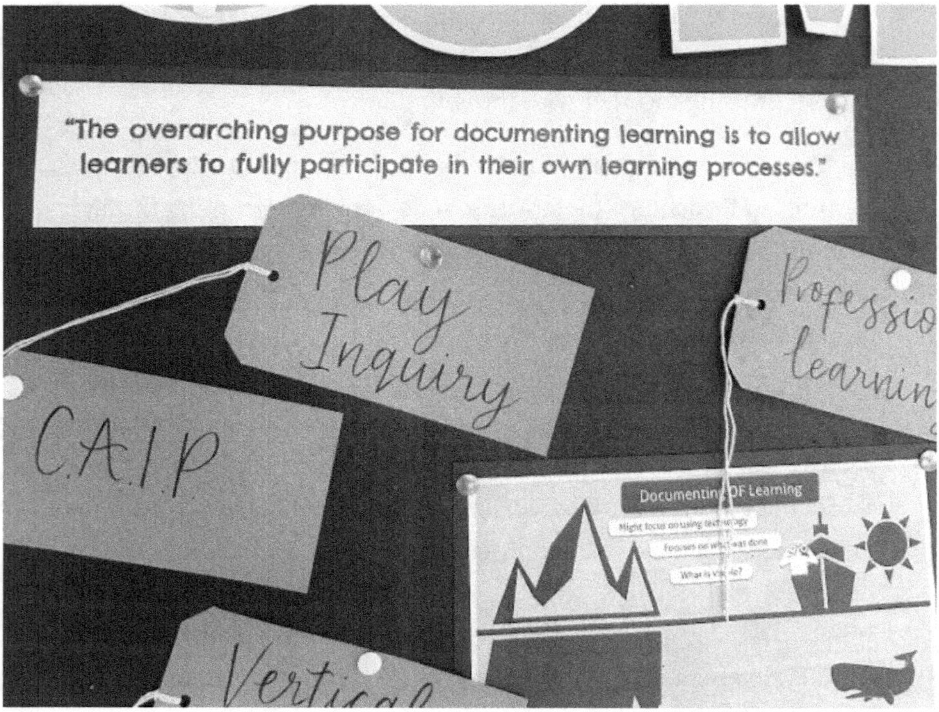

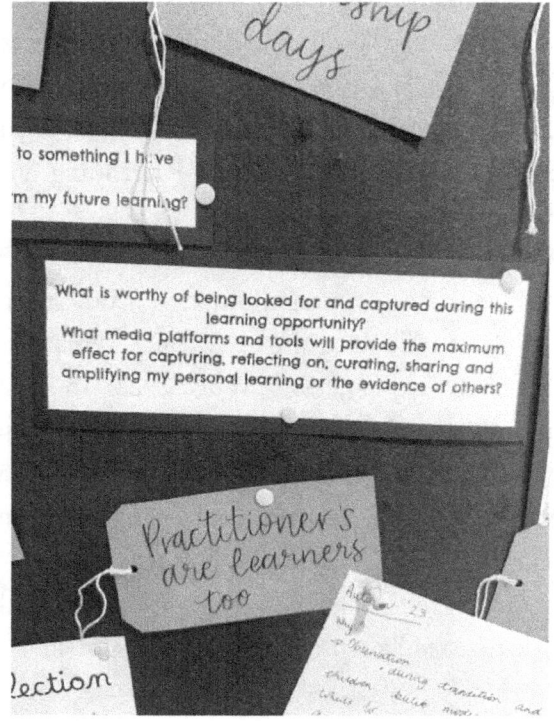

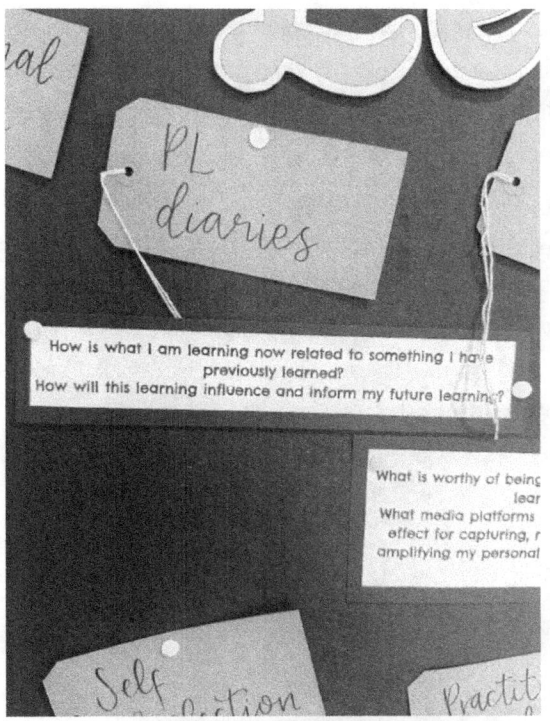

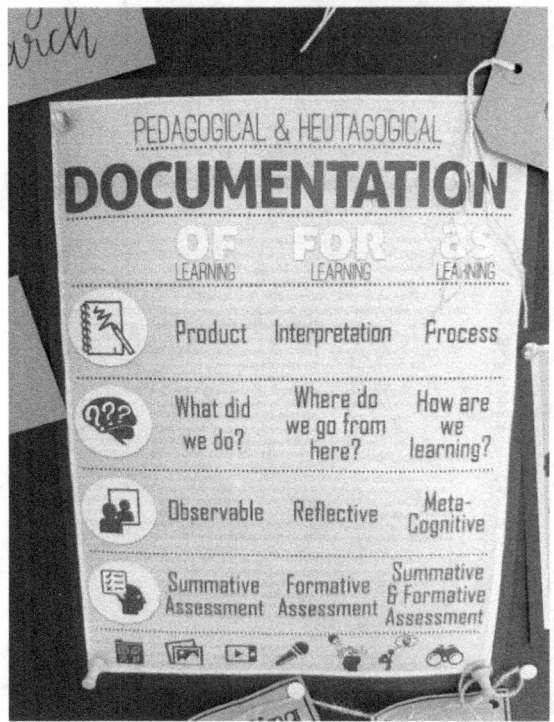

As a learning organization, we place great emphasis on the importance of self-reflection. We provide our teachers with the space and time to reflect on their planning for learning and recognize the crucial role they play in children's learning. It is important that this also provides opportunities for teachers to consider how this reflection will influence future learning. The process of reflection has developed in sophistication and honesty and has contributed to the trust and agency that teachers have across our school. By displaying examples of teachers' reflections, it encourages openness and values the role of self-reflection within our learning.

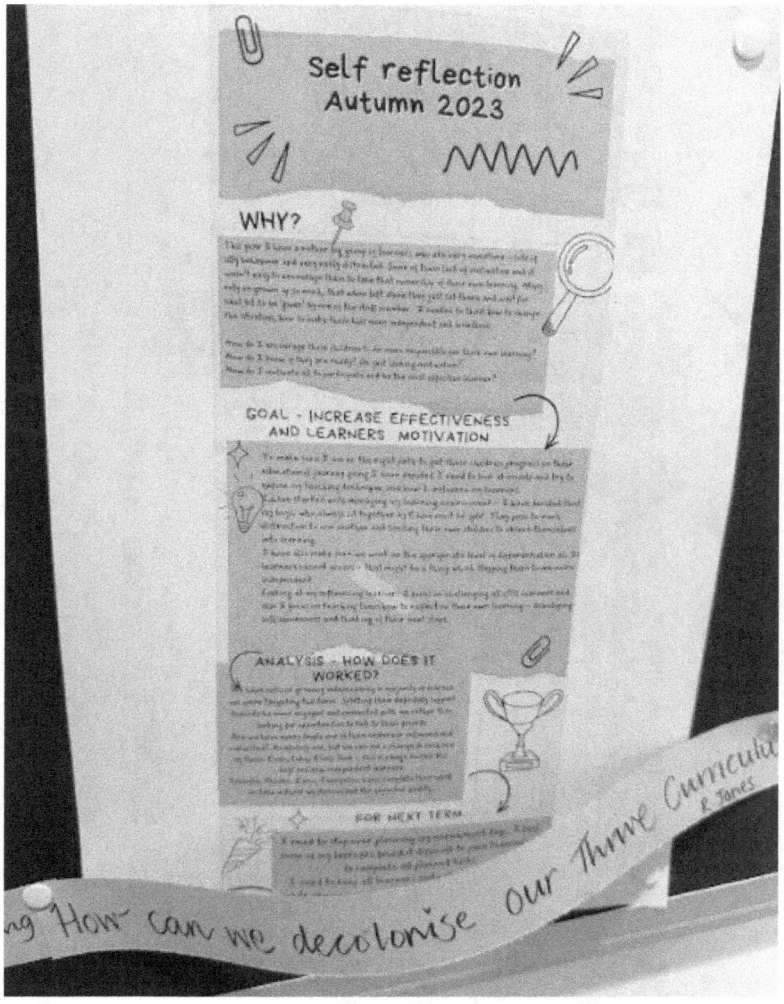

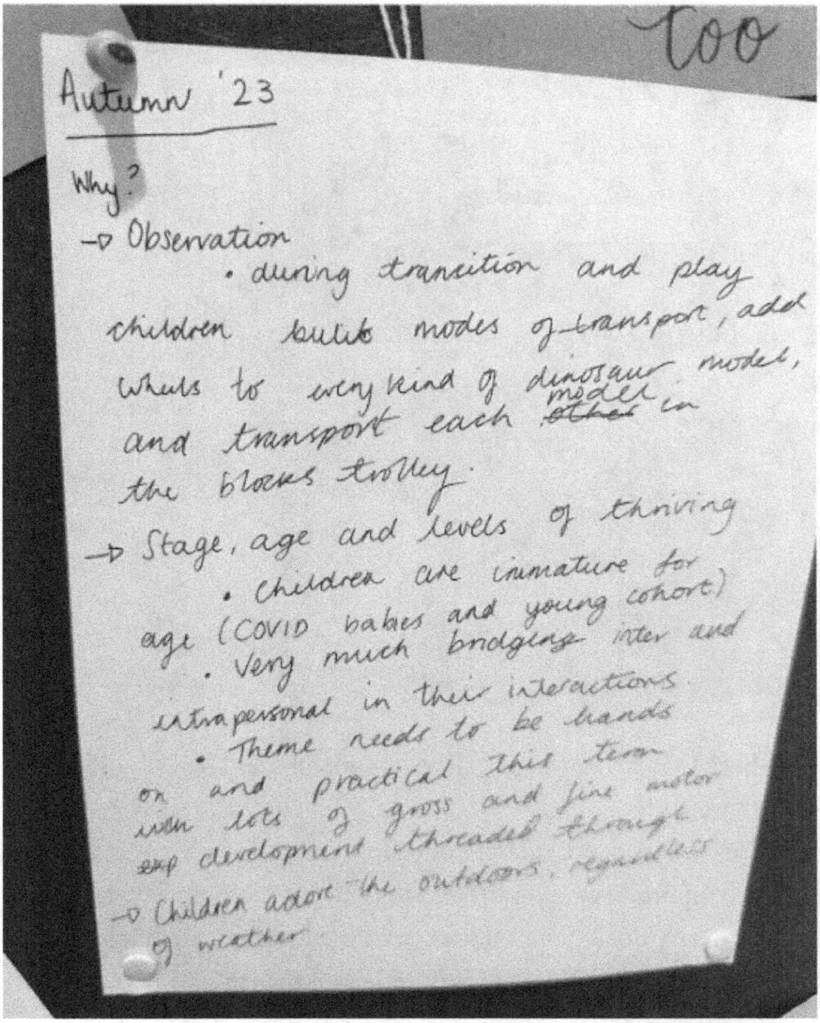

too

Autumn '23

Why?

→ Observation

- during transition and play children build modes of transport, add wheels to every kind of dinosaur model, and transport each ~~other~~ in the blocks trolley.

→ Stage, age and levels of thriving

- children are immature for age (COVID babies and young cohort)
- Very much bridging inter and extrapersonal in their interactions.
- Theme needs to be hands on and practical this term with lots of gross and fine motor exp development threaded through

→ Children adore the outdoors, regardless of weather.

So what? Using a learning wall to document adult learning has been very powerful!

The process of articulating our professional learning and development is important for all staff and for student teachers who are based within our school for their initial teacher education. Highlighting this information on our learning wall indicates that this offer is available for all staff, regardless of their role. It also demonstrates the high priority we place on professional learning and development to any visitors to our school.

The sharing of key information, models, and provocations from our professional learning and development sessions enables all staff to reflect and keep these in mind, particularly as the board is located in a busy corridor that most staff walk through every day!

Across the school, all staff undertake individual professional inquiries—passion projects. These are developed throughout an academic year, and the working titles of many of these projects are displayed on the learning wall. This has enabled staff to know more about the inquiries that are being undertaken by others and has encouraged the sharing of related research and ideas.

Staff are often found looking at the board or commenting about something that a member of staff is learning or inquiring about. This has enabled learning-focused dialogue between staff and supported the sharing of pedagogy and practice.

Through documenting adult learning, it became clear that there is significant professional learning for all staff across the school. There are clear connections in the offering that reflect both our vision principles and our school improvement priorities.

Now what? We are going to continue documenting adult learning. We will ensure the learning wall is regularly updated and responsive to our professional learning offer. We will continue to provide the space and time for staff to reflect on their own learning and share examples of this on our learning wall.

Erica Thompson
District Consultant
Beaufort Delta Divisional Education Council | Inuvik, NWT, Canada

Learning wall intention: My intention for my learning wall was to create an area where I could make my thinking visual and consistently reflect on that thinking as I design training and teaching and learning experiences. I wanted a collection of thoughts, questions, and structures to develop a series of concepts that I believe guide my work as a district consultant. My learning wall has been developing throughout the school year. The foundational thinking and concepts are key elements of my portfolio and the guiding vision for the district. I check in with the learning wall in my office consistently when I am in there working and add elements roughly bi-weekly. I have been scheduling in time to reflect using the wall since my return from the winter holidays.

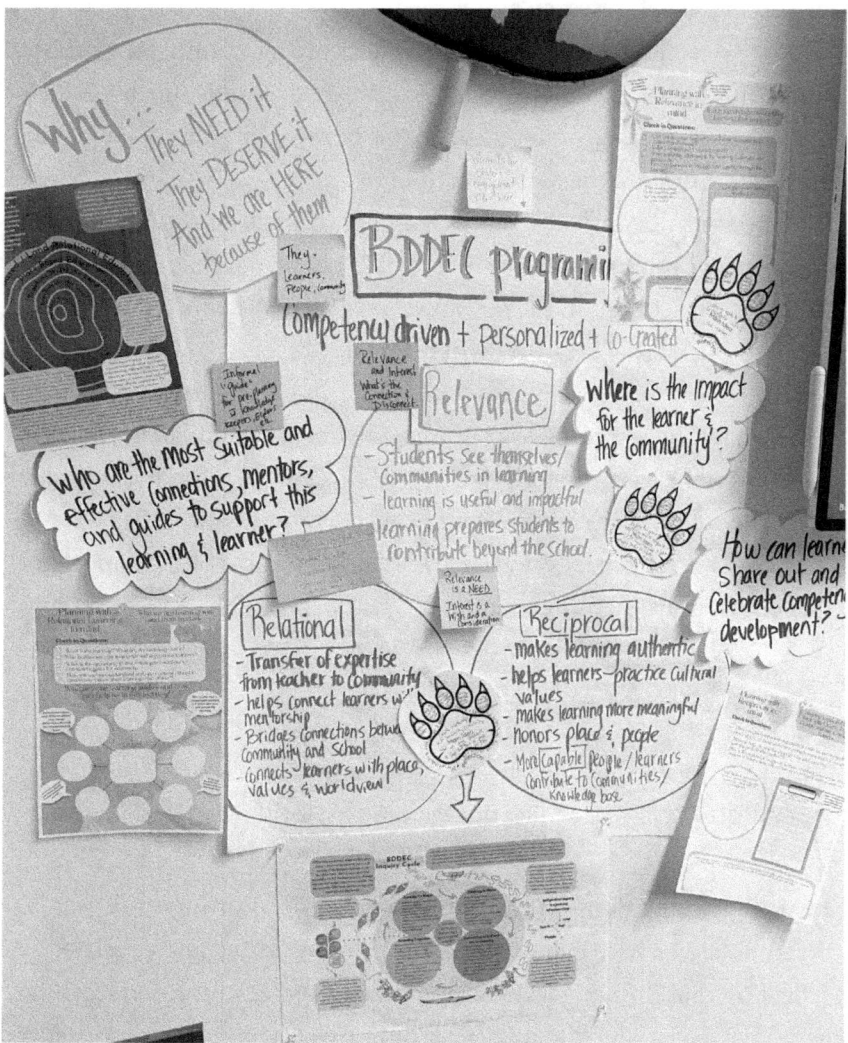

What? This learning wall is a compilation. It started with a chart paper model of the three foundational elements I see as being priorities in lesson/unit design for the learners in the district where I am a consultant, and it has developed into a central place for thinking about Indigenizing teaching and learning. For each element of the original programming design model—relevance, relationality, and reciprocity—I have designed resources to use with educators and colleagues. These resources are informed by the key points in each area.

I have also developed guiding questions for each of the elements that can be added to planning templates to help teachers check in and design with these in mind. I have used these questions in coaching with teachers throughout the district and in the co-facilitation opportunities I have when working with schools. These questions have been very helpful in my work throughout the year.

Most recently, I used a place-inspired thinking routine for synthesizing and reflecting, which is inspired by the structure and function of a polar bear's paw, to help me concentrate on actions to deepen each element of our instructional design. The practice of working through the thinking routine and aligning each "paw" to the right element of planning and design clarified the actions needed next. On the wall itself, these tracks make a path from element to element, and I like that the visual effect mimics the developmental process.

So what? When I plan for the elements on my learning wall, the teaching and learning is engaging, effective, and meaningful for students. When lessons are designed for relevance and include relational elements as well as teachings, nudges, and perspectives about reciprocity in the learning process, students connect with the content and seem to be willing to take risks in their learning. This tells me that familiarity is safe and increases access.

When I consider the guiding questions on the wall and plan for them, my lessons and units are purposeful and relevant for learners. Units planned with the resources and thinking from the learning wall will have a greater impact on the communities beyond the school—because it involves elders, experts, and knowledge keepers whose wisdom and perspective are foundational to the worldview of the students in the classroom. I also love the way that the place-based thinking routines that are developed in the region are useful for student thinking as well as district-level thinking. When I sat down and worked through the Polar Bear Paw routine, it helped clarify and focus my work through each element on the wall.

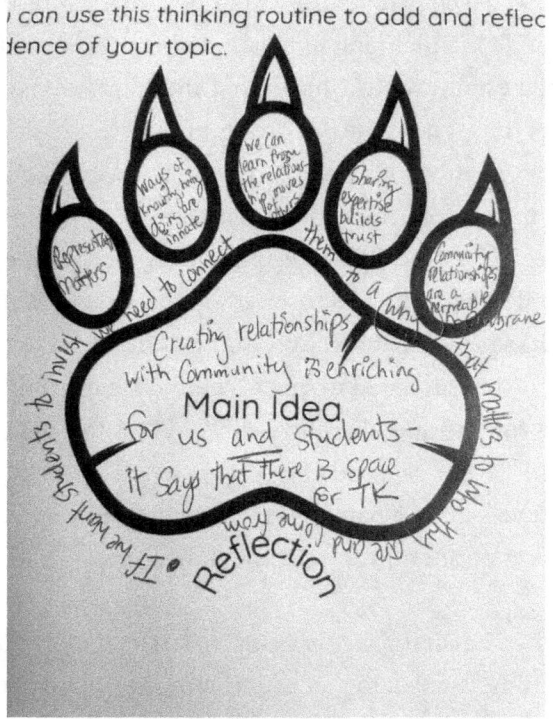

I noticed that as my wall grew—and I added to and engaged with it more—more people who stopped by or worked with me in my office began commenting, contributing, and starting conversations inspired by it. In this way, it is acting as a provocation. This is perhaps my favorite part of the process thus far, because it helps other consultants and teachers begin to develop their thinking along those elements.

Now what? The next steps along my learning wall journey will be to compile the successful elements of planning and implementation of lessons and units I have seen and facilitated throughout the year. I want to create a suite of resources to help schools tune into relevance, relational thinking, and reciprocity in teacher pedagogy.

I will continue to use the wall to inform my thinking, and I plan to add visuals of the learning in action that I have witnessed. I am

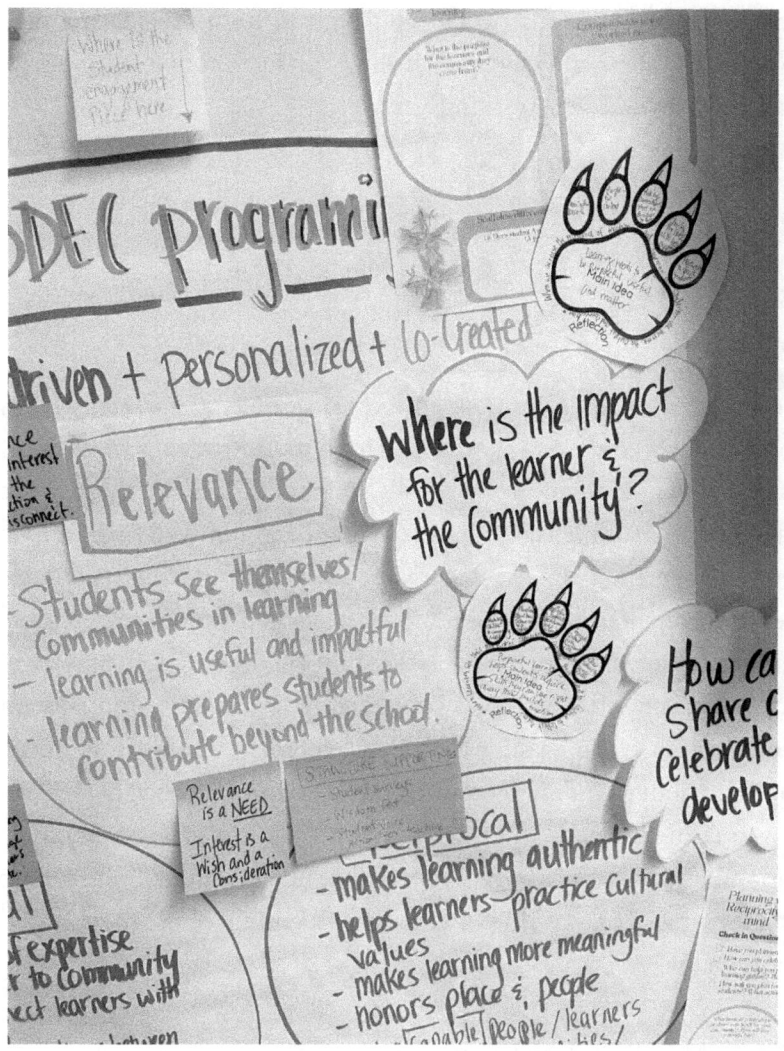

debating about moving the wall because I am limited on space—I have considered moving it into the virtual space and then using printouts for the proximal visual referent, which is pretty important for me as a learner. I think that if I use a FigJam, Canva Whiteboard, or another virtual platform, I can grow it in a new way and share it more intentionally and more widely.

I am now wondering how I can facilitate this kind of professional inquiry journey made visual through an interactive learning wall with other leaders in our district. Related to this, I am considering highlighting the steps and elements of the construction of a learning wall that captures a professional inquiry.

Kristen Martin

IB Coordinator (PYP and MYP)
Paso Verde School | Sacramento, California

Learning wall intention: As an inquiry leader on my campus, my intention with my learning wall is to support our collaborative conversations and planning time by highlighting the values and the practices that we have committed to as a learning community. By making our work visible and connecting with the learning wall artifacts and evidence throughout our conversations, I am modeling for our teachers and team the power that comes from making the language of learning accessible and relevant in our work together. As an IB coordinator, my work includes helping support the development of our program and building understanding by connecting colleagues to the values that we have outlined for our learning community. With this lens, my learning wall is more of a responsive tool that builds on our conversations and learning goals within our community, and therefore there is not a set timeline.

What? My office is the hub of our collaborative meetings on our campus. These meetings are focused on developing our instructional practice. This wall was built from collaborative conversations around identified goals that each of our teams had identified as their "one thing" that they want to focus on for the trimester. As teams set their intentions for their own professional focus and learning, we worked to organize and consider the categories that these goals might fall into and added those to the wall. We ended up with *Evidencing Learning, Curiosity, Co-construction, Agency,* and *Action.* Organizing our goals into categories helped to highlight themes and connect colleagues to one another for support and resources. As our teachers began working on their "one thing," they invited me into the learning and shared documentation with me of progress toward their goal.

These moments that were captured and celebrated with colleagues are added as artifacts for our wall. In addition to the photographic evidence, I also added tools or resources that teams used in their implementation. Whether it was an image of scholars in action, a learning wall in a classroom, or a research mat that was built to nurture curiosity, the artifacts added to my learning wall serve as exemplars and inspiration to support the work happening on campus that is directly aligned to our identified goals. In addition to our goals, I added three questions that were modeled from an inspiration wall that Jess had shared with me during our coaching. These questions were used to nudge our collaborative conversations and center our thinking around the work. These questions were, *What intention can we set for ourselves? How do*

you want to show up today? How can we model our thinking/language?
In an effort to model the model with my team, I added artifacts to the
wall that I have used during PD or other collaborations that lift up key
routines and practices that are aligned to these questions. Whether it
was using a Chalk Talk routine to provoke and capture thinking and
make it visible or the I Used to Think, Now I Think routine that powerfully nudges reflection around our thinking and consolidates the
learning, both routines provided structures that explicitly aligned with
the goals identified by our team.

So what? As the wall grew and was added to throughout the trimester,
I found myself taking moments to pause during my day to reflect on
the work our team was committed to as a community. It was in these
moments of pause that I considered my role as a coach to provide support and connection and to nurture next steps in a way that created
a culture of learning on our campus and built capacity and collective
efficacy on our team. In some cases, grade-level teams shared evidence
that was celebrated and yet still provoked curiosity around how we
might design intentional next steps to foster even more independence
and ownership for our scholars.

In these situations, the evidence on the wall provided a foundation for my coaching conversations, and I found myself adding sticky
notes to the wall with questions that bubbled up for my teams and
nudged them toward targeted next steps in their practice. It was in
using this wall as a provocation for my own professional reflection that
I found myself entering into the collaborative conversations with more
intentionality and anticipation that undoubtedly supported the growth
and development of my practice as a coach and the work of our team
toward their goals. On one occasion, I was late making it to our collaboration meeting, and I entered my office to find a team of colleagues
standing at the wall and sharing reflections and aha moments that connected to their goal. They were sifting through the artifacts posted and
making connections to the work of another grade-level team around

a similar goal. Rather than transitioning to sit down at the table to collaborate, I joined them at the wall, and we had discussions around the evidence and goals that were both rich and meaningful. It was at that moment that I realized the incredible power of sharing the story of our learning and growth through our wall and the momentum that having our story visible generated. The work was not just happening in isolation anymore in classrooms or even grade-level buildings; it was living and breathing through connection to context and our shared values in action as a community.

Now what? After reflecting with colleagues on the powerful ways that our learning wall provoked thinking and reflection for our team around our goals, I am inspired to move the wall out of my office and into a more visible and shared space on our campus. If the learning wall supported us in communicating our purpose and kept us anchored to the beliefs and values that aligned to our goals, shouldn't it be somewhere that would be more consistently accessible for our team? I am curious how this one little shift might inspire a ripple effect for our team and encourage more interaction with the wall outside of collaborative conversations during structured meeting time? How might this movement of the physical placement of the wall invite others to engage in the conversation/thinking, and what impact might this have on their ownership of the work? How may this collaborative and co-constructed wall support teachers with understanding the value of the learning wall in their own spaces? As I consider my planning for this next iteration of the learning wall for our community, I am reminded of the power that comes from making our process of learning visible, and I am excited for how this shift may inspire more engagement and lead to a deeper connection with the work for our team.

Paige Driscoll

Vice Principal and Instructional Coach

Mangilaluk School | Tuktoyaktuk, NWT, Canada

Learning wall intention: My goal as an inquiry leader is to advance teacher agency, and the goal for the school principal was to be more intentionally playful. My goal for the learning wall was to document each staff professional development meeting and to ensure that we were being responsive to teachers' needs. This learning wall is intended for teachers and support staff at our school but is also a great model to show our students. My role as the instructional coach is to support teachers with inquiry moves, Indigenizing education, making thinking visible, creating learning walls, using thinking routines, and maximizing key cultural events. We want to support teachers in connecting with the local community and providing students with relevant, meaningful, and engaging learning that is connected to their culture. A whole-school approach supports new teachers in connecting with the community and allows a safe space for collaboration, where we can all share our strengths and gifts to best support students. This inquiry unit lasted approximately seven weeks. It involved some planning initially between Jessica Vance, the principal, and me to make a timeline and identify goals for each staff meeting. All classroom teachers and students participated. Some classes made a whole unit with it and also created learning walls within their classroom, and some classes did a few lessons and contributed to the whole-school inquiry wall. The actual dog sledding took place the week of April 1, and the school/community share-out took place on April 24.

What? This learning wall is just about completed and reflects the various staff meetings, professional development, collaboration, co-designing, and reflection of our staff. At the top right (see photo below), you can see the pre-meeting we had with Jessica. In the meeting, she worked with the principal and me to go over some of our strengths and challenges as a school. I shared my experience with the whole-school inquiries last year and shared my thoughts on what the next steps could be. We talked about our values as a school and how we want to support the Northwest Territories key competencies and

all parts of the Beaufort Delta Education Council Indigenized Inquiry cycle. I also shared that one of the biggest challenges is time, especially juggling my two job roles. Jessica created a timeline for us, and we backwards planned for the unit's key dates. This was a vital part of our learning wall and helped ground us in our goals and values as inquiry leaders in our school.

We started the first staff professional development with a celebration and lifted up all the awesome work being done at our school. Next, we did a Compass Points thinking routine. This was to gather data from teachers about the support they would like for the next whole-school inquiry. From this routine, we gathered that teachers needed more support with essential questions and making the topics/ themes of the whole-school inquiry accessible to all grades and levels. At the next staff meeting, we did a question sort. We provided teachers with a Google Drive folder of place-based provocations (dog teams, dog races, dog mushing, houses, food, puppies, etc.) and asked them to come up with questions. We had teachers work with a similar grade teacher to do a question sort, thin to thick. This worked really well because the questions were geared to the students, and it really demonstrated to teachers how they could do a similar activity with their students to make the inquiry unit more accessible.

My favorite artifact to collect was in the last staff meeting, when we were planning for the "coming to know" section and co-creating the share-out. When we asked teachers to share some examples of sharing-out from their classrooms, it was really heartwarming to hear about the variety of ways they are supporting student voice, choice, and agency. I enjoyed learning more about micro-celebrations, and we had great discussions about how celebrations don't always need to be these big events, as long as they are meaningful for the students. I also liked seeing some common themes such as reciprocity, inviting in the learning guides and families, food, and students getting to share and present their inquiry learning journey.

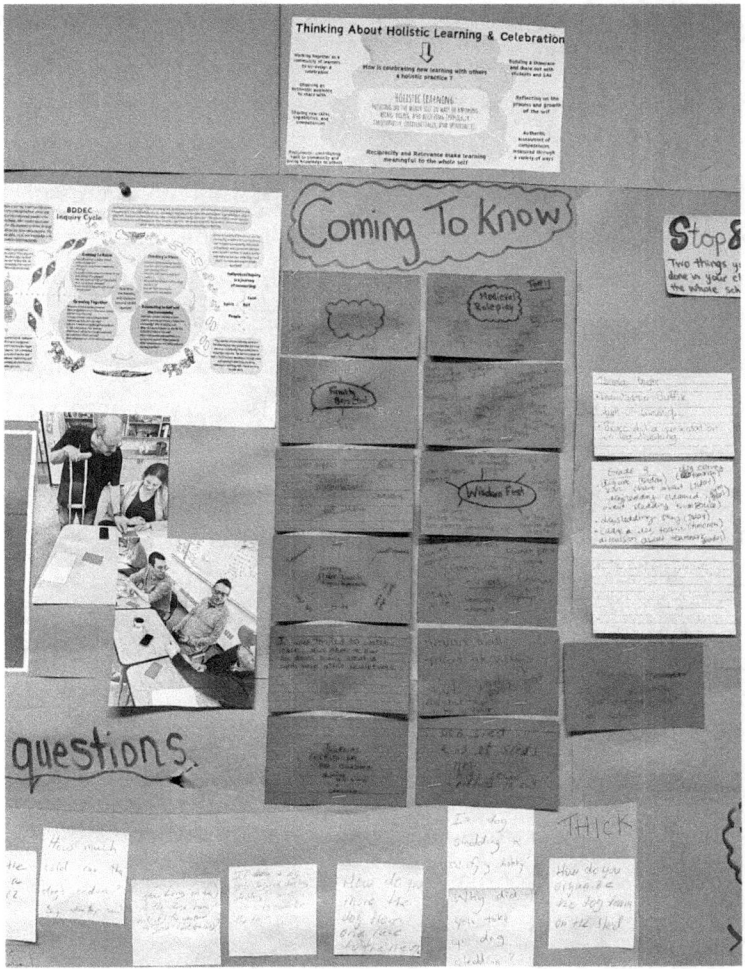

So what? After each staff meeting, we collected some kind of visible thinking evidence from the teachers. The evidence demonstrated to me how we are all stronger and more capable together. It showed me the power of collaboration and co-planning and also showed me what can happen when we give teachers more agency in the planning process. Before each staff meeting, I had some ideas and assumptions about what would arise, but I was always left surprised by how much great teamwork was occurring. There was one staff meeting in which we scaffolded teachers in planning with the key competencies; they got to work with a partner and co-designed lesson ideas that aligned with these competencies. I was blown away by the lesson ideas and how the ideas were further developed by sharing and working with a colleague. I was also impressed with the range of lesson ideas, from mathematics to STEM, coding, and SEL learning.

In general, I was very surprised with staff engagement! The thought of weekly staff meetings was a bit daunting, and I was unsure about how teachers would feel. Each meeting was planned to have a purpose and a goal, and they did not drag on. They were dynamic and involved lots of discussions and collaborations. Teachers saw the value of the professional development sessions. Teachers enjoyed viewing our learning wall, and I think it modeled to them some ideas about how to document and evidence. Additionally, students noticed and wondered about our admin learning wall! They thought it was so cool that teachers participated in learning walls too. The whole-school learning wall was also a welcome surprise. It turned out even better than I could have imagined. We had tried two whole-school learning walls before this, but we didn't get nearly as much participation. I think the scaffolded approach we took this time was really helpful for teachers.

Now what? In wrapping up this unit of inquiry, next we have our big community share-out that was co-designed by staff and students. After that, we will create a Google Form to gather some data from teachers on their experience with this whole-school inquiry. Looking ahead to next year, we have started planning some ideas for our school improvement plan (SIP), "blue days," with teachers. We will be more intentional with school-based SIP days, maximizing the time we have together and especially involving the support assistants.

Next year we will have a bigger teacher turnover, and to best support them, we will plan a whole-school inquiry for the fall. This will offer a great opportunity for older staff to mentor new staff and really support community connections for new teachers. This will help teachers make connections between the SIP sessions and what it could actually look, sound, and feel like. We will collaborate with the two Indigenous language educators to plan ahead for this fall-time fish inquiry unit. We would like the adult learning wall to be more interactive and offer more responsibility for teachers to add to and adapt the learning wall. Depending on the renovations, we will place the adult learning wall somewhere more accessible to all the teachers.

It makes me wonder how we could use the SIP time to facilitate collaboration with the support assistants, because they are great learning guides and experts in the local culture and traditions. It would be great to involve them more in the adult learning wall and allow more time for them to collaborate with the teachers.

Stories of
Conceptual Understanding

Tiffany Keske

Kindergarten Teacher

Tarvin Elementary | Leander, Texas

Learning wall intention: In my kindergarten classroom, we use our learning wall as a living document that tracks our learning journey through a concept every nine weeks. Our district divides our school year into four nine-week grading periods. Each nine weeks, our class explores a new concept. During this nine-week period, we are conducting an inquiry on cycles.

What? This nine weeks, we are focusing on the word *cycle*. To start our inquiry into cycles, we employed a Tug-of-War thinking routine. I asked my learners to tell me whether they thought the statement *Cycles repeat* was true. They then used a sticker to indicate their thinking: if their sticker was by the check, they thought the statement was true; if their sticker was in the middle, they weren't sure; if their sticker was by the X, they thought the statement was false. This thinking routine helps me assess the prior knowledge that my learners might have. After our Tug-of-War, we had a discussion in which we determined what a cycle was. Through that discussion, we identified seasonal cycles, human life cycles, moon cycles, butterfly life cycles, plant life cycles, and patterns, and I also had a learner wonder whether the word *bicycle* had anything to do with cycles. This discussion helped my learners see the cycles around them.

From this point, we started looking for cycles across content areas and began to see cycles in math, science, and language arts. In math, while observing a hundreds chart, students noticed that the numbers followed a pattern and repeated. While creating graphs, learners noticed that we had a cycle: come up with questions, gather data, sort data, create a graph. In language arts, during our author study on Eric Carle, we noticed that he had a process for creating books: paint, create, write. We then tied that to our own writing process: come up with

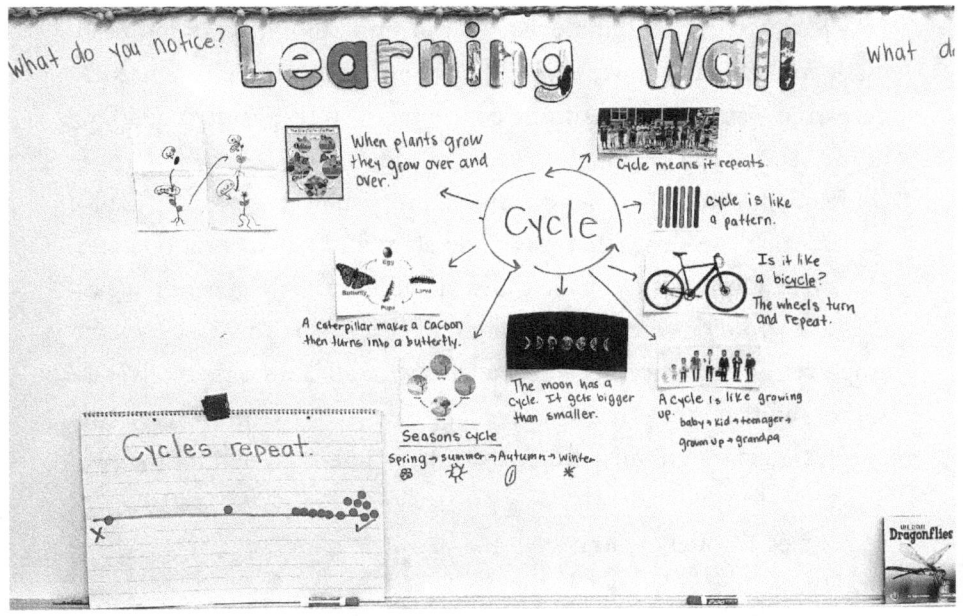

an idea, create, publish. We also recognized cycles during our science units. We observed cycles as our plants started to grow, and we stumbled on the water cycle. As we proceeded through this inquiry, I used pictures of work samples, pictures of anchor charts, pictures of experiments, and See, Think, Wonder thinking routine charts to help build our learning wall. Our learning wall became a living document that we added to and changed as our learning continued to move forward.

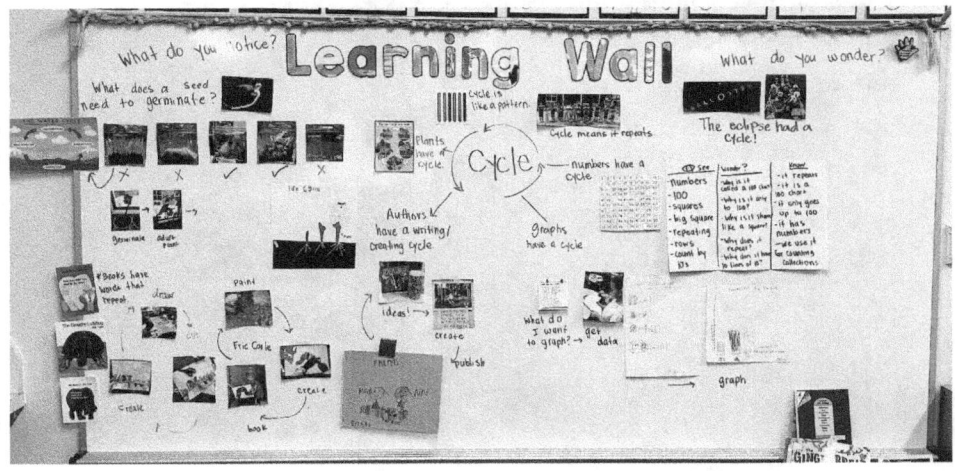

So what? My learners embraced our learning wall this year and used it as a tool to both showcase thinking and to pose questions. Our kindergarten team started planning conceptually in the last two quarters of the school year. Through the lens of inquiry, we were able to find connections throughout our day and in every subject. My favorite connection that learners made was understanding that writing operates in a cycle. Our class created an idea jar to use to help generate ideas; then we wrote out our stories and published them. This was such an empowering revelation because students were able to see themselves as authors and often referred to where they were in the writing cycle as we progressed through our writers' workshop time. Throughout the two quarters, learners identified cycles throughout the day. They frequently asked to add cycles to our wall, which continued to grow and change over the period. During our student-led conferences at the end of the year, students were able to select a cycle, illustrate it, and explain it to their loved ones. It was empowering for both my learners and me to see how our learning wall became so much larger and how it helped students make connections across the curriculum.

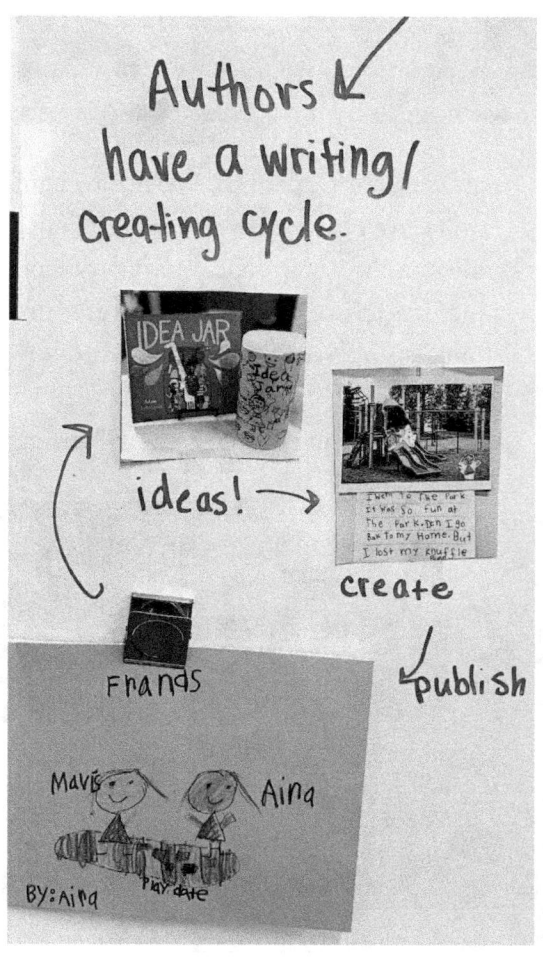

Now what? Transitioning to conceptual planning with a learning wall has been a game-changer in my classroom because it has enabled me to assist my learners in asking bigger questions and thinking more deeply. It has allowed our learning wall to encompass many different subjects that we are learning about at one time. The learning wall has also helped to put student voice and thinking in the forefront of our classroom. I hope that it helps my learners to feel and see that I value the learning they are doing. As I progress through my inquiry journey, I plan to continue implementing various thinking routines to facilitate deeper thinking, and I also would like to incorporate more student wonderings as we delve into different concepts. Additionally, I aim to include more documentation created by students, such as work samples, copies of their work, and photographs of students engaging in provocations.

Lindsey Hofheins
Pre-Kindergarten Teacher
Laurel Mountain Elementary | Austin, Texas

Learning wall intention: I work with a diverse group of four- and five-year-old pre-kindergarten students, most of whom are emergent bilingual students. The intention for this learning wall is to co-create a space to document students' growing knowledge and connections around stories. Although our units are typically about a month long, we explore the concept of stories throughout the school year, so this learning wall will stay on display, and we will add to it over the year.

What? I started by choosing questions to add to the wall that would provoke students in analyzing stories and expressing their thinking. Once the questions were on the wall, I added examples of work by authors and artists that students have been interested in and inspired by. Next I added student artifacts under each question. Students created

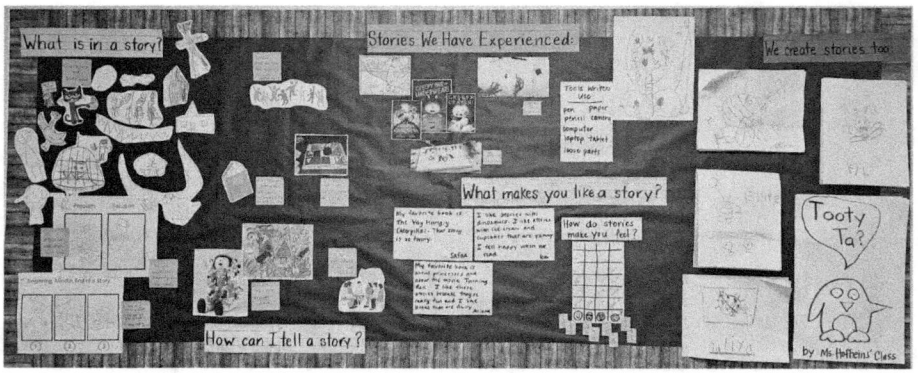

examples of story elements (character, setting, problem/solution) and expressed what they liked about stories and how stories made them feel. We created a class book modeled after a book we read and added that to our wall. As students created stories, I added to and edited the wall so it remained a living documentation of their understanding of stories.

Students were particularly enthusiastic about creating story elements to add to the wall. Drawing was an effective way to include emergent bilingual (and other) students whose written language is less advanced than their understanding around concepts.

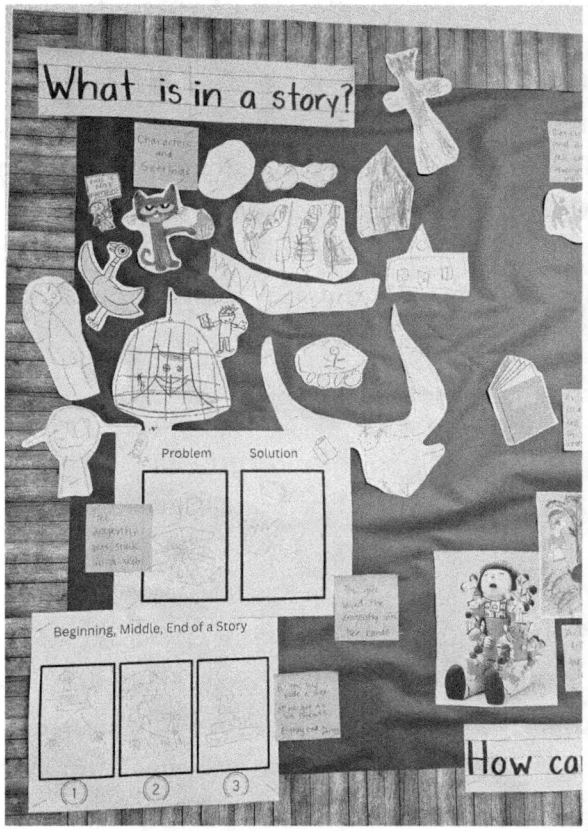

So what? Since adding student-created work to the learning wall, I often hear students using vocabulary from the wall (*character, setting, villain*) during play or while they create art. Once I began adding their stories to the wall, students also became excited to create more stories to share with classmates.

When we created the graph for the question *How do stories make you feel?* I included the feelings *bored* and *confused*. I had noticed some students struggling to understand the words and plots of some of the books we read together, and I wondered whether they would feel safe to name those feelings. Several students did so, and I reflected on what steps I could take to support them in better understanding the words in stories. I began creating targeted vocabulary lessons and taking more time to teach the language necessary for those connections to form. I have been pleased that it is helping those students.

Now what? So far I have focused on adding stories that students have written on paper to the wall. I am planning for opportunities to create stories with loose parts, video/audio, and through co-writing a script for a play we will perform, adding documentation of these to the learning wall. In a few weeks, we will have student-led conferences, and I am also planning to have students use the learning wall to help convey what they've learned about stories to their families.

Miho Vargo

Elementary School Japanese Language Teacher

The American School in Japan | Tokyo, Japan

Learning wall intention: My intention for my learning walls is to make the students' thinking and learning visible, illustrating their learning process. Also, I want it to foster a sense of belonging within the classroom, encouraging students to take ownership of their learning journey. By involving students in the decision-making process regarding what they learn, how they learn it, and what our next steps are, the wall becomes a collaborative space that reflects their curiosities, thoughts, questions, and discoveries. As I often gather my students in front of our learning wall to start the class, it also facilitates their reflection on their learning and thinking, addressing their Portrait of a Learner (PoL) competencies, as well as the Japanese language content.

I teach the Japanese language to students in grades one through five who are learning it as a heritage language. The common language used for communication and instruction in class is Japanese, but the students naturally flow in and out of both English and Japanese (or other home languages when there are students who speak them) and use their full linguistic repertoire in order to support their own conceptual understanding and meaning-making.

I'm sharing the Grade 5 unit called "Money and Consumption" in which students explored the concepts of value, perspectives, empathy, and their choices and responsibilities toward consumption and sustainability.

What? This photo was taken at the beginning of the unit (the tuning in phase). This unit was launched with a guest speaker sharing their stories of ethical consumption. It played the role of provocation to activate their curiosity and to share their prior knowledge and experiences related to the topic/concepts. My students are familiar with the thinking routine See, Think, Wonder, so they used it during their Turn and Talk, jotting their questions and wonderings on sticky notes. I listened to students' conversations, writing down their prior Japanese knowledge and skills and focusing on the vocabulary and the complexity of their sentence structures. At the end of the session, they also used a modified version of 3, 2, 1 Reflection to share three things they learned from the session, two feeling words in Japanese to describe their feelings based on what they learned, and one burning question they for sure want to explore. My anecdotal notes, what students wrote on their sticky notes, and their 3, 2, 1 Reflections were the artifacts collected because they told me what differentiated goals and instructions my students would need since their Japanese proficiency levels, including their abilities of kanji usage, vary. Also, these artifacts indicated what students were interested in, the connections they made, and what ideas and problems resonated with them, and they gave me some ideas for the next possible inquiry steps my students might want to engage in.

So what? The artifacts and evidence I collected from the thinking routines showed what ideas and problems resonated with the students from the guest speaker session. This gave me ideas about the topics my students might want to inquire into and possible resources to begin gathering for their inquiries. When I guided my students to make a decision on which forms of guided inquiry they preferred, they chose small group inquiries with others who had similar interests. Then they shared their questions and sorted them into shallow/deep questions using the inverted pyramid question routines as a group. For their Japanese language learning, I learned what extended vocabulary and sentence structures they needed to learn from the thinking and question routines and group discussions. I formed small groups who had similar language learning needs and integrated lessons during the finding-out phase.

The learning wall became their learning resource and a space where students naturally shared their learning, found connections, and discovered different perspectives. Since some artifacts were layered due to limited wall space, students often took them off of the wall to reflect on their learning and thinking and to give each other helpful feedback

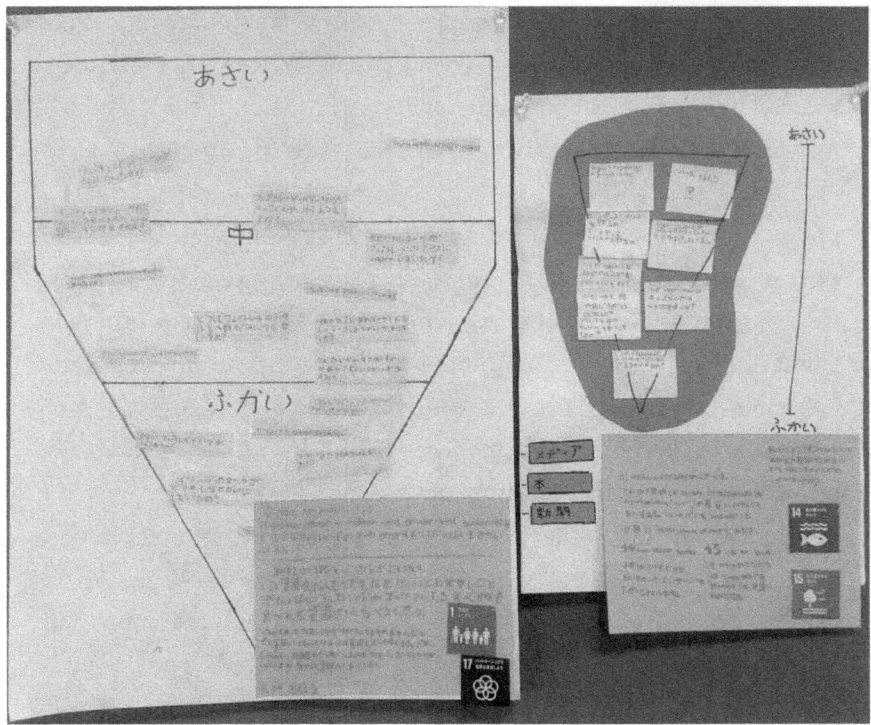

on other possible ways to deepen their learning. Also, reviewing the artifacts and evidence helped students recall their learning from the previous day or week. They used it to reflect on their learning journey, which helped them build a deeper understanding.

Since I teach different grade levels and they each have their learning wall, it's been fascinating to see how students from different grade levels are interested in other grade levels' learning walls. They enjoy finding connections with their own learning and also notice how everyone is working to develop the PoL competencies, regardless of their age. The learning walls with students' work, visuals, and photos help the students in different grade levels to deepen their understanding of how each competency might look in different contexts.

Now what? The next step after the question routine was to explore what resources and methods might help students gather information. Some mentioned interviewing experts within our school community and giving surveys to their classmates, parents, and guardians to collect data. They wrote letters and emails to people requesting interviews and asking for information (data collection), which turned out to be very authentic writing activities that will also help them in real-life situations. These showed me some of their writing abilities that weren't evident in other tasks planned for the unit. This is one of the reasons why I like learner-driven and teacher-guided/facilitated learning. Students can display what they can do with language that otherwise might not be apparent if I don't offer such an opportunity. As a result, I was able to adjust and prepare reading materials and videos that were more appropriate for their Japanese language proficiency levels and ages as they continued their investigation.

My students often find connections in their current units to their learning and thinking in previous units. I wish there were enough wall space to keep all of the learning walls visible. Since that's impossible, I'm thinking about leaving up photos of learning walls from previous units throughout the school year. Also, my students enjoyed sharing their learning journey and growth using their learning walls during the Leaders of Our Own Learning conferences (student-led conferences). I want to explore possible ways to co-construct learning walls with my students on digital platforms, such as Google Slides or the Seesaw app, for them to share their learning with their families concurrently with it happening in class.

The learning wall photo at the end of the unit

Stories of Assessment

Shannon Mills

Grade 2 Teacher

Colwood Elementary | Victoria, BC, Canada

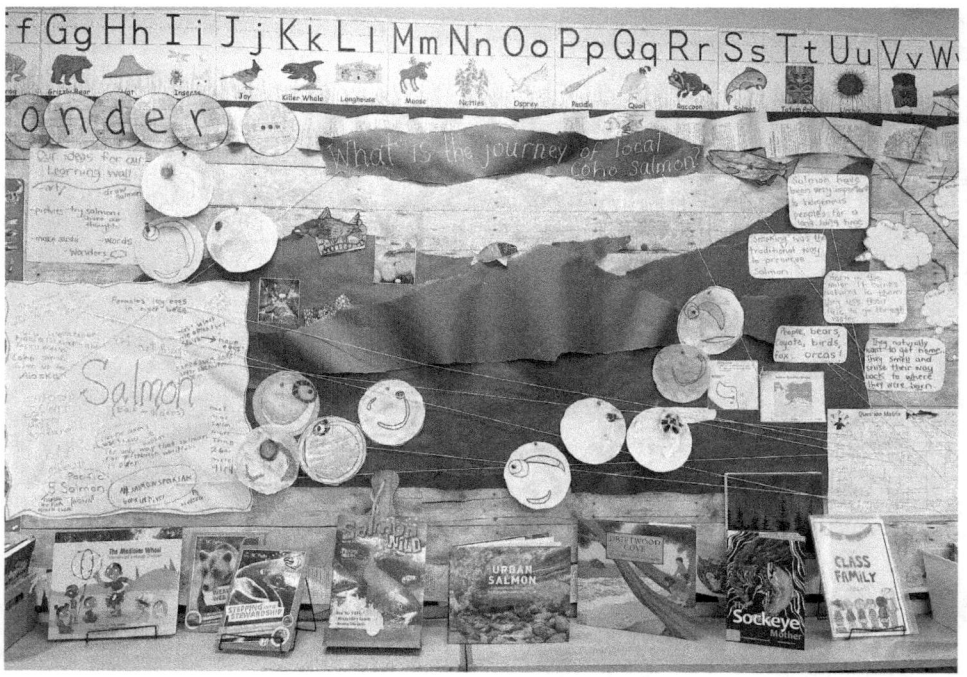

Learning wall intention: I am currently a Grade 2 teacher, in my seventh year of teaching but only my third full school year with the same class. I am very new to learning walls, but the inspiration was instant. Each year I teach, I have set intentions for myself focused around *What can I do better?* I never want to be stuck in a rut, teaching the same lessons with faded student examples from years past. The lessons I remember as a child are the creative, hands-on, "fun" lessons. *How can I bring the elements of fun and creativity into each day?* For this unit on salmon, I wanted the students to really understand and dive into each stage of the salmon life cycle, rather than just memorize it. I knew we would be going to see the salmon spawning in a local river, so our overall inquiry question was *What is the journey of our local coho*

salmon? We dug into this learning for about six weeks. I had taught a salmon inquiry last year with one of my first, very basic learning walls, so I had an inquiry plan and resources ready, but quickly drifted away from that as we explored the questions these students asked.

What? With any new skill or goal, you can't go in full force or you'll likely fail. My first few learning walls were very much teacher-created displays for the students, but I was incredibly proud of them! My intention of *What can I do better?* was being fulfilled by allowing the students to visualize more than a couple of days of schoolwork. I have two useable boards in my room, and due to time, I didn't change them very often. Using the space for learning walls allows the students to see that learning is a journey.

For my personal growth, my intention for the "Salmon" inquiry was to include more student voice. I began by asking the students what we should put on our learning wall. That was also the first time I started with the Question Matrix (which was a complete fail the first go, but we sought big buddy help, and we were able to foster some fantastic wonders). We discussed ways in which we could gather information (videos, experts, reading, prior knowledge). From there, salmon video provocations to create excitement, engaging livestreams of bears feeding on salmon in Alaska, and the reading app, *Epic!,* were always the go-to for research. When we came across something in a book or video that answered a wonder, I recorded it and connected it on our learning wall. (A future goal is to get students to do this more.) Because I wanted them to really understand each stage, we completed a directed draw of each part of the life cycle throughout this inquiry. Each one was finished with a different style of art (pastels, watercolor paint, pencil crayons, etc.) and, I feel, it was a beautiful way to connect subjects as well!

So what? This inquiry was a learning opportunity for me because we quickly learned most of our local salmon are chum, not coho, so we crossed out and edited our big question! In my past salmon inquiry,

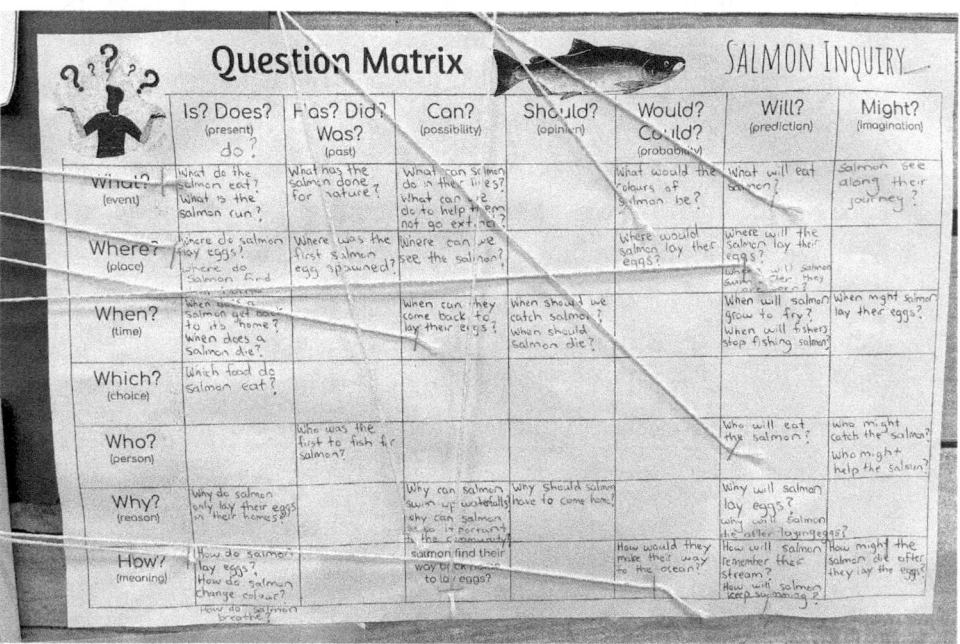

we just learned the life cycle and answered our wonder questions. This inquiry felt very different. The kids were truly invested. I felt we connected more to the land and our local area, and the field trip was a hit. They could name all of the stages through a full understanding rather than memorization.

To showcase our learning, I wanted to also try something new and build a classroom museum rather than just a final project. I shared some YouTube videos about what a museum is for some kids who hadn't been to one. They were over the moon excited to build our own! Throughout our learning, we brainstormed exhibits we could create for our families. We made clay salmon in our school kiln for art, which became an exhibit. One of our lessons was a salmon board game, so we set that up to play. We had watched many videos and documentaries, and they chose one to have playing quietly.

When I do an inquiry, I attempt to have it cross all subject areas the best I can. Throughout our journey, we recorded learning in an inquiry booklet and wrote reflections on our field trip; these were also set up for our families to read. The kids were buzzing with excitement to have their families in. As each day inched closer, as we made museum tickets to bring home. As the students built and set up habitats around the room, they were not only deepening their understanding but also growing more excited to share their learning. The learning wall was a massive part of our museum, and the students were able to walk their families along our journey.

Now what? The unit ended smoothly. Because it was focused around learning about the stages of the salmon life cycle, it ended as we learned about the spawning stage. Parents knew through our digital portfolios that we were learning about salmon, but they were glowing with pride seeing their children excited to show off and interact with the exhibits. I share with the kids that learning is never fully complete, so I do always leave some wonders unanswered. Not out of laziness or lack of time, but to be able to sit with some thoughts, to accept that we don't need to have everything answered. Much of my learning came through the students—watching how they interacted with the wall and considering what next steps I want to do for my growth. I am beyond proud of this inquiry; the kids are able to recall and make honest learning connections. When an Indigenous Elder came to visit four months later to share knowledge, the students were able to remember all five types of salmon.

I've made adjustments to my next learning wall. I am using thumbtacks instead of staples, because our garden inquiry is going to be a few months long. Artifacts will go up, be moved around, and come down for new ones to be added. I've added a space for more ongoing student connections, too, because I want students to be able to read and add at their own pace. This learning wall and museum inspired two of my close colleagues to begin their own journey with learning walls. A third colleague recently reached out asking for tips and where to begin. Start where you feel comfortable and grow each new learning wall slowly. Remember, I was very proud of my "teacher-created displays" for the students.

Sarah Scott

Primary Teacher (Years 1 through 6)

Scone Grammar School | Scone, NSW, Australia

Learning wall intention: The intention of our learning walls is to create a "third teacher" in the classroom. Our walls create a visual, and sometimes sensory, representation of our learning journey to help students make links throughout their investigations and spark emotive connections to experiences that support memory retrieval, helping to eliminate the "doorway effect." Our walls are used to create and display anchor charts with working examples that can be accessed, referred to, and transferred across different lines of inquiry or curriculum areas, providing a resource that promotes independence and agency within the classroom. Our walls symbolize our view of learning as a journey, our collaborative classroom culture, and the reflection that learning is not something we have to do alone.

What? Students co-construct purposeful learning that is displayed with the intention of it being shared, accessed, and used by everyone. Our walls guide our curriculum, provide insights into students' wonderings, interests, and understandings, and allow me as the teacher to plan for learning experiences that break down misconceptions and build up foundations of knowledge. Our walls give my students a voice, allowing their questions and curiosities to guide the learning process, and provide an outlet for them to celebrate, share, and contribute their discoveries.

As a primary teacher, I work with students aged five to twelve years, teaching across all curriculum areas, with class sizes ranging from twenty-four to twenty-eight students. This learning wall originated from our Year 1 (six-year-olds) English unit focused on themes of planet preservation and the environment. As we delved into various texts, students became increasingly curious and developed thought-provoking questions, ultimately leading to our overarching inquiry question: *What impacts do trees have on our environment?* This wall was co-constructed not only to visually document our learning journey but to help teach our younger learners the process of inquiry, including routines, structures, dispositions, and skills that they can refer to, build on, and practice throughout their schooling. The lengths of our units are dependent on student interest; however, this particular inquiry line continued for ten weeks.

So what? These photos were taken in the first weeks of our learning journey with these intentions:

1. Spark curiosity.
2. Tune in to establish student prior knowledge and existing theories.
3. Use student wonderings to develop questions.
4. Establish background knowledge, context, and foundations for students to build on.
5. Begin collaborative research to determine areas of interest and lines of exploration.

Because our younger students are still learning the inquiry process, routines, structures, dispositions, and skills required to be successful, this learning wall evidenced our co-constructed anchor charts. It included photographs, working examples, and student quotes that the children to refer to throughout the year.

Our previous English unit served as a fantastic provocation for igniting curiosity and wonder in our students, prompting them to draw connections to their past life experiences. The tuning in phase acted as a pre-assessment to gauge what my students already knew, exploring existing theories and identifying any misconceptions. For this, the students used loose parts to answer the question *What could the life of a tree look like?* Working in pairs, students were encouraged to collaborate and share their ideas, fostering teamwork and communication skills. Through play, they intentionally created stories that illustrated their understandings, expressed their thoughts and insights, and deepened their comprehension of the topic.

Our next step was to turn student wonderings into rich questions that could be used to guide our inquiry. We introduced a new questioning routine called the Question Formulation Technique in which students learned how to ask *thin* and *thick* questions. Using a picture provocation, students used their new co-constructed anchor chart and question starters to help craft rich questions that were explored together as a class. We incorporated student voices, pictures, and co-constructed examples onto the learning wall to serve as memory triggers, facilitating recall of the experiences whenever students referred to the wall.

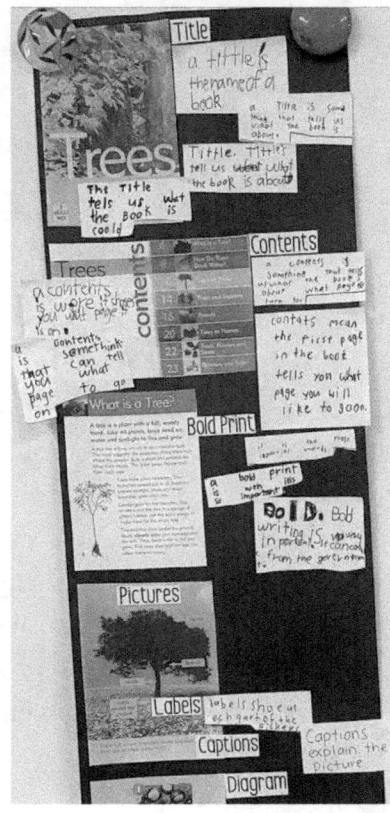

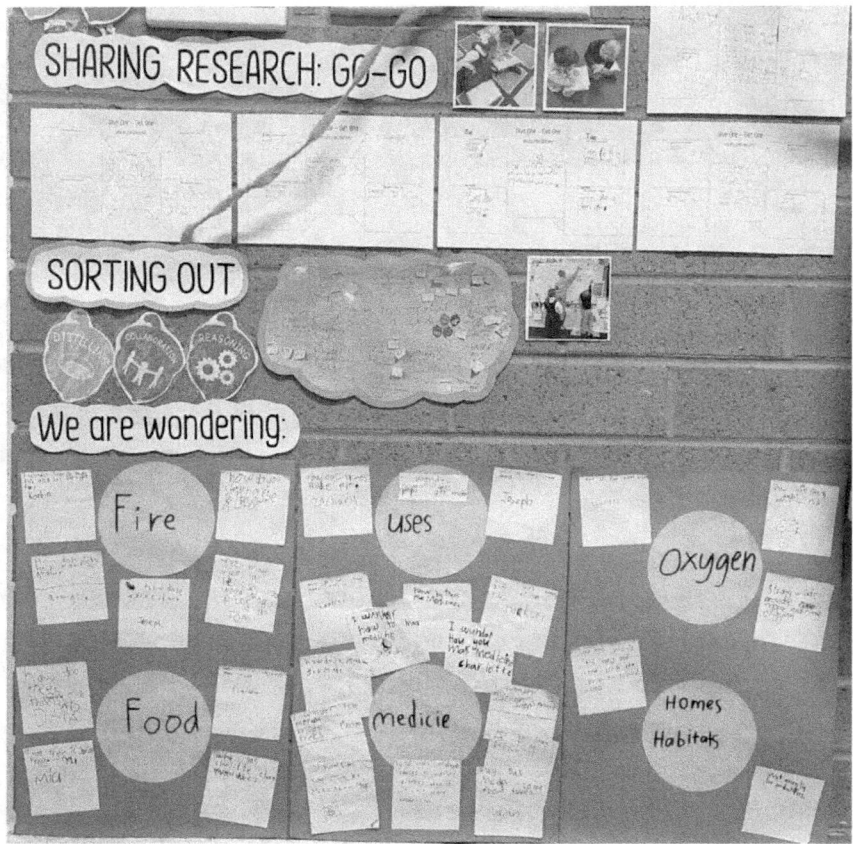

After reviewing the questions, the students chose *Why are trees so important?* to investigate. Students began to do some research, using note-taking and brainstorming skills learned in previous investigations. Embracing a student-centered approach, we took this opportunity to teach the students how to effectively use informative texts for research purposes, highlighting key features to look for when gathering information. A co-constructed anchor chart was placed on the wall next to student research notes. Student research was shared using the Give One, Get One visible thinking routine. Because this sharing prompted so much curiosity and wonder, students were asked to write their top two wonderings on sticky notes. As a class, we grouped the sticky notes into topic categories that determined our lines of investigation for the following weeks.

Now what? The evidence collected provided authentic insights into my students' understanding of the topic, enabling me to assess and plan for learning. The tuning in activity raised theories around life cycles, food, shelter, habitats, fire, and oxygen production, highlighting connections to previous units and life experiences. However, it also revealed some misconceptions for us to discuss and explore. The Give One, Get One routine not only allowed me to assess student research, comprehension, and communication skills but also highlighted topics sparking wonder and curiosity. Sorting class wondering questions with the Give One, Get One generated both data collection and a visual representation of student interest. These topics and student wonderings laid the foundations for our inquiry journey.

Although the wall's evidence highlighted a lot of interest around medicine, the students wanted to investigate fire first. We engaged in a What I Think and Wonder visible thinking routine to establish existing theories, misconceptions, and curiosities before embarking on a five-week investigation. Throughout this period, we addressed

and explored the students' questions while meeting syllabus requirements. Before diving in, we established context and foundational
understandings about fire to support ongoing learning. I provided
intentional investigative lessons that allowed students to research and
develop understandings, which they contributed to our research wall.
Positioned at student height, this learning wall enabled students to
add "quality" evidence they deemed important to the class's learning
journey. These interactive elements provided students with a sense of
voice, connection, and ownership over their learning, empowering
them to add, remove, and improve their learning over time.

It was fantastic to witness the students constantly referring
to and drawing connections with the foundational research as we
explored student questions and investigated various topics, including
Aboriginal and Torres Strait Islander uses for fire, the science behind
Burning Mountain, plants that require fire for survival, impacts of fire
on communities, cooking with fire, and fire safety. The students frequently interacted with their learning walls, retrieving evidence from
the wall and bringing it back to their desks or even dragging chairs or
mini whiteboards over to the wall to support their learning. Whenever
a student had a question, peers often directed them to the learning wall
first to seek answers. When visitors or parents came to the classroom,
students eagerly took them on "learning walks," sharing their learning
journey and celebrating their contributions.

As the teacher, my next step was to plan provocations for potential learning experiences. Because we were integrating our inquiry
unit with English, I reflected on the student questions about fire and
reviewed my syllabus to identify possible connections. I discovered a
variety of literacy texts that explored different aspects of fire, providing
excellent opportunities for creative and informative writing pieces. I
also considered provocations that would facilitate reflective and pro-
cedural writing experiences.

To ensure our inquiry journey was authentic, rich, and meaningful, I organized excursions that took students out of the classroom,

allowing them to engage with learning in different contexts. I wanted students to physically experience the learning, creating emotional connections and lasting memories. I arranged hands-on investigations, experiments, and experiences that contextualized learning and enabled students to play, explore, prove, and challenge their theories and ideas. We also explored the local community to investigate local connections, perspectives, and events, enriching our learning and providing deeper purpose. Most importantly, I prioritized giving my students time to play, question, learn, share, reflect, and draw connections between their experiences, ensuring their writing pieces were rich and meaningful reflections of their learning journey.

It was inspiring to witness how the students accessed and used the interactive components of the learning wall. Their engagement fostered a sense of ownership and connection that I am eager to enhance with learning walls. I'm left wondering about the most effective methods to display our learning to continue promoting and encouraging purposeful interactivity.

> Use this QR code to see Sarah's classroom and learning wall!

Tania Steenholdt
Prep/Early Years Teacher
Glen Huon Primary School | Glen Huon, Tasmania, Australia

Learning wall intention: To gather information about what the children are interested in or notice in a setting that we hadn't accessed regularly at that point. Collating artifacts on the board gave me the opportunity to reflect by myself and with the children at the end of our sessions and find common threads in terms of the pictures the children are drawing. The photos I have taken of what they are doing, finding, and are interested in, as well as snippets of conversations that we have had, provide me with useful data. Currently the interests and

learning are centered around classification of things we find out in the country—insects, animals, and plants. The children are also collecting data on birds they see when we visit.

I found a smaller board that I could transport and move to be with us Out on Country (in the bush or forest), so the coalition is immediate, and children can pin things to the board as/if they like. I also like the idea that I can place the board outside the classroom once we return so parents can see it and children can talk to them about it before and after school, sharing their learning experiences and ideas with their parents. It is impossible to ignore right at the entrance of the classroom, and parents are engaging with it. As drawings and photographs get moved off the wall because space is limited, they go into a

scrapbook for children and families to access inside the classroom—
bringing the outside learning into the classroom.

What? Initially I included on the board prompts for myself and the
children to enable me to link the learning inside with the learning outside. I printed a copy of an Acknowledgement of Country poster which
we reference to begin each week within the classroom. Including a copy
on the board means I can link this with the acknowledgment of the
traditional owners of the land on which we meet (Melukurdee people,
Aboriginal Tasmanian group) that I give when we are Out on Country.
During this time, we thank Country for what we can see, hear, touch,
taste, and feel around us. When we are outside, my Acknowledgment

tends to be less formal and more heartfelt, talking about custodianship and respect of the land we are sitting on, trying to include things that we see in nature as we sit together. I initially included the words to a song that we sing that is about respect for Country. We have been singing this together at the beginning of each week in class, but it is more poignant when we sing it outside amongst the trees, insects, and incredible birdlife of Southern Tasmania. These prompts also serve as information for families as they access the learning wall, and I include information about this in my daily communication to families.

On the first day, I pinned to the wall a data collection sheet with photos of local birds, so children could easily begin to collect data on what they were seeing in the space. They were very used to collecting data as part of our inside learning, so the link was relevant. I also offered the children drawing materials on the first visit with the wall, and their drawings and paintings went straight onto the wall that day. These additions to the wall gave us things to reflect on together at the end of the time there.

So what? The children have been encouraged to add things to the wall: leaves, flowers, or pictures of birds or insects they have seen. We round out our time on Country sitting in front of the wall reflecting on what we have seen together. Children are invited to collect an artifact to bring back to a basket for items to thank Country for. The children explain why it is meaningful to them as part of our oral language program. Later I add photographs of the children engaged in the outside space for them to reflect on with their families. One day a lot of pictures of insects and natural objects appeared by the end of the session. We talked about these together and spent some time sorting/classifying them—plants, animals, insects. This sparked meaningful conversations about their features, brought in numeracy through shapes and counting legs, literacy through initial sounds, science through habitat discussions, and the history of our traditional custodians.

For me, after the children go home, I spend some time reflecting on the wall, making transcripts of conversations we have had during our reflection time—I use voice memo to capture these because I am not fast enough to write down the conversations these days because the children's oral language and sharing of thinking with one another has just exploded! Sitting in front of the wall and the collection of artifacts in our "Thanking Country" basket, coupled with the voice memo recording, gives me an insight into what the children are interested in and thinking and learning about. The visual representation makes my planning of provocations a breeze because it is all laid out in front of me.

Now what? When I first took the children down to the bush space, my intention was that I would let them play and discover, and I would light a fire with them, tell stories, and teach them good techniques to make cubby houses. We have done none of those things because the children have shown clearly through their drawings, questions, and conversations that what they are interested in are the creatures that inhabit our bush space. This was surprising to me because I had never witnessed any interest in the insects that inhabit our kindergarten playground space. On reflection, the kindergarten playground space possibly doesn't lend itself to that kind of investigation.

My next steps will be to support them to explore the insects that we are seeing and help identify them. I will invite the children to explore and consider the habitats each creature prefers and offer them materials to allow them to show their understanding by making their own insect habitat, based on some we have found. I can easily incorporate numeracy and literacy into the learning as the opportunity arises— names of creatures, numbers of legs, keeping data of how many we have found. The children are *so* engaged in this learning, all I hear is my name being called to race over and see their latest discovery, or requests for magnifying glasses to inspect more closely their finds. The time goes so quickly, and I look around the space and see heads down, exploring, drawing, looking through books to identify their finds, and intense discussions. It is so authentic and purposeful.

What has also been interesting is the spontaneous drawings that have been occurring from members of the class who are usually reticent artists. I am surprised not only that they are choosing to draw but also by the skill they have shown in drawing their insects and creatures, compared with what I have seen of their drawings in the classroom.

The children have shown interest in a Melukurdee counting book, and a couple of children have suggested we make our own book based on what we have found in the bush space. I have tucked that idea away to explore closer to the end of the year. This may or may not happen, but it is an idea that we have parked, which has come from the children.

Erin Stewart
Teacher and MYP Coordinator
Somers High School | Lincolndale, New York

Figure 1: Connecting the Minds—Genre Study

Learning wall intention: This is my third year to teach tenth-grade English using an embedded honors model, meaning all students have an opportunity to seek honors distinction throughout the school year. Students have five tiered assessments, one essential learning summative, and one enrichment learning summative. If they choose to complete three of five enrichment option assessments, they can earn the honors distinction for the year.

My class also happens to be a co-taught class. What began as simply offering tiered summative assessments has evolved into tiered lessons and formatives. The goal is that all students have access to the enriched option through intentional instruction. My students complete a STAR (Standardized Testing and Reporting) examination multiple times each year, and I've learned that in addition to ten-plus individualized education program (IEP)/504s in my class, I also have a wide variety of reading and writing levels. We often provide further differentiated options.

Initially, my intention began as a way to use the learning wall as a third teacher and reinforce prior knowledge. *How does my environment support the values of a co-taught embedded honors model? How can all students access learning and practice the rigor and sophistication of skills needed for English pathways offered in eleventh- and twelfth-grade levels? How can I overcome the barrier of not "owning" the classroom space?* I often teach in multiple classrooms, and often different classrooms from year to year. I started my inquiry into learning walls in the 2022–2023 school year. What is in this document is the product of two years of action and reflection.

What? In this image, you can see students reflecting on skills and attributes (far right; this remains up throughout the school year); students maintain portfolios, and we conference often on growth in these skills and how we nurture learner attributes in successfully choosing strategies, setting, and achieving goals in English. The blue poster is for collaborative notes by students on their self-selected independent reading. Our community studies *The Catcher in the Rye* by J.D. Salinger, "Brutal" by Olivia Rodrigo (song), and *CODA* (film). We use this wall as a method of identifying text features, sharing the codes and conventions of the coming-of-age genre, and practicing skills of comparing and contrasting. Alongside the "Connecting the Minds" poster is a mind map or one-pager students completed to build consensus and explain patterns found within the genre.

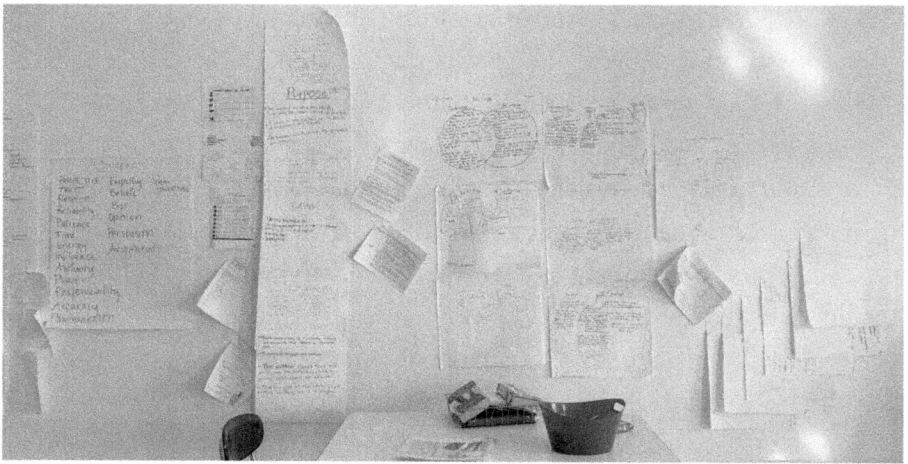

Figure 2: Rhetorical Analysis Unit (half way through the unit)

This collection of artifacts is made up of visible thinking routines (Venn diagrams, 3-2-1 Bridge, SPACECAT), a list of ongoing concepts that arise from classwork and discussion, as well as any and all handouts given out during class. The decision to include handouts is recent. I've noticed students, while technologically savvy, are not using our online platform well (absent or absent-minded/disorganized). Students are universally struggling with executive functioning, and the inclusion of these documents helps them recall prior knowledge as well as locate the correct documents from their folders. Furthermore, I notice more and more students feeling at liberty to leave their seats to refer to the wall as they begin to realize that the wall reflects our entire unit of study and supports them as they complete formative and summative assessments.

These newsletters are ungraded, student-generated work. I offered a model of September and often take pictures throughout the unit. When it comes time for select students to create the newsletter, they may choose what platform to use to create, how it will look, and what

to include. They often refer to the wall, and I sometimes provide them with a list of learning experiences (if requested) as well as pictures (students are not permitted to use their phones during class time).

I intended to share these newsletters with parents, but because this was brand new to our classroom culture, I decided to wait until next year to implement sharing with our larger community and include students in how to roll that out, using feedback from students this year as well as co-constructing this activity with students next year.

So what? My biggest takeaway has been watching students unlearn the rule of "sitting in desks" and how much the learning wall increases agency to use the room. I notice students practicing implicit skills to recall learning. I notice students in need of executive functioning support benefit from visual cues. The learning wall naturally includes this. I noticed students happily creating class newsletters and how accurate their recollections were when using the wall to support their reflection and documentation. I was surprised by the student newsletter led by students who often seemed off task!

I noticed the linear approach (Figure 2) seemed more accessible to students than the skills-based approach (Figure 1). They understood the objective and used the learning wall because they saw the progression of the lessons as opposed to seeing analysis and organization skills at work.

Now what? For two years, it has taken students almost five months before they feel at liberty to move freely about the classroom. It makes me wonder how else the space affects them and how we might provide resources for learning that de-center the classroom. I wonder about flexible seating in a secondary education classroom and how often collaborative routines are used to support the use of the space. I wonder what routines and rituals might further support executive functioning in the space and how to intentionally use the learning wall within daily instruction.

I wonder about including students in the construction of the learning wall. What would they have it look like if I explicitly shared what the wall was for? How could this be another opportunity for co-construction and student-driven learning? I wonder about how to make intentions/objectives of the wall more clear from day one. How to scaffold it to promote student use of the wall faster? I wonder how to use the wall more proactively as formative assessment for instruction. What protocols can I put in place as an educator? How might I use this with my collaborative teacher team? How can I include students in this type of assessment? Next, I will ask students to review and reflect on our year of learning together. We've been using Harvard's Project Zero Ladder of Feedback every unit, but I'd like them to offer me feedback about the class itself. Another protocol I like to use is Keep, Cut, Create. Perhaps we can conduct a gallery walk of various artifacts and newsletters. I often have them write a letter to next year's class. I wonder how I might include this feedback.

Stories of Virtual and Digital Learning Walls

Beth McCord

Lead Practitioner, Cross School Curriculum
Development and Training

Rachel Smith, Anne Davidson, Rhodri Smith

Heads of Digital Learning and Innovation
Thomas's London Day Schools | London, England, UK

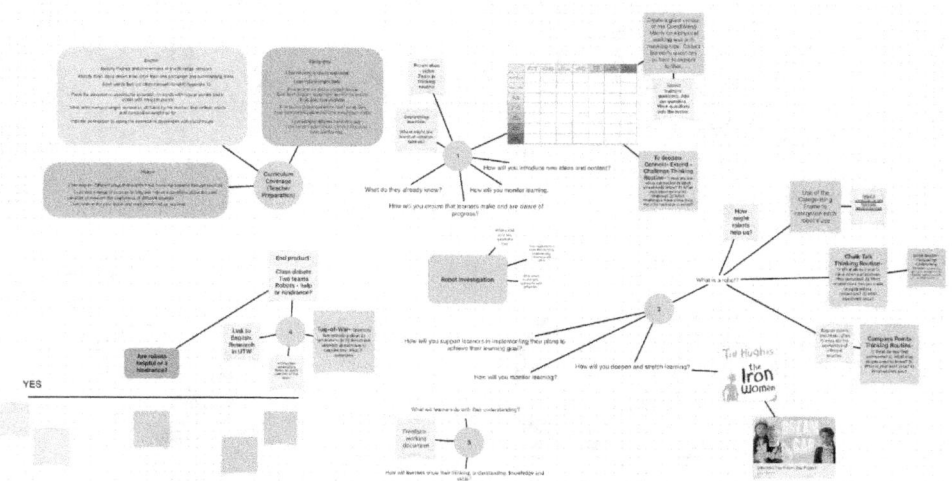

Learning wall intention: Part of my role at Thomas's is to help to bridge the gap between an enquiry mindset and digital technology so that these aspects of the curriculum are interwoven and not seen as two separate entities. This is achieved while working alongside the Heads of Digital Learning at Thomas's: Rachel Smith, Anne Davidson, and Rhodri Smith.

At Thomas's, we believe strongly that effective digital learning is intrinsic to creating successful twenty-first-century learners both in school and beyond the world of education. The digital vision is to see all pupils and teachers using technology to create engaging and innovative materials to support the development of thinking, questioning, and applying in an Enquiry Mindset curriculum. We want children to become problem solvers by considering the society in which they exist and collaborating to create design-oriented responses to local and global issues. Effective and meaningful use of iPads across the Enquiry Mindset curriculum has allowed us to take teaching and learning beyond the classroom walls, develop higher-order thinking skills, and design and deliver authentic learning experiences while ensuring the learning is accessible for all.

Once the idea to introduce digital working walls was born, we found that teachers were encouraged to plan with an enquiry mindset, but some were struggling to implement this effectively because of the constraints of traditional planning methods such as linear Word documents. We also noticed that teachers were more hesitant to use digital working walls with their learners because they were not fully confident in using them themselves. Digital working walls can be an effective way to build on teachers' thinking as well as to harvest ideas in a practical and collaborative way while building on their own digital skills. In the UK, the school year is broken up into three terms. The investigations/units of enquiry vary in length depending on the learning journey. This could range from a one-day to a one-week "Quest" or a longer investigation lasting five to fourteen weeks. For context, Quests are often standalone points in the academic year that focus on a "big" question or contemporary problem, and investigations have a big idea in the form of a catchy title and an essential question that prompts the learners to think deeply. These are centered around curriculum content that is relevant, significant, and empathetic. The example below was used to plan an investigation lasting approximately eleven weeks.

What? The photo above was taken of a digital working wall produced on Freeform during a collaborative planning session with the Year 4 teaching team at Thomas's Kensington. This was used by adults to explore and collect ideas for a new investigation/unit of enquiry around robots. The information collected was drawn from a group discussion using key questions as well as an awareness of the knowledge and skills to guide this piece and drive the unit. The digital working wall was broken down into five sections, which mirrored the learning journey.

Part of this discussion was around which thinking routines would be most beneficial to be used with the class to help make the learning visible and engaging, as well as to scaffold and support student thinking. The Question Matrix, a tool used to enable one to frame deeper questions, was already in place, and it was decided that the routine Connect, Extend, Challenge would be used to scaffold the conversation around the questioning. This would enable teachers and pupils to co-construct and guide learning as the investigation evolved by collecting and revisiting learners' questions. This would therefore work as an information harvest as well as inviting new thinking and challenges. Chalk Talk and Compass Points were suggested to deepen and stretch the learners. The latter would also assist learners with their next steps and ensure that it supports learners in implementing their plans to achieve their goals. Finally, Tug-of-War would pose the question *Are robots helpful or a hindrance?* This would enable a class debate that would help the children to draw on the knowledge and skills learned in the unit.

The provocations collected (book and video) were relevant and contemporary, and they would enable real-world links. They made the research meaningful while developing enquiry and digital skills.

So what? When teachers used the digital working walls to collect ideas, it was evident that it brought the learning journey to life, beyond the classroom walls, making the vision visible to all and removing the pressure of having to make planning perfect. When working on this digitally, it allowed for planning to be presented in an adaptable layout. Furthermore, it meant that one could add and refine information and ideas in real time, allowing one to tap into different viewpoints. It also allowed the ability to connect different types of media, such as photos, videos, website links, and PDFs with ease, which helped teachers to think about the learning as a moveable exploration rather than rigid and linear.

Creating a digital working wall with adults made evident that it ignited excitement and curiosity, which could then be transferred into the classroom setting to further engage the learners. The rich discussions were truly special and enabled connections between ideas to be formed. Clearly it honored both choice and voice while enabling increased motivation and engagement with the unit. Collaboration was a key focus of this; it provided each teacher with an active role in deciding what they would place on the working wall and how, thus demonstrating teacher agency. Through using the digital working wall, the understanding was considerably deep and reflective while making the learning journey adaptable, relevant, transferable, and personalized, because it helps to facilitate seamless adjustments based on feedback and evolving requirements while ensuring the learning is accessible for all.

The evidence demonstrates that teachers' use of technology in this meaningful way helps to create engaging and innovative materials to support the development of thinking and questioning. It also allows for teachers to build confidence in their digital skills while making the planning process visual, flexible, and versatile.

Now what? During collaborative planning sessions, it was noticed that although teachers were encouraged to use the physical wall space with their learners to produce working walls/learning walls, some were finding it more challenging to implement these effectively, primarily because of lack of space.

Although the idea is to use digital working walls collaboratively as teachers for lesson planning, the goal is to further embed the use of the digital working wall space with our learners across the curriculum. These can be an effective way to build on a learning journey because their portability ensures versatility and transferability between different subjects while addressing challenges with space.

Furthermore, it enhances accessibility for all learners, contributes to an environmentally conscious space, and seamlessly enables one to incorporate multimedia elements while still fostering collaboration with increased flexibility.

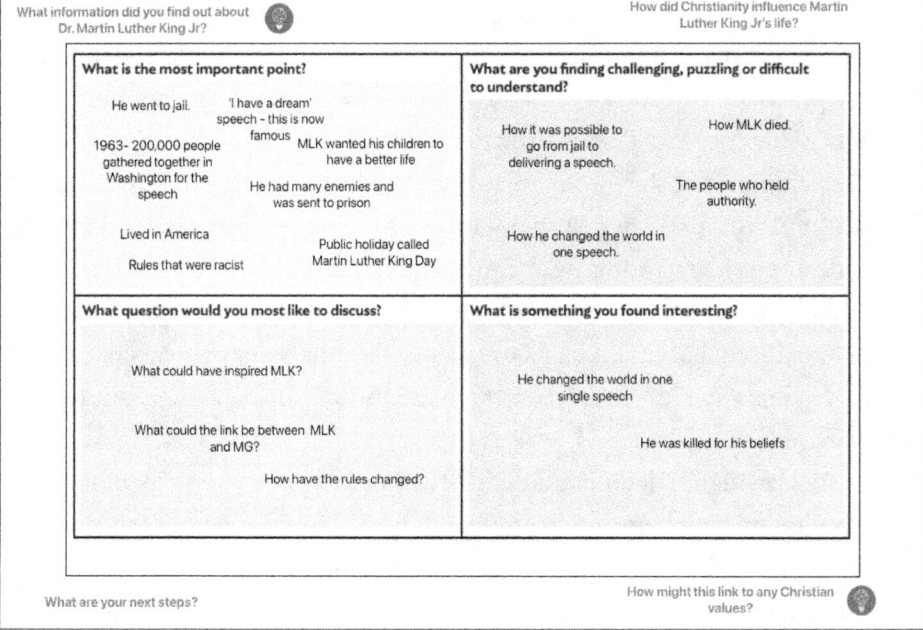

The image above uses the Take Note thinking routine to reflect on a video stimulus about Dr. Martin Luther King, Jr. The template was created by the teacher, and the children then built on this, as their digital working wall, as part of their learning journey. This was achieved with a Year 5 class at Thomas's Fulham.

Angela Stockman

Executive Director of Distance Education and Faculty
in the Department of Education

Daemen University | Amherst, New York

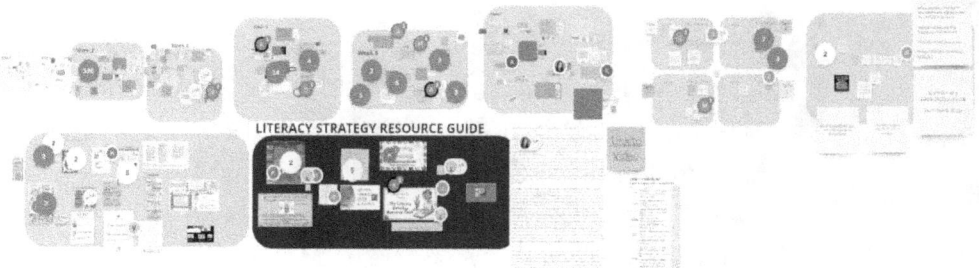

Sometimes we need to see things in color, zoom in a bit closer to notice the details, and pick up the nuances that help us try something new. Scan the QR Code to get a closer look at all of the learning walls featured in this book, including this one!

Learning wall intention: This learning wall was constructed for my SED 535/635 students. Inclusive Practices in Elementary Literacy is a hybrid graduate-level course that preservice and newly practicing teachers take online at Daemen University in Amherst, New York, to fulfill New York State requirements for their master's degrees in education. It was my intention that learners would use this wall to document, reflect on, and synthesize their learning as the semester unfolded. Our course was grounded in Duke and Cartwright's Active View of Reading (AVR), and the wall supported our exploration of that model as well as our findings as we did additional research and tested approaches in classrooms. Our learning wall was built in Miro. It was fifteen weeks long and spanned from September to December of 2023.

What? Our work on the wall began the first week of class, as learners were asked to research Duke and Cartwright's AVR, view some associated videos, and then capture artifacts of their own learning to add to our digital board, housed in Miro. Questions and expectations shifted a bit from week to week, but in general, our work on the learning wall was guided by prompts like these:

1. *How has your thinking, learning, or your work in the field changed this week as a result of your learning?* Share a photo, a screenshot, a video, or any other artifact that captures this important learning moment or how it has changed you.
2. *How will you know if you've done high-quality work?*
   - The images or videos you share on Miro will help viewers understand how your thinking, learning, or work in the field is changing as a result of your learning.
   - The written reflection that accompanies your Miro post will speak to this shift or change and reference the learning experiences that caused it.
   - You will have submitted thoughtful questions—related to each of our reading selections—that might be used to drive next week's discussions and reflections on our learning wall.
   - You will feel confident that you are prepared to engage in an evidence-based discussion that references these works and the content shared on our learning wall in next week's class.

Early in the semester, the artifacts added to the board were the work of single learning moments that did not yet connect to others. You may notice how, over time, their reflections become more thoughtful, evidence-based, and connected to previous learning and work. If you look at week seven, for instance, you'll see how they are copying content from prior work on the wall and recontextualizing it. Although our wall is a bit more linear than those I use on the ground, in my face-to-face courses, learners still made connections between pieces of it. You will notice how arrows can be added from the menu on the right. During many classes, groups worked together to use those arrows, much as we might use string on the ground. They connected elements of the board together and reflected those connections. Arrows were eventually removed so we could see the content clearly again.

So what? I've invited my students to document their learning in a variety of ways over the last several decades. We've used portfolios, scrapbooks, notebooks, reflection journals, Google Slides, Google Drive, Storypark, SeeSaw, Unrulr, and now, Miro.

I've learned much that is surprising about the influence of tools on how learners document, organize, and interpret their learning. They truly matter. Tools that invite the collaborative creation of a wall invite a sort of shared curation, synthesis, and interpretation that I haven't experienced before. The *wall* matters. It becomes a community square of sorts—we are all gathered in the same space at the same time, and we can see one another. We face one another. That's not how Slides or Instagram or Seesaw or other tools work.

What's more, using a digital tool like Miro invites the use of multimedia documentation, and this has deepened our inquiry work as well as our ability to represent our thinking in just-right ways. When I build walls in my physical classroom, using physical tools, I notice that we rely on print a great deal. We still do in the digital space, too. However, students were more inclined to drop links out to other artifacts, include photos they themselves took, and comment more frequently and freely. I feel that the digital wall is more efficient to build, and it allows for the quick and painless addition of content. The example I've shared [on the next page] is one that a student drew and then linked to sources.

This semester, I've built a physical wall in another class. Because I share this room with many other instructors, the wall has been hard to maintain. People keep taking it down, and when they do, items are torn. Sticky notes fall off and are lost. I don't like taping them down because I want them to move. It's been a bit of a nightmare. So . . . I asked students to return to the wall and pull down or otherwise document the elements that we need to preserve as we move to a digital wall. I've made this choice because the physical wall is not sustainable in this space. I said, "This wall has served our beginnings in this class. Our early thinking is documented well here. Now, it's time to start the last leg of our journey in this class. We're going to take this wall down. We will be carrying just a few pieces of it into this third and final act of our course. . . . We're moving to Miro to do that, for the sake of my sanity."

Source: Allison Jahr

Now what? All of this leaves me wondering about the impact of the learning environment, space, and tools on the quality of our collective inquiry and collaborative learning. As I explained above, I noticed that the *wall* seems to matter. Not a feed. Not a stream. The wall. If it's my purpose that learners will not only document their learning but engage in collaborative learning, work, and interpretation—especially if they're going to seek diverse perspectives—we need a space that invites to "circle up" or "circle around" and not just post in a feed, stream, or in an otherwise isolated and linear fashion. Digital spaces like Miro also invite diverse perspective taking. For instance, I can invite you or others in my learning community into the room to apply different lenses, from different vantage points, to our work. I plan to continue using Miro to build learning walls in the future. I also intend to continue using Unrulr—a tool that functions differently and in a more linear/feed sort of fashion—to invite my students to document their learning. It seems to me that for my purposes, all learning walls in my world include documentation of learning. Not all documentation efforts are about creating a shared, collaborative learning wall, though. I wonder which experiences serve learners best. Do we need to do both? Is the wall enough? I'm curious about this now.

You've read personal accounts and honest sharing from school leaders modeling thinking routines and inquiry moves that empower their adult learners, classroom teachers with many years of experience in facilitating an inquiry practice, early years educators who've carefully balanced opportunities for independence and agency with mindful modeling skills and lesson objectives, as well as educators just getting started with their inquiry practice and leveraging learning walls as a way of stretching their practice in new ways.

By now, you must recognize that reflection is a main driver of learning walls and what makes these vertical spaces stand out from a traditional display of learning. Anchoring the inquiry cycle helps us make sense of the interactions, experiences, questions asked, and conversations before us. As you reflect on the stories of learning journeys generously included in this section, I wonder what new connections you are making with the tenets of a learning wall and the sketchnote I introduced to you in Part Two of this book. What plans you have for your process and systems of documentation? How will you use the resources here to support you in your next steps on your journey with this refreshed process of documentation? Throughout this publication, I have asked you to share your process with a wider audience using #learningwalls. I encourage you to do that as you dig into these resources and apply ideas from the examples into your own setting.

Concluding with a Call to Action

The moment you decided to build a learning wall, you chose to value the process of learning. You accepted the truth that it is within your control to approach your practice in a manner that engages scholars in meaningful ways. You know deep in your core that although *tasking* and *telling* are easier, those actions lead to disengaged students and surface-level thinking.

Learning walls transform our classrooms by empowering scholars to drive the learning, thereby reducing cognitive resistance.

Learning walls tell all learners they are capable.

Learning walls nurture cultures of thinking, encourage mindsets of awe, and bring schools together as communities.

Learning walls bridge different generations, experiences, and backgrounds by offering a communal language that invites and extends conversations and connection.

Learning walls lift the weight of *not doing enough* that educators so often carry.

One of the biggest mistakes we make as educators and leaders is assuming that we have to do it all alone. We strive to check all the boxes and cover all the material, hoping we'll eventually, finally *arrive*. We mistakenly believe that creativity only lives in in *fun* spaces—art and music rooms, Makerspaces, early years halls, or Genius Hours—and that there's too much work to do for that kind of messy learning. Feeling the pressure to get it *all* done, we tell ourselves, *Yeah, but standards simply don't allow space to pause.* Or, *Yeah, it would be great to add a little playfulness to the classroom, but we have to stay focused and master those disciplines to be ready for the assessment.*

These *yeah, but . . .* hesitations are, in fact, the very indicators we need to create and explore more. They are why we need to model a sense of playfulness. We must rediscover what passion for our craft and balance as a human means—because the better attuned we are to ourselves, the better we can tune in to our learners' needs. The more we push pause to reassess deliberate moves we make to demonstrate that we value student agency, creativity, collaboration, communication, and community, the more our learners can push play.

Although the title of this last chapter is "A Call to Action," my hope is that while you've been reading you've been tinkering with ideas. I hope you've already experienced some success with what you've applied, learning through trial and error as you've befriended the lessons and shared new practices with peers. Perhaps you've been inspired, as I have, by the other educators featured within these pages to try something new. While drafting this manuscript, I revisited chapters, pinned photos for reference, and used the structures and steps outlined in each of the steps to building a learning wall to guide my understanding and reflection. In the same way, I hope you'll return to this book to support your learning journey the same way you would seek out a critical thought partner and friend.

As you conclude your reading, consider the story of learning you are telling with your documentation. If storytelling is about human connection, what do the artifacts, the placement of evidence, and the collection of thinking reveal? How do they illustrate your values and what's worth learning? Just as importantly, using the evidence before them, what stories of self-discovery, insights, growth, or aha moments might your learners tell?

 Use this QR code to download the Story of a Learning Journey resource whenever you need clarity in your documentation process, want to reflect on progress over time, or are collaborating with thought partners. Whether you use the prompts to spark conversations or for quiet reflection, I'm confident you'll uncover a clear path forward in your documentation journey!

This book, these educators, and the inquiry community are here to support you. But as with all good stories, your journey will have unexpected twists, relatable themes, and moments of tension that bring just the right lessons to the surface at just the right time. I have a quiet confidence that by the time this book has found its way into your hands, it will be the vehicle you need to craft a learning story that's bursting with a plot, filled with agency, curiosity, community, reflection, and self-awareness.

I look forward to hearing your stories—the ones you rewrite for yourself, the ones you co-author with your students, and the ones that bring the magic and wonder back into your habits, thinking, and actions.

What are you waiting for? It's time to turn the page . . . and start building.

Bibliography and Suggested Reading

Agarwal, Pooja K, and Patrice M Bain. *Powerful Teaching: Unleash the Science of Learning*. Jossey-Bass, 2019.

Berger, Warren. *A More Beautiful Question: The Power of Inquiry to Spark Breakthrough Ideas*. Bloomsbury USA, 2014.

Boyden, Joseph. *Three Day Road*. Penguin Canada, 2005.

CODA. Apple Original Films, 2021.

Costa, Arthur L, and Bena Kallick. *Discovering & Exploring Habits of Mind*. Association for Supervision and Curriculum Development, 2000.

Duke, N. K., and K.B Cartwright. Active View of Reading Graphic: "The Science of Reading Progresses: Communicating Advances Beyond the Simple View of Reading. *Reading Research Quarterly*, 56(S1), S25–S44. 2021. https://doi.org/10.1002/rrq.411.

Dweck, Carol S. *Mindset: The New Psychology of Success*. New York: Random House, 2006.

Frith, Alex, and Alice James. *Big Questions About the Universe*. Usborne Publishing, 2022.

Grant, Adam. *Hidden Potential: The Science of Achieving Greater Things*. Viking, 2023.

Grant, Adam. *Think Again: The Power of Knowing What You Don't Know*. Penguin Books, 2021.

Halbert, Judy, and Linda Kaser. *Leading Through Spirals of Inquiry: For Equity and Quality*. Portage & Main Press, 2022.

Hammond, Zaretta L. *Culturally Responsive Teaching and The Brain: Promoting Authentic Engagement and Rigor Among Culturally and Linguistically Diverse Students*. [S.l.]: SAGE Publications, 2015.

MacKenzie, Trevor, and Rebecca Bushby. *Inquiry Mindset: Elementary Edition—Nurturing the Dreams, Wonders, & Curiosities of Our Youngest Learners*. Elevate Books Edu, 2019.

MacKenzie, Trevor. *Inquiry Mindset: Assessment Edition—Scaffolding a Partnership for Equity and Agency in Learning*. Elevate Books Edu, 2021.

MacKenzie, Trevor. *Inquiry Mindset: Questions Edition—Cultivating Curiosity and Creating Question Competence*. Elevate Books Edu, 2024.

Murdoch, Kath. *The Power of Inquiry: Teaching and Learning with Curiosity, Creativity and Purpose in the Contemporary Classroom*. Seastar Education, 2015.

"Project Zero." Homepage | Project Zero. http://pz.harvard.edu/.

Ritchhart, Ron, and Mark Church. *Power of Making Thinking Visible: Using Routines to Engage and Empower Learners*. Jossey-Bass, 2020.

Ritchhart, Ron, Mark Church, and Karin Morrison. *Making Thinking Visible: How to Promote Engagement, Understanding, and Independence for All Learners*. Jossey-Bass, 2011.

Robinson, Ken, and Lou Aronica. *Creative Schools: The Grassroots Revolution That's Transforming Education*. Penguin Books, 2015.

Rodrigo, Olivia. "Brutal." *Sour*. Geffen Records, 2021.

What Ed Said (blog), https://whatedsaid.wordpress.com/.

Salinger, J.D. *The Catcher in the Rye*. 1951. Reprint, Little, Brown and Company, 2009.

Silvia Rosenthal Tolisano, and Janet A Hale. *A Guide to Documenting Learning: Making Thinking Visible, Meaningful, Shareable, and Amplified*. SAGE Publications, 2018.

Wieber, Frank, et al. "Promoting the translation of intentions into action by implementation intentions: behavioral effects and physiological correlates." *Frontiers in Human Neuroscience* Vol. 9, 395. July 14, 2015, https://pmc.ncbi.nlm.nih.gov/articles/PMC4500900.

Wexler, Natalie. *The Knowledge Gap: The Hidden Cause of America's Broken Education System—and How to Fix It*. Avery, 2019.

Wheatley, Margaret J. *Turning to One Another: Simple Conversations to Restore Hope to the Future*. Berrett-Koehler Publishers, 2002.

Wheatley, Margaret J. *Who Do We Choose to Be?: Facing Reality, Claiming Leadership, Restoring Sanity*. Berrett-Koehler Publishers, 2017.

Wiggins, Grant, and Jay McTighe. *Understanding by Design*. 2nd ed. Alexandria, Va.: Association for Supervision and Curriculum Development, 2005.

Yeager, David. *10 to 25: The Science of Motivating Young People; A Groundbreaking Approach to Leading the Next Generation—And Making Your Own Life Easier*. Simon and Schuster, 2024.

Acknowledgments

Writing a book for the second time may come with a sense of familiarity, but it is by no means without its challenges. The process still brings unease, self-doubt, and the ongoing task of collecting evidence, refining ideas, and *thinking again*—something author and organizational psychologist Adam Grant reminds us to do often.

Though my name stands alone on the cover, this book is far from a solo endeavor. It exists because of the countless individuals I've had the privilege of learning from, the experiences I've gathered as a school leader and educational consultant, and the books that have shaped and inspired me. Everyone who has played a part is woven into these pages.

To my house full of boys—your loving patience, unwavering encouragement, and boisterous zest for adventure continue to inspire me. You remind me daily of what it means to live out loud and embrace curiosity.

Never did I imagine that my work would reach the far corners of the world, let alone that it would be met with the energy and passion that Tania Steenholdt brings to children in the early years. Tania, thank you for your fearless dedication to creating richly curious spaces for students, for your Tasmanian moon photos, and for being both a critical thought partner and a dear friend. Our ongoing exchanges are a gift.

To Erica Thompson—our hours of co-working, co-writing, and exchanging wonderings have been invaluable. Your ability to synthesize ideas into the most beautiful one-liners, your tireless effort to create space for more voices, and your deep love for words never go unnoticed. Wherever your next journey leads, I look forward to continuing to learn alongside you.

Kristen Martin, your unwavering commitment to putting learners first is truly inspiring and a testament to the power of leading with a lens of inquiry. Your leadership strikes a masterful balance—challenging learners to stretch beyond their edges while fostering a thoughtful culture where everyone feels their expertise is honored and valued. Beyond that, you have been a critical thought partner, pushing ideas further with insight, curiosity, and care. Your dedication creates an environment where learning and growth flourish, and I am deeply grateful for the impact you make every day.

Thank you, Ryan Bear, for continually bringing such playful and vibrant images to life in a way that allows big concepts and ideas to stick a little longer. Your illustrations add depth, joy, and wonder to each page, making this body of work and research not just something to read, but something to experience.

Bringing the curiously brilliant minds of Becky Carlzon, Trevor MacKenzie, and Kath Murdoch into my world has pushed my practice and thinking to whole new heights. I'm so grateful for the way you challenge, inspire, and stretch my ideas while keeping curiosity at the center of it all. Learning alongside you has been an absolute gift!

To the educators, outdoor spaces, students, and families at Laurel Mountain Elementary—you have given me the opportunity to stretch toward new edges. The time spent in this not-so-little neighborhood school has been nothing short of magical.

And to those who have so vulnerably opened the four walls of your vertical spaces in this book—thank you. Erin Boughner, Sarah Scott, Matt Fletcher, Fiona Hudson, Graham Laing, Trevor MacKenzie, Alona Yildirim, Becky Carlzon, Catherine Place, Erica Thompson, Kristen Martin, Paige Driscoll, Tiffany Keske, Lindsey Hofheins, Shannon Mills, Tania Steenholdt, Erin Stewart, Beth McCord, Rachel

Smith, Anne Davidson, Rhodri Smith, William Polan, Mary Rimbey, Lousia d'Arille, Miho Varga, Amanda Carroll, Megan Cera, Angela Stockman, Colleen Ruplinger, Amy Osborn, Nicole Levitan, Ashley Bodnar, Karen Myrick, Amy Ing, Samantha Jorgans, Taylor Meister, Continental Colony Elementary, Beaufort Delta Education Council, Tarvin Elementary, and Natomas Unified School District—your willingness to share your questions and inquiry-driven practices has expanded my thinking, nudged me to research further, and reinforced the power of leading with a lens of inquiry.

This book is a reflection of all of you. You have my sincere gratitude.

More From
Elevate Books EDU

Leading with a Lens of Inquiry
Cultivating Conditions for Curiosity and Empowering Agency
By Jessica Vance

Typical models of training and professional development focus on telling. It's a model that far too often
trickles down to classrooms where the traditional way of "doing school"
limits the way educators teach and students learn. Fortunately, there
is a better way to learn: through wonder, agency, and inquiry. From
Leading with a Lens of Inquiry, administrators, educational instructors,
and peer leaders learn how to cultivate learning spaces that ignite curiosity and inspire critical thinking in adult and student learners alike.

Dive into Inquiry
Amplify Learning and Empower Student Voice
By Trevor MacKenzie

Dive into Inquiry beautifully marries the voice and
choice of inquiry with the structure and support
required to optimize learning. With *Dive into Inquiry*,
you'll gain an understanding of how to best support your learners as
they shift from a traditional learning model into the inquiry classroom
where student agency is fostered and celebrated each and every day.

Inquiry Mindset: Elementary Edition
Nurturing the Dreams, Wonders, and Curiosities of Our Youngest Learners
By Trevor MacKenzie and Rebecca Bushby

Inquiry Mindset: Elementary Edition offers a highly
accessible journey through inquiry in the younger

years. Learn how to empower your students, increase engagement, and accelerate learning by harnessing the power of curiosity. With practical examples and a step-by-step guide to inquiry, Trevor MacKenzie and Rebecca Bushby make inquiry-based learning simple.

Available in English, French, Latin American Spanish, and European Spanish

Inquiry Mindset: Assessment Edition
Scaffolding a Partnership for Equity and Agency in Learning
By Trevor MacKenzie

Trevor MacKenzie takes another deep dive into inquiry as he examines the role of assessment in education through the lens of co-designing and co-constructing with students. In *Inquiry Mindset: Assessment Edition*, he outlines the beliefs, values, and frameworks that allow teachers to scaffold assessments infused with student voice, understanding, and autonomy.

Inquiry Mindset: Questions Edition
Cultivating Curiosity and Creating Question Competence
By Trevor MacKenzie

The Question Routines and teacher insights in *Inquiry Mindset: Questions Edition* provide a framework that you and your students can use to craft, organize, and justify questions. Effective across grade levels and subject areas, the strategies MacKenzie provides will empower you to bring fresh excitement and engagement to the learning experience.

Getting Personal with Inquiry Learning
Guiding Learners' Explorations of Personal Passions, Interests and Questions
By Kath Murdoch

In *Getting Personal with Inquiry Learning*, world-renowned inquiry expert Kath Murdoch draws on decades of experience to offer a thorough, practical guide to supporting young learners' investigations into their passions, interests, and questions. Following on from the best-selling Power of Inquiry, this book invites teachers to take their thinking about inquiry to the next level and to truly honor both their own and their students' agency.

From Agency to Zest
A Journey through the Landscape of Inquiry
By Kath Murdoch

The delightfully thought-provoking words in this exploration of inquiry-based learning embody the essence of inquiry. Designed to be used to initiate reflection and to provoke professional dialogue amongst educators, *From Agency to Zest* offers insight into inquiry as an approach to teaching and learning. In addition to the explanations provided throughout, Murdoch offers practical advice on how to support and deepen professional learning experiences within and across schools.

Outsmarted
The Changing Face of Learning in the Era of Smartphones and Technology
By Lisa Green

In *Outsmarted*, educator Lisa Green considers the impact of today's rapidly advancing technology on children's and teens' mental and emotional development. Green navigates the complex journey of preparing learners to succeed in a high-tech world. She offers practical approaches to smartphone management, skill-building, and assessment in today's classroom.

Leveraging Deep Learning: Strategies and Tools for Assessment of Conceptual Understanding
By Tania Lattanzio and Andrea Müller

This indispensable guide, coauthored by the expert consultants at Innovative Global Education (IGE), empowers you to transform assessment practices. You'll discover tools and strategies to empower assessment-capable learners as you shift the focus from assessing knowledge to evaluating and transferring conceptual understanding.

Taking the Complexities Out of Concepts
By Tania Lattanzio and Andrea Müller

This practical resource designed by Innovative Global Education (IGE) helps educators shift from a content-based curriculum to a conceptual curriculum. Teaching through concepts provides context that leads to the transferability of knowledge. Using the strategies and ideas in *Taking the Complexities Out of Concepts,* students will develop connections to and a deep understanding of the material.

The AI Infused Classroom
Inspiring Ideas to Shift Teaching and Maximize Meaningful Learning in the World of AI
By Holly Clark

With the right mindset, the right questions, and the right strategies, you can use AI to create and broaden meaningful learning experiences for every student. In *The AI Infused Classroom*, Holly Clark points out that students need well-trained educators now more than ever to ensure they are prepared for the world of AI. This book equips you to navigate the latest iteration of edtech.

The Google Infused Classroom
A Guidebook to Making Thinking Visible and Amplifying Student Voice
By Holly Clark and Tanya Avrith

This beautifully designed book offers guidance on using technology to design instruction that allows students to show their thinking, demonstrate their learning, and share their work (and voices!) with authentic audiences. *The Google Infused Classroom* will equip you to empower your students to use technology in meaningful ways that prepare them for the future.

The Microsoft Infused Classroom
A Guidebook to Making Thinking Visible and Amplifying Student Voice
By Holly Clark and Tanya Avrith

Packed with ideas you can use in your classroom tomorrow, *The Microsoft Infused Classroom* equips you to use powerful tools that put learning first. Edtech experts led by Holly Clark and Tanya Avrith show you how to use technology to increase engagement in your classroom and provide authentic opportunities for students to share their work and their voice.

The InterACTIVE Class: Creation in a World of AI
Empowering Educators to Inspire Creativity and Innovation in an AI-Driven Classroom
By Joe and Kristin Merrill

Whether you are a seasoned educator or just beginning your teaching journey, this guide has the tools and insights you need to nurture the next generation of thinkers, creators, and innovators. With 40+ lesson plans and unlimited possibilities, you'll be prepared to navigate the ever-evolving technological landscape with confidence!

The InterACTIVE Class
Using Technology to Make Learning more Relevant and Engaging in the Elementary Classroom
By Joe and Kristin Merrill

In this practical and idea-packed book, coauthors, classroom teachers, and edtech experts Joe and Kristin Merrill share their personal framework for creating an interACTIVE classroom. You'll find new ways to inspire young learners to grow and to develop grit as they stretch their thinking and abilities.

Sketchnotes for Educators
100 Inspiring Illustrations for Lifelong Learners
By Sylvia Duckworth

Sylvia Duckworth is a Canadian teacher whose sketch-notes have taken social media by storm. Her drawings provide clarity and provoke dialogue on many topics related to education. This book contains 100 of her most popular sketchnotes with links to the original downloads that can be used in class or shared with colleagues. Interspersed throughout the book are Sylvia's reflections on each drawing and what motivated her to create it, in addition to commentary from other educators who inspired the sketchnotes.

How to Sketchnote
A Step-by-Step Manual for Teachers and Students
By Sylvia Duckworth

Educator and internationally known sketchnoter Sylvia Duckworth makes ideas memorable and shareable with her simple yet powerful drawings. In *How to Sketchnote,* she explains how you can use sketchnoting in the classroom and that you don't have to be an artist to discover the benefits of doodling!

40 Ways to Inject Creativity into Your Classroom with Adobe Spark
By Ben Forta and Monica Burns

Experienced educators Ben Forta and Monica Burns offer step-by-step guidance on how to incorporate this powerful tool into your classroom in ways that are meaningful and relevant. They present 40 fun and practical lesson plans suitable for a variety of ages and subjects as well as 15 graphic organizers to get you started. With the tips, suggestions, and encouragement in this book, you'll find everything you need to inject creativity into your classroom using Adobe Spark.

The HyperDoc Handbook
Digital Lesson Design Using Google Apps
By Lisa Highfill, Kelly Hilton, and Sarah Landis

The HyperDoc Handbook is a practical reference guide for all K–12 educators who want to transform their teaching into blended-learning environments. *The HyperDoc Handbook* is a bestselling book that strikes the perfect balance between pedagogy and how-to tips while also providing ready-to-use lesson plans to get you started with HyperDocs right away.

About the Author

With a professional teaching and leadership background in both private and public international schools (IB PYP Educator and PYP Coordinator), **Jessica Vance** brings a unique perspective to her role as enrichment and environment coordinator. Her passion for student-centered learning, collaboration, and coaching stems from the students themselves, finding inspiration in their natural curiosity as they authentically engage in learning experiences inside and outside of the classroom. Jessica strongly believes in the power of leading with a lens of inquiry, facilitating innovative professional learning opportunities, and coaching sessions that provide the space for educators to collaborate and reflect while supporting their professional growth as inquiry practitioners.

Her journey and experience as an inquiry educator in IB schools and place based education fuels her passion and global work in coaching both teachers and leaders in their roles, as well as supporting schools in implementing inquiry-based learning. Jessica understands the power of curiosity to guide next steps, creating the space we all need as learners as we actively engage in a reflective practice. In her published book, *Leading with a Lens of Inquiry*, she outlines the ways in which we, as leaders, need to support and facilitate our teachers in the same ways in which we want our teachers to engage with their students.

LinkedIn and Instagram @jess_vanceedu
Website: LeadingWithInquiry.com

About the Illustrator

Ryan Bear is a visual storyteller currently based in Portland, Oregon. With a background in animation and digital media arts, his focus is in illustration and motion art. He's been a part of many projects ranging from personalized family commissions, whimsical children's books, thoughtful commercial work, and zippy animations to preproduction in storyboards and character design.

Through his mastery of technique and vivid imagination, he prides himself on delivering quality work. Every piece has an intentional balance of craft and his clients' authenticity. With a big emphasis on the creative process, he dives deep with clients to bring their vision to fruition. He is known for being immaculate and putting in the extra mile for the project to reach its full potential.

Instagram @ryanbearart
Website: RyanBearArt.com